B   Hirsch, H. N.   STORAGE
FRANK
FURTER   The enigma of Felix
       Frankfurter

14 95

DATE			

THE ENIGMA
OF
FELIX
FRANKFURTER

THE ENIGMA OF FELIX FRANKFURTER

H. N. Hirsch

Basic Books, Inc., Publishers

1628

NEW YORK

Grateful acknowledgment is made for permission to reprint the following:

Excerpts from *Felix Frankfurter Reminisces: Recorded Talks with Dr. Harlan B. Phillips,* copyright 1960 by Harlan B. Phillips, by permission of William Morrow and Co.

Excerpts from *Roosevelt and Frankfurter: Their Correspondence, 1928–1945,* copyright 1967 by Max Freedman, by permission of Little, Brown and Co.

Excerpts from the Columbia Oral History Collection, copyright 1972, 1975 by the Trustees of Columbia University in the City of New York, by permission of the Oral History Research Office.

Excerpts from the correspondence of James F. Byrnes, by permission of Clemson University, Clemson, South Carolina.

Excerpts from the correspondence and diaries of Henry L. Stimson, by permission of Yale University Library.

Excerpts from the correspondence of A. Lawrence Lowell, by permission of Harvard University.

Library of Congress Cataloging in Publication Data

Hirsch, H N
    The enigma of Felix Frankfurter.

    Includes bibliographical references and index.
    1. Frankfurter, Felix, 1882–1965. 2. Judges—
United States—Biography. I. Title.
KF8745.F7H57   347.73'2634   [B]   80–61884
ISBN: 0–465–01979–X

For Lawrence Street

CONTENTS

PREFACE   *ix*

CHAPTER 1   *One Man Among Nine*   *3*

CHAPTER 2   *1900–1919: The Development of
             Self-Image and Political Style*   *11*

CHAPTER 3   *1919–1929: The Decade of Triumph*   *65*

CHAPTER 4   *1932–1939: The Cambridge-to-Washington
             Shuttle*   *99*

CHAPTER 5   *1939–1943: The Unexpected Challenge*   *127*

CHAPTER 6   *Dénouement*   *177*

CHAPTER 7   *Conclusion*   *201*

NOTES   *213*

INDEX   *249*

PREFACE

THIS is an interpretive biography of a much-studied and highly complex man. It does not claim to be exhaustive, but rather explores what I perceive to be unanswered questions concerning both Frankfurter's behavior and the Supreme Court as a political arena composed of flesh-and-blood human beings.

Frankfurter left us a treasure of words—thousands of letters, scholarly articles and books, a remarkably revealing reminiscence for the Columbia Oral History Collection, and, of course, hundreds of Supreme Court opinions. I have attempted to let him speak for himself as much as possible, so that the reader might discover, as I did, psychological clues and repetitions that are impossible to ignore.* For those who find the use of psychological theory as a tool of interpretation unsettling, I ask only for a suspension of disbelief until the evidence is presented.

·   ·   ·

My debts are many and a pleasure to acknowledge. This book began at Princeton, and I must first thank my teachers and fellow students there for making my years in graduate school a time of extraordinary fulfillment. The members of my dissertation committee—Walter F. Murphy, Fred Greenstein, Robert C. Tucker,

---

* In reprinting Frankfurter's correspondence I have retained his own punctuation and spelling, which is, at times, awkward or incorrect. The reader should keep in mind that many of these letters were written by hand and that English was not Frankfurter's native language. I have inserted *sic* only where the language is unusually cumbersome.

and Sanford Levinson—provided guidance and faith in my abilities in a manner for which I shall always be grateful.

For comments, criticism, encouragement, or aid at different stages, I would like to thank many individuals: Jerold Auerbach, Alan Betten, Jennifer Brown, John Burke, Erika S. Chadbourn, Jack Chapin, Morris L. Cohen, Sidney Davis, Richard and Eleanor Freeman, Susan Goodman, Gerald Gunther, Paul Hefron, Morton Horwitz, J. Woodford Howard, Jr., Pnina Lahav, Irving Lefberg, Alpheus T. Mason, Joel Migdal, Bruce A. Murphy, Yvonne Quinlan, Peter Rofes, Glendon Schubert, Martin Shapiro, James Sharaf, Judith Shklar, Marion Smiley, Henry Steiner, Philippa Strum, Sidney Verba, and David Wigdor. I owe a special and enormous debt to Nancy and Richard Rosenblum. I must also make special mention of Michael Parrish, whose generosity made it possible for me to use quotations from the Frankfurter papers at the Harvard Law School.

For expert counsel at Basic Books, I would like to thank Martin Kessler, Maureen Bischoff, and Julia Strand.

H.N.H.
Cambridge, Massachusetts
September 1, 1980

THE ENIGMA
OF
FELIX
FRANKFURTER

CHAPTER 1

One Man Among Nine

H E WAS perhaps the most influential jurist of the twentieth century. As a professor of law at Harvard, he trained a generation of lawyers and legal scholars who have, in turn, continued to spread his influence so that it remains almost as potent today as during his lifetime. As a justice of the Supreme Court for nearly a quarter of a century, he was a persistent spokesman for one of constitutional law's most durable theories: judicial self-restraint. He was one of the first academics in American history to play the role of intimate advisor to a president of the United States. Jewish immigrant, child of New York's Lower East Side, scholar, Ivy League professor, defender of Sacco and Vanzetti, he was labeled everything from radical to liberal to conservative. In every phase of his life, Felix Frankfurter was a phenomenon.

. . .

The marble walls of the Supreme Court have been the last edifice to succumb to the weight of psychological realism. The secrecy protecting the Court's deliberations and the reverential awe usually accorded by the general public to both the Court and its decisions have helped shroud the members of the Court in a mystery almost as black as their robes.[1] Yet the very structure of the Court as a

political arena seems strongly to suggest that careful psychological analysis of its members is necessary for a full understanding of
the workings of the institution. These nine men must reach a collective decision, and therefore interact and bargain with each
other; they enjoy life tenure and are shielded from publicity, and
thus are subject to fewer formal demands than is the case with most
political roles. Nine men, locked in a conference room with only
their notes, their law books, and each other—if ever there was a
political forum where personality would have an impact, surely this
is it. This need to examine judicial personality seems especially
acute for the analysis of periods of transition within the Court,
when constitutional precedent gives way to doctrinal confusion.
It is during such periods of uncertainty that personality may become a particularly important determinant of judicial outcome.[2]

Felix Frankfurter was appointed to the Supreme Court in 1939,
during just such a period of transition. The Court had renounced
its self-assumed role as the protector of the laissez-faire economy
of the nineteenth and early twentieth centuries but had not yet
adopted its role as the protector of individual rights, which it was
to play in the years to come. Frankfurter, as a close friend of
Franklin Roosevelt's and a legal scholar of great repute, was expected by the White House to lead the Court through a period of
calm after the stormy Court-packing controversy of the mid-
thirties. Calm, however, was hard to produce in a period marked by
unsettled doctrine and dynamic judicial personalities. FDR placed
on the Court highly complex and extraordinary men—Hugo Black,
William O. Douglas, Frank Murphy, Robert H. Jackson, and Felix
Frankfurter—whose combined volatility made it impossible to
achieve the judicial peace he sought.

Of the men Roosevelt put on the Court, Frankfurter was perhaps the most unusual; the force of both his personality and his
philosophy made him the center of the Court's deliberations during his twenty-four years on the bench. Brought to this country
at the age of twelve, he had risen to the summit of the Yankee-
dominated, anti-Semitic legal establishment.[3] Frankfurter was a
vibrant personality: witty, charming, warm, energized, sparkling.
He had scores of friends whom he loved and who loved him, in-

cluding men prominent in politics, the academy, and the legal profession. Few men in the twentieth century have had the devoted
loyalty of so many.

But, upon closer examination, there is a darker side to his character as well. Other, less flattering adjectives have been used to describe him: intense, nervous, arrogant, domineering. His correspondence with FDR, published in 1967, reveals a sycophantic
flattery; [4] his more recently published diaries reveal an obsessive
concern with the motives of his judicial opponents mixed with
high-pitched anger at their behavior and doctrines.[5]

There are, moreover, some puzzling questions about Frankfurter's judicial performance. When he was appointed to the Court,
many expected his long-time commitment to civil liberties to
translate into judicial philosophy; instead, Frankfurter demonstrated an austere commitment to judicial self-restraint. Yet despite this credo, Frankfurter willingly extended protection to
values he considered essential in a manner hard not to perceive as
contradictory or hypocritical. Everything about Frankfurter, in
fact, suggests a complex personality at work; there was about
him an unmistakable psychological spark.

The central hypothesis of this study is that Frankfurter can
only be understood politically if we understand him psychologically, and that we can understand him psychologically as representing a textbook case of a neurotic personality: someone whose
self-image is overblown and yet, at the same time, essential to his
sense of well-being. Because of delays and difficulties in psychological maturation—because for several crucial years he could not
decide who and what he was and thus suffered from severe self-
doubt—Frankfurter, I will argue, was led to develop a compensating, "idealized" self-image in which he exaggerated his political
skills and talents. His political style, which he applied throughout
his life, resulted from that self-image; it emphasized what he perceived as his ability to handle other people.

The key aspect of Frankfurter's personality as it affected his
public behavior was his attitude toward political opposition. Because his self-image was inflated, and because his psychological
peace rested upon that self-image, Frankfurter could not accept

serious, sustained opposition in fields he considered his domain of expertise; he reacted to his opponents with vindictive hostility. Unconsciously, such hostility was a projection of his own self-doubt.

Until his appointment to the Supreme Court, Frankfurter had been able to beat his opponents and to dominate every personal and professional situation in which he found himself—the various government bureaus in which he worked, the organizations to which he belonged, the Harvard Law School, the circle of advisors in the Roosevelt White House. When he was appointed to the Court, Frankfurter quite naturally expected to dominate yet another situation. This expectation was buttressed by his many years as a scholar of the law and by the intimate knowledge of the Court he had acquired through two of his mentors, Holmes and Brandeis.

The Supreme Court, however, was an environment unlike the ones in which Frankfurter had triumphed; he was formally committed to sharing power with strong-willed individuals who had ideas of their own. Frankfurter could not lead the Court and, much to his surprise, found himself faced with an opposing "bloc." He was thus confronted, late in life, with a serious challenge to his self-image; he reacted in a manner affecting both his relations with his colleagues and the content of his jurisprudence.

In the chapters that follow, I seek to document and substantiate these propositions. In doing so, I draw upon the work of both political scientists and a particular school of psychological theory.

. . .

Political scientists and historians have had mixed success applying psychological theory to biography.[6] Particularly useful, however, has been the concept of "style" developed in the study of the American presidency. In the formulation of James David Barber,[7] an individual's style involves his manner of handling the three things that appear in any political role—words, work, and people, the "three broad dimensions of life as an enterprise in which the individual receives from and acts upon his world."[8] Barber finds that the balance among these three elements of style varies from one individual to the next: "One . . . may put most of himself into rhetoric, another may stress close, informal dealing, while still another may devote his energies mainly to study and cogitation." [9]

Several corollary points flow from this concept of style and its application to political biography. The first is that an individual's style may conflict with the requirements of his office; it is just such a condition that may lie at the base of political failure.[10] The possibility of such "misfit" between style and role is greatest when an individual comes to a new and demanding office—like the presidency or the Supreme Court—late in life, after a successful career. The White House—or the Court—is the last achievement of a man's life; it is the final prize, the ultimate confirmation of the self. Men in such positions do not find it easy to change the successful practices and habits of a lifetime. It is thus crucial to examine the fit between an individual's style and the requirements of his political roles, and whether those requirements change as the individual moves through his career.[11]

Moreover, the use of the concept of style makes it imperative to examine that point in a subject's early life at which his style was first formed and applied successfully—his "first independent political success." [12] It is at this point that we may find the key to an individual's later political behavior. This creation of a political style will often be part of an identity crisis in young adulthood;[13] the individual's psychological equilibrium may therefore depend upon the creation and successful application of a particular style.

Concern with political style thus leads the biographer inevitably to a concern with the psychological development of the individual, particularly his sense of identity during his social and political maturation. The tools necessary for an understanding of the psychological mechanisms involved in the formation of an individual's sense of self can be found in the school of thought that has been termed "ego psychology." In the theories of psychologists Erik Erikson (who uses the term "identity") and Karen Horney (who uses the term "self-image") the biographer can find carefully elaborated propositions, based upon clinical evidence, useful in the quest for an accurate psychological assessment of his subject.[14]

In his seminal work Erikson has presented a by-now familiar theory concerning the stages of ego growth. At every stage of childhood, adolescence, and young adulthood, Erikson has found, the individual is faced with a form of psychological crisis; the successful resolution of these crises—in their proper sequence—leads to the formation of a firm identity in late adolescence or early adulthood. If an individual becomes "stalled" at any given point, however, he will not be able to complete the cycle of growth Erikson describes as essential to psychological well-being.

Horney, on the other hand, is concerned with describing the particular type of neurosis that develops when an individual creates for himself an "idealized" self-image to compensate for low self-esteem. An individual in desperate need of self-confidence, Horney finds, creates it for himself through an act of imagination. He unconsciously exaggerates his talents or skills and then identifies himself with this exaggerated image; he thus compensates for what is in fact a negative self-image. "Self-idealization always entails a general self-glorification," Horney writes, "and thereby gives the individual the much-needed feeling of significance and of superiority over others." [15] By "idealizing" his self-image, the individual solves his problems by one daring and fateful act.

When a self-image is created and used for such purposes of compensation,[16] certain psychological consequences inevitably follow. The individual will feel a constant need to "prove" the validity of his self-image in action, and thereby convince himself that he is who and what he thinks he is. At the same time, his self-image, because essentially false, is never really secure. The individual will thus react with particular vehemence to any challenges to his self-image; such challenges will be psychologically painful because they call forth his self-doubt or self-hatred. Such self-hatred, however, will often be projected or "externalized"—that is, directed outward, toward those who offer the challenge. Instead of hating himself, the neurotic individual will hate those who challenge him; instead of seeing his own faults, he will see his own faults in others. Thus if an individual's self-image seems inflated, and if he reacts with particular vehemence to challenges to that self-image, this may be a clue that his self-image is functioning in the neurotic manner Horney describes. A strong public self-image may mask a weak, private one; public aggressiveness may compensate for private insecurity.

The interpretation of Frankfurter to be presented here, resting upon this theoretical framework, is not an attempt to reduce his jurisprudence to the content of his psyche. Although in some cases "personality" and "ideology" are posed as mutually exclusive alternatives, in many cases psychological processes and ideological predispositions will in fact reinforce one another. Personality thus becomes, in the language of social scientists, a contributory variable, the strength of which, given its interaction with other variables and the highly delicate nature of psychological evidence, is impossible to measure with mathematical precision. As Alexander George argues, "faced with the play of multiple, complexly interacting causal variables, the investigator is bound to have great difficulty in assessing the weight of any given factor. . . . Often the most that can be said is that personality needs or other personality characteristics were among the many contributing factors." [17]

Personality needs may explain *how* an individual's ideology is translated into specific political acts; they may account for the manner in which the subject interacts with other individuals in his environment; they may explain an inability to adapt personal style to the requirements of an office, role, or situation. Personality most often interacts with ideology; seldom does it completely supplant it. "Ideology" will often explain the general direction of a subject's behavior; "personality" may then explain his precise route, speed, and means of reaching his destination.

Thus, I will not argue that Frankfurter's personality forced him to take positions on the Supreme Court completely at odds with his pre-Court political ideology; rather, I will argue that his personality led him to harden his stands, to behave in a certain way toward his colleagues, to emphasize certain strands in his philosophy and to exclude others when they were adopted by his enemies, to ignore and rationalize certain contradictions in his legal theory. By systematically examining Frankfurter's personality, this study seeks to explain certain characteristics of Frankfurter's behavior that are difficult to account for in a purely "ideological" explanation—for example, the manner in which he dominated those around him; the extreme anger with which he attacked the motives and abilities of his political opponents; the degree to which he projected his own behavior onto others. The hypotheses offered here do not deny the importance of Frankfurter's political beliefs;

they are not meant as a substitute for traditional ideological analysis, but rather as its complement.

It must be remembered, moreover, that the process by which an ideology is adopted is itself strongly influenced by personality factors. Ideological commitment can provide a powerful sense of self; the value system of respected and admired mentors—who provide crucial approval and acceptance to a young adult—can be easily internalized. As Erikson argues, "Whatever else ideology is . . . and whatever transitory or lasting social form it takes . . . it [is] a necessity for the growing ego. . . ." [18] Thus an important theme of this study is the degree to which Frankfurter, an immigrant much in need of acceptance, clung to the promise of American democracy and gladly accepted—and sometimes confused— the political values of a remarkable trio of elder mentors: Henry L. Stimson, Louis D. Brandeis, and Oliver Wendell Holmes.

•   •   •

Hanging in the library of the Harvard Law School, where much of this book was written, is a famous portrait of Frankfurter by Gardner Cox. Unlike most portraits of famous men it is done in both charcoal and oil; it is so unusual that one notices it immediately among the many canvases surrounding it. Although the famous Frankfurter face is visible—sharp, almost piercing eyes, prominent nose, bold forehead—the lines are nevertheless somewhat obscure, the tone oblique. Many have commented that the portrait has the look of being unfinished or a rough draft. Much has been written that captures the clear, sharp lines of Frankfurter's public personality—the man Frankfurter himself wanted history to record. But, like the portrait, this study will seek to explore the shadows and the shades of the man as well.

CHAPTER 2

1900–1919: The Development of Self-Image and Political Style

I N 1919 Felix Frankfurter attended the Paris Peace Conference as a representative of the American Zionist Organization headed by his friend and sponsor, Louis D. Brandeis. He was thirty-seven years old. After a long and difficult courtship, he had won the promise of Marion Denman to marry upon his return. He had spent most of his adulthood as a young lawyer in New York and Washington, except for a brief and, in his own mind, tentative period on the faculty of the Harvard Law School before the war. After Paris, he would return to Cambridge to marry and to begin a long tenure at the Law School that would continue until his appointment to the Supreme Court in 1939.

Paris was, for Frankfurter, a triumph. Surrounded by the world's greatest statesmen, he found himself an effective and admired cog in the machine of world diplomacy. In his letters to Marion from Paris, he speaks of his admiration for the men of power who surround him, men to whom, he repeatedly says, "I'm only a boy." [1] He quickly notices that he is making an impression upon these men, a fact that obviously pleases him. He repeatedly talks about going through a "fundamental change" of attitude, and calls himself a "not yet moulded personality." He often says he feels he is entering a new period in his life. And he continually writes Marion about his ability to handle the men around him, a process he calls *personalia*:

> I don't remember ever having been less free as to time and circumstances than here and now. . . . The job is incapable of standardization or of definite working hours. . . . So much of it is personalia. . . . For instance today I thought I'd have an hour or so at noon . . . instead Weizmann * was in the deep dumps and so I had to pull him out of it. It's an amazing mixture of personalities that has to be handled, with all sorts of backgrounds and personal prejudices. Much of my work is this kind of mediation—nursing and mediation.[2]

What emerges clearly from Frankfurter's often candid letters to Marion from Paris is a self-image, and a style of behavior that results from, and reinforces, that self-image. Frankfurter at this precise moment of his life is a man realizing that he is a success, that he is admired by men of influence and power, and that he can handle people with his charm, wit, and intelligence. In psychological terms, Paris is the culmination of a period of identity formation. This chapter will explore the events and the emotional trail of that process. My underlying hypothesis is that Frankfurter's period of identity formation was both overly prolonged and torturously difficult, and that he did not form a coherent self-image until his mid-thirties, after a period of intense psychological stress. This delay was due to a fundamental ambiguity in his choice of an identity and the emotional complications attached to that ambiguity.

.   .   .

Frankfurter was born to Jewish parents in Vienna in 1882, the third son in a family of six children. His family had been socially prominent within the isolated Jewish community; for centuries

* Chaim Weizmann, the international Zionist leader, with whom Frankfurter worked closely at Paris. Weizmann and Brandeis would later clash over the leadership and direction of the Zionist movement.

members of his father's family had been rabbis. Frankfurter's uncle became the head librarian of the University of Vienna and was a scholar of some repute. Frankfurter's father, Leopold, prepared for the rabbinate but did not complete his studies; he abandoned the seminary in his final year to marry and to become a businessman. He was not, however, successful in business, and like many of his culture and generation, Leopold Frankfurter decided to abandon Vienna for America. He left Vienna in 1893, and brought the rest of his family to join him the following year.[3]

Felix was brought to New York City—via steerage—when he was twelve, in August of 1894. He spoke no English when he arrived, although he is reported to have learned the language in six weeks.[4] Frankfurter remembers himself coming home and saying, "This man Laundry must be a very rich man because he has so many stores."[5] The family settled first in a German-Jewish neighborhood on the Lower East Side of Manhattan. Later, when Leopold prospered a bit, they moved uptown to a better but still modest neighborhood in the East Seventies, a common move for German Jews at the time.[6] Frankfurter's father sold linens, using the family apartment as his shop; during the summer he peddled door to door.[7] The two eldest sons, Fred and Otto, went immediately to work to help support the family; the two youngest sons, Felix and Paul, entered P.S. 25.[8]

It is within this cultural configuration of immigrant Jewry that we must begin to understand Felix Frankfurter. Although this world consisted of several subcultures,[9] all of them emphasized education as a means of survival and advancement in the New World. On New York's Lower East Side, young men like Felix enjoyed an environment bursting with a crowded, stimulating, rough-and-tumble intellectuality.

Frankfurter's reminiscences about his youth provide an important insight into this environment. In this excerpt, Frankfurter identifies a personality trait to which he will call attention throughout his life: his unreflectiveness, his inability to analyze himself.

The neighborhood was one a lot of German-speaking people moved into. . . . I had such a good time, I was so extrovertishly busy, that I wasn't thrown in upon myself to reflect upon things. Every day was full. . . . Right near where we lived I discovered Cooper Union. . . . Cooper Union was a very important part of my education. There were classes. There were courses over the week—courses in history, in geography, and in the natural sciences. Downstairs was the famous red-chaired hall in which Lincoln made one of his great addresses. In that same hall Friday night there was always some public topic under discussion. . . . The meeting lasted from eight to ten, and at ten o'clock sharp the lights went out. . . . The discussion would continue outside, sort of late night Hyde Park stuff.[10]

Frankfurter remembers himself as being "more bookish than others in my family, although I came in part from a bookish family." [11] He quickly discovered the reading room of Cooper Union, where he sat for hours reading daily newspapers from around the country, developing an interest in politics and current affairs. He was, he proudly recalled, a child prodigy, and, in his remarks, does not hesitate to compare himself to great men.

Just as Fritz Kreisler began to play the violin when he was very young, and Mozart composed when he was four, to make irrelevant comparisons, and John Stuart Mill read Greek when he was four, in me there was no such precocious gift, but early, certainly in the early teens, it became manifest that I was interested in the world of affairs. Why that shouldn't be as pronounced a predilection as playing the fiddle or reading Greek I don't know. Anyway, in my case it was. It began very early. . . .[12]

One of Frankfurter's early heroes was William Jennings Bryan, nominated for the first time when Frankfurter was fourteen. "Here was a fellow who could entrance people by the quality of his voice, the beauty of his speech. It was all so fresh and romantic and the voice of hope." [13] Frankfurter recounts playing hookey from school to attend a Bryan campaign stop in New Jersey; he also remembered that his family "was all for McKinley." [14]

The available evidence, although somewhat meager, indicates that Frankfurter's family structure fits squarely within a fairly typical immigrant pattern: weak, unsuccessful, gentle father; strong, dominant mother. Matthew Josephson, one of the earliest and most astute observers of Frankfurter's character, reported for the *New Yorker* in 1940 that Frankfurter's father was "remembered by his neighbors as a man of frail health, a dreamy and charitable soul who enjoyed giving baskets of fruit to poorer neighbors. It was Mrs. Frankfurter who was the backbone of the family, ruling its economy...." [15]

Irving Howe, in his recent study of immigrant Jewry, provides an interpretation of family dynamics that finds the origins of characteristics such as these in the shock of transition to the New World, a shock that was much greater for the father than for the mother of the family. The moral authority of the father in the old country had been based on the importance of tradition and religion for daily life; the transition to the New World thus led to an inevitable loss of status and self-respect for the male as these traditional patterns were broken. For the woman, the transition was not as severe; her role as the emotional center of the family remained intact. The psychological dislocation resulting from the male's loss of authority, together with his failure to provide adequate income for his family in an economy he was unequipped to enter, led, in Howe's words, to "a flow of power toward the mother." [16]

All of the evidence available to me indicates that this pattern applied to the Frankfurters. Throughout his correspondence, Frankfurter stresses the tenderness of his father and the strength of his mother; in a letter to Marion, he describes his parents in this way:

There are two distinct deep strains in me—I know the qualities I have from Father and those that are mine through mother. My father loved *life*—he thought we were here for joy; joy was his emphasis. Mother's accent, from childhood when the burdens of her parents' household fell not a little on *her*, marriage only making a transfer of the immediate interests of her cares, is duty.[17]

Beyond this familiar and typical pattern, there is strong evidence of emotional stress within the family. Frankfurter's relationship with his mother, after his father's death in 1916, produced a powerful source of emotional strain and guilt. His mother's emphasis on "duty" proved to be a major source of tension, as Frankfurter found it difficult to ignore her feelings about his relationship with a non-Jewish woman. In the struggle within his own mind between his mother and the woman to whom he was attracted, Frankfurter was forced in dramatic fashion to face the question of who he was.

This evidence of tension with his mother contrasts sharply with Frankfurter's public pronouncements about his parents, whom he always attempted to describe in glowing terms without giving any hint of strain. In the following excerpt from his reminiscences, Frankfurter is clearly trying to paint a pleasant picture of his family, and yet, between the lines, there is a hint of resentment at having been neglected.

If you were to ask me what I think as I sit here, without any analysis, if you were to ask me as I sit here in my chair, without having me stretched out on a couch behind you, I would say, at least the picture in my mind of me and my family, is that they took me for granted—more particularly my father and mother, and more particularly my mother who saw more of me than anybody else—they just somehow or other saw that they didn't have to bother about this kid, that he was doing all right, and why bother about him. I was a sociable creature. I didn't give them any trouble, but please don't infer that I was a goody-goody. I've said, and I've said this when I was nearer in time and feeling to my youth and my relations to my family, that the greatest debt I owe my parents is that they left me alone almost completely.[18]

Elsewhere in his reminiscences, Frankfurter clearly attempts to avoid the subject of conflict with his parents, using language quite uncharacteristic of him: "I never had any Weltschmerz. Maybe that makes me out a little prig, but I can assure you contemporaneously I didn't feel like a prig. Maybe I just ain't got no memory for things like this. In short, it's not a profitable vein of exploration." [19]

Frankfurter's private comments—especially in his letters to his wife—suggest that his family relationships were not as free of conflict as his usual public portrait indicates. The point that should be stressed here is simply that there *is* some evidence of tension within the Frankfurter family. Although it is not clear how far back into childhood this tension extended, by his young adulthood—the period crucial to the consolidation of his identity—the tension is clearly present and in the open.

. . .

Frankfurter was ready for high school two years after arriving in New York. He took an examination for entrance to Horace Mann, but could not attend for lack of funds. In a passage reeking of self-embellishment, he recounted the incident.

One day I had a letter from Virgil Prettyman, the principal of the Horace Mann School, asking me to see him in his office. I went up there. He said that I came very, very close to being one of the winners in this contest throughout all the public schools in New York. I came so close to it that they would very much like to have me as a pupil. They would take me for the first year as a pupil at half the tuition fee, I think $100 then. The promise of my examination was such that there was a good chance that I would get a scholarship for the other years. I said I, of course, would have to take that up with my parents. So there was a family council. Horace Mann seemed a little sweller than something else. Horace Mann sort of led to Columbia. I'm quite sure I said, "No, why should you spend $100 on me? It would be nice if I had a scholarship." That was that.[20]

Frankfurter entered City College when he lost his chance to attend Horace Mann. "In those days," he recalled, "City College was an intensive course which crowded into five years high school and college. . . . It was a fantastic thing really. For five days a week, four hours a day, there was classroom work. . . . There were several fellows on the faculty who were very congenial to me." [21] He continued to immerse himself in the rich culture of his environment.

I made friends there particularly with one fellow who was a loquacious talker and a gluttonous reader of everything. . . . I'd sit hours and hours and hours in East Side teashops, coffee rooms, and drink highball glasses of tea with some rum in it, or lemon, and a piece of cake, and jaw into the morning about everything under the sun.[22]

At some point during these early years, Frankfurter discontinued his association with religious Judaism; [23] later, Frankfurter would call himself an agnostic. He nowhere discusses the degree of religious observance in his home, or the effect of his attitude on his parents, although he described the moral atmosphere of his home this way: "Certainly I was brought up in what might be called an ethical tradition. You were decent. You were respectful. You believed in certain verities. You were supposed to be truthful. Now where I got these from, I might say my mother's milk, except I know damn well that milk carries no ethical instruction." [24]

At City College Frankfurter developed skill as a public speaker and debator. He was vice president of the senior class, an assistant editor of a college magazine, and a member of both the chess club and the debating society.[25] The debating society once changed its rule that only seniors could represent it in its yearly debate tournament to allow Frankfurter, who was only a junior, to participate.[26] The perceptive comments of Joseph Lash concerning Frankfurter's developing oral skill and intellectual power point to an important conclusion: "Short of stature—he was less than five feet, five inches—he needed eloquence and intellectual power to keep the world of taller men from overlooking him. He succeeded, graduating from City College at nineteen, third highest in his class." [27] Compensation, in one of its many forms, would be a psychological coping mechanism for Frankfurter throughout his life.

Frankfurter had long been interested in the law. It was a natural choice for a bright, ambitious, verbally capable Jewish adolescent with an interest in public affairs. "I do not remember," he later said, "the time when I did not know I was going to be a lawyer." [28] Lacking the money to enroll in law school immediately after his graduation from City College in 1902, Frankfurter took a civil service examination and got a job as a clerk in the just-established New York City Tenement House Department for a year. He also did private tutoring, and he considered night law school.

I first started in the New York Law School, and that was so bad I couldn't stand it. Then I went over to the New York University Law School, and that was pretty bad too. I knew what bad law schools were. So I quit. I worked very hard that year doing all these things. One day I started to go up to Morningside Heights to matriculate in the Columbia Law School for the next year. . . . So I started to walk up to Morningside Heights on a nice spring day with ten dollars in my pocket with which to matriculate. On the way up I ran into a buddy of mine, a classmate from City College. He said, "Where are you going? What are you doing?" I told him I was going to Columbia to matriculate. "Oh," he said, "you can do that some other day. It's a lovely day. Let's go to Coney Island. If you're going to matriculate, you must have some money on you." So we went up to Coney Island. The whole course of my life was changed by that diversion.[29]

Before he could enroll at Columbia, Frankfurter became ill with a serious case of the flu. A doctor advised him to get out of New York City and to attend law school in the country. He first thought of the University of Michigan, but an acquaintance's brother (Sam Rosensohn, later a close friend) went to Harvard, and Frankfurter spoke to him. In this passage, like many others, Frankfurter seems to be overplaying the nonchalance of his family life.

I told my parents that I was going to Cambridge, to Harvard. I don't remember any discussion about it. I had enough money to go. . . . Sam Rosensohn was a first-year man, . . . and he said that next year we could live together. It was fixed up like that. I don't agonize over things. I don't consult a thousand people. I don't dramatize life. You know, you just go.[30]

Up to this point—his twentieth year—Frankfurter's identity was with the intellectual elements of his culture and environment most congenial to his personality and his abilities. This was an identity easy for someone in his position to assimilate. Except perhaps for his rejection of religious Judaism, his choices engendered no conflict with the culture of which he was a part. Frankfurter had been recognized as an intelligent, diligent student and as a capable and lively speaker and friend by people of his own kind. By outward appearances he was, at this point, typical of his generation.

Harvard, however, was a new world; Frankfurter entered it with fear, awe, and a determination to succeed. It was at Harvard that Frankfurter began giving shape and substance to his identity and to add to it in ways that changed him profoundly. These changes, moreover, would prolong and make difficult the final definition of Frankfurter's self.

.   .   .

Frankfurter entered the Harvard Law School in the fall of 1903. Because he was still working at the Tenement House Department and wanted to receive a full month's salary, he arrived a week after everyone else. It was the first time he had lived away from home; his mother had packed his suitcase.[31] He had never seen Boston or Cambridge, and the world he was entering was new and frightening. "The first day I went to my classrooms," he later said, "I had one of the most intense frights of my life. I looked about me. Everybody was taller. . . . I was a little fellow. . . . There were a lot of big fellows . . . robust fellows, self-confident creatures around." [32] Throughout this period of his life, Frankfurter was self-conscious about his appearance, especially his small size.

At first, Frankfurter exalted in the life and freedom of Cambridge.

In no time I revelled in the place. I ate up not only the law, but attended lectures of other people, went to concerts. My roommate was by this time a second-year man. . . . He thought I wasn't studying law hard enough, which I didn't in the first few months at the Harvard Law School because I was rejoicing in its freedom. . . . I went to this and that, went to the library, read, roamed all around, and just satisfied a gluttonous appetite for lectures, exhibitions, concerts.[33]

At mid-year, Frankfurter did poorly on a series of tests. "That was the necessary jolt. I buckled down and ended up by being first in the class, which I continued to be the three years that I was there, but which I did not know about at the time." [34]

Frankfurter's success at and love of the Harvard Law School is a well-known phenomenon; he described his feelings about Harvard as "quasi-religious." [35] The vague image of himself as an intellectual that Frankfurter had absorbed from his surroundings in New York was concretized at Harvard through his worship of the law. The law—as taught at Harvard—would become the object of his energies, the root of his pride, an immensely important source of his self-esteem. And, equally important, Harvard provided an environment that allowed him to break the bounds of his culture and gain acceptance—of a certain kind—from the American establishment, so foreign to him thus far.

There was a dominating atmosphere, first, of professionalism and what I think is an indispensable quality of true professionalism, the democratic spirit. What mattered was excellence in your profession to which your father or your face was equally irrelevant. And so rich man, poor man were just irrelevant titles to the equation of human relations. The thing that mattered was what you did professionally.[36]

"Your father or your face"—two aspects of himself about which Frankfurter had deeply ambivalent feelings—became unimportant at Harvard. And Harvard was an environment that allowed Frankfurter to turn his intellectual powers into an objective measurement of worth.

Election to the *Harvard Law Review* followed academic rank, an automatic affair. All this big talk about "leadership" and character, and all the other things that are non-ascertainable, but usually are high-falutin' expressions for personal likes and dislikes, or class, or color, or religious partialities or antipathies—they were all out. . . . If one fellow got 76 and another 76.5, there's no use saying, "The 76 man is better." Maybe so, but how do you know he's better?[37]

It was, moreover, an environment in which Frankfurter's academic success was translated into a certain degree of social acceptance from Brahmin, Yankee culture; he proudly recounts in his memoirs being asked to tutor one of his classmates, "a tall, gangling, six-foot-three fellow. . . . He was . . . well-to-do."[38]

Frankfurter adored the faculty at Harvard—men like Samuel Williston, John Chipman Gray, Joseph Beale, and most of all, James Barr Ames, the dean. "You would sort of walk off on clouds as a result of a talk with Ames. . . . I have a reverent feeling about him. . . ."[39] Frankfurter excelled at the classroom repartee required in the case method. During one of his summers in law school, he was asked to serve as a research assistant to Gray; it was a letter from Gray that introduced him to Oliver Wendell Holmes. Commenting about the faculty as a whole, Frankfurter said:

Giants they were, and I revere their memory because they seem to me to represent the best products of civilization—dedication of lives of great powers to the pursuit of truth, and nothing else, complete indifference to all the shoddiness, pettiness and silliness that occupies the concern of most people who are deemed to be important or big.[40]

The faculty at Harvard were the elect, the elite—men to be worshiped and emulated.

During the spring recess of his third year in law school, Frankfurter went job hunting in New York, armed with letters of introduction from Dean Ames. "These notes Dean Ames wrote for me," he said, "commended me to them in very strong terms. I was such a shy and sensitive kid . . . that I was a little ashamed to hand out letters that put me in such a favorable light." [41]

Frankfurter's search for a job from law firm to law firm in New York was a jarring and disturbing experience; it was a reminder that outside the walls of the law school, good grades were not an automatic guarantee of success. "I went from office to office, and it was not a pleasant experience because I was made to feel as though I was some worm going around begging for a job." [42]

Frankfurter recounted several incidents from his New York trip in his reminiscences; he encountered a lawyer who was sure he had forged Ames's signature, and one who reminded him "that the life of a lawyer in New York is not an intellectual life. . . . He induced me to feel that the fact that I did very well at Harvard Law School really didn't amount to very much. . . ." [43] He finally met Dwight Morrow, later his good friend. "When he got through talking with me," Frankfurter recalled, "he said, 'Well, I don't know whether we'll have room for you in our office, but just remember that a good office needs a good man just as much as a good man needs a good office.' " [44]

For Frankfurter, "that was a revelation from heaven. That put the thing in proper perspective, that I wasn't a mendicant, that I had something they wanted as much as they something I wanted." [45] He continues:

There was one office, Hornblower, Byrne, Miller and Potter, that was one of the best offices at the time. Lots of Harvard people were in there. I'd heard that they had never taken a Jew and wouldn't take a

Jew. I decided that that was the office I wanted to get into not for any reason of truculence, but I was very early infused with, had inculcated in me, a very profoundly wise attitude toward the whole fact that I was a Jew, the essence of which is that you should be a biped and walk on the two legs that man has. . . . You should take that ultimate fact that you were born of some parents instead of these other parents as much for granted as the fact that you've got green-brown eyes instead of blue eyes.[46]

Frankfurter regarded his religion as a mere accident of birth, and was determined to succeed in the Brahmin world. At Harvard, his skill as a student had brought a degree of acceptance he could never have dreamed possible earlier. Yet as his life unfolded, Frankfurter revealed a growing bitterness toward those who did not agree that religion was merely an accident of birth. As he moved further and further into the establishment, and came to be more fully, but not completely accepted by it, he came more and more to resent religious intolerance.

The result of this process—substantial, but not complete acceptance—helped produce a fundamental tension in Frankfurter's identity. As he moved through his career, Frankfurter continually tried to resolve the question of whether he was an insider or an outsider. He wanted profoundly, almost desperately, to be an insider—someone at ease in and accepted by the world of Boston Yankees and Wall Street lawyers. Yet he was never fully accepted by this world and was continually reminded of his background—of "his father and his face." Even after his triumphant storming of a New York law firm that had never accepted a Jew, Frankfurter was told by a senior partner of the firm that he ought to change his name.[47] As he left the protective walls of the Harvard Law School and ventured into New York and soon into Washington, Frankfurter bore the confidence of a successful and respected student. That confidence, however, was never complete; there always remained a lingering doubt about whether he really would be accepted where he was headed.

Thus once again the completion of Frankfurter's identity was delayed. It had first been delayed by his decision to go to Harvard and thus to explore new possibilities for his self-image; it was now delayed by a subtle ambiguity about what the results of that process had been. He could not completely adopt the identity of an elite Harvard lawyer, yet he was no longer a typical son of the Lower East Side. As he began his legal career, Frankfurter was not yet certain who he was or to what group he belonged; he was still exploring these fundamental questions.

This type of prolonged process of identity-formation, psychologists have found, has two results: an increase in self-consciousness and difficulty in forming intimate relationships.[48] In the years after leaving Harvard, Frankfurter would manifest both characteristics. At the same time, the struggle to free himself from his old identity—represented by his parents—and to complete his new identity—represented by Harvard and by his attraction to a non-Jewish woman—would produce both psychological strain and guilt.

.   .   .

Frankfurter did not spend much time at the Hornblower office. He soon had an offer to join the United States Attorney, who had been given his name by Dean Ames. The United States Attorney was Henry L. Stimson, and in 1906 Frankfurter began his association with this man who was to figure prominently in his life for forty years.

Stimson offered Frankfurter a smaller salary, but Frankfurter was immediately attracted to the idea of public service. "I knew at once I wanted to do that," he said, "because that solved my problem. I could practice law without having a client. There it was. Perfect." [49] Frankfurter's desire to practice law without a client suggests a characteristic he would manifest throughout his life: a need for control of his situation, or, in his own words, a need for "a sense of freedom." In many different situations, Frankfurter will avoid commitment to an institution that might bring him under the direct power or influence of another individual.

Frankfurter summoned up the courage to leave the Hornblower firm and began his apprenticeship to Stimson. It was a remarkable relationship, one that would introduce Frankfurter to Theodore Roosevelt, bring him to Washington, and eventually help provide him with a faculty position at Harvard. Decades later, their positions reversed, it was a relationship that would bring Henry Stimson into Franklin Roosevelt's cabinet.

Frankfurter quickly became something of a personal assistant to Stimson, who was prosecuting several antitrust cases and often relied upon Frankfurter for research. Frankfurter was given legal cases concerning immigrants to take care of; Stimson told him, "You are likely to have more understanding of their problems than some of the other lads in the office." [50] "I began in the fall of 1906," he said, "and I had nothing but a wonderful time being Mr. Stimson's personal assistant in one important litigation after another." [51] Frankfurter brought his first case to trial, prosecuting a man who had falsely posed as a secret service agent. "It was really a very rich life. Professionally it couldn't have been better." [52]

Frankfurter observed carefully the relationship between Stimson and President Roosevelt, a man Frankfurter was coming more and more to respect. It was his first contact with men wielding national power, and it was a heady experience. "I'll never forget the excitement in me to hear Mr. Stimson tell the President of the United States, 'This is what I'm going to do. If you don't like it, you can do what you want to do.' " [53] The relationship between Stimson and Theodore Roosevelt would, much later, provide Frankfurter with a model for his own relationship with FDR. At the same time, the antitrust cases he saw passing through the office began to raise Frankfurter's political consciousness and to crystallize his progressivism. When asked, "Why did you decide not to become a leading member of the bar of New York?" Frankfurter, in a revealing passage, recounted watching the investigation of E. H. Harriman of the Union Pacific Railroad.

He had a retinue of lawyers. He was handling the matter himself. He knew more about his business than his lawyers did. There were the lawyers, some of the greatest of the day. . . . The way Mr. Harriman spoke to his lawyers, and the boot-licking deference they paid to him! My observation of this interplay between the great man, the really powerful, dominating tycoon, Harriman, and his servitors, the lawyers, led me to say to myself, "If it means that you should be that kind of subservient creature to have the most desirable clients, the biggest clients in the country, if that's what it means to be a leader of the bar, I never want to be a leader of the bar. The price of admission is too high." [54]

Frankfurter in this passage displays another lifelong characteristic: the ability to notice and criticize in others what was a characteristic of his own—in this case, the propensity to flatter.

In the spring of 1909, both Roosevelt and Stimson left office. Stimson returned to private practice and took Frankfurter with him. In a short time, however, Frankfurter was asked to return as a special assistant to Stimson's successor, in order to handle cases that had originated under Stimson's regime. But when Stimson ran for the governorship of New York in 1910, Frankfurter again left the United States Attorney's office and became a campaign aide. Frankfurter was being thrown about in his career; his ties to Stimson made it difficult for him to settle anywhere and feel at home.

Roosevelt campaigned for Stimson—a disastrous campaigner himself—and Frankfurter had many opportunities to see the ex-president. It was Frankfurter's first taste of behind-the-scenes politicking, and he loved it. Frankfurter was once summoned by Roosevelt.

I rode down Fifth Avenue with him. . . . After he asked me the questions he had on his mind pertaining to Stimson's work as United States Attorney, he then turned toward me—mind you, I was a kid of about twenty-seven then, and this was the ex-President of the United States talking, who was my hero—and he said, "Tell me, what do you hear about my speeches? Are they all right? Am I making the right kind of speeches for Harry?" [55]

Stimson lost the election. By this time the Taft-Roosevelt breach in the Republican party was widening and, seeking to soothe the nerves of Roosevelt supporters, Taft invited Stimson to become secretary of war. Stimson accepted, with Roosevelt's blessings. Frankfurter went with his mentor once again, and entered the world of Washington for the first time.

•　　•　　•

Henry Stimson influenced Frankfurter in many ways. There was, first of all, an ideological influence: Stimson, the archetypical Progressive, was idolized by Frankfurter. Although he would later, largely due to the influence of Brandeis, adopt the philosophy of the New Freedom, with its distrust of big business and abhorrence of economic concentration, at this point in his life Frankfurter embraced the Roosevelt-Stimson New Nationalism, which accepted economic concentration as healthy and inevitable.[56]

There were also influences on a deeper level. Stimson had a profound influence upon Frankfurter's self-confidence and his style of behavior; it was probably his most significant relationship at this time of his life. The Stimson-Frankfurter relationship fits precisely within the model of the mentor-mentee relationship recently offered by Daniel J. Levinson and his associates.[57]

Crucial to the psychological functioning of a young man during his twenties and thirties, Levinson finds, is the presence of a mentor, someone eight to fifteen years his senior. The younger man internalizes the value system of the mentor and depends upon his approval for an important part of his self-esteem. The younger man "feels admiration, respect, appreciation, gratitude and love for the mentor." [58] The relationship ends after it has served its purposes, and the process by which a mentee pulls away from the mentor—becoming one's own man—is an important and *necessary* psychological step. "The relationship is lovely for a time, then ends in separation arising from a quarrel, or death, or a change in circumstances." [59]

Stimson was fifteen years older than Frankfurter and a representative of the Brahmin culture toward which Frankfurter felt intensely drawn. He was a profoundly attractive figure—intelligent, sincere, respected, cultured. "I don't see how a young fellow coming to the bar," Frankfurter later said, "could possibly have had a more desirable, more deepening, and altogether more precious influence during his formative years than to be junior to Henry L. Stimson." [60]

In some interesting ways, Stimson's personality and style were quite similar to Frankfurter's, and it is a plausible hypothesis that Stimson influenced Frankfurter to adopt these modes of behavior.

Stimson was, first of all, possessive about people and, in the words of his biographer, apt to "jack them up for his own good." [61] He was, furthermore, prone to arrogance; he was convinced that once he had the necessary facts about any given situation, only one decision was possible.[62] Both were traits that Frankfurter would manifest in later years. Frankfurter himself acknowledged the influence of Stimson upon him. "I'm sure he must have had a good deal of influence on the exactions I make of my young men, what my standards are." [63] Frankfurter also attributed his attitude toward proper criminal procedure in part to Stimson.

This was an incredibly effective and wholly scrupulous man. When he went out to raid a place with a search warrant—not only wouldn't he do it without a search warrant, but he'd send youngsters like me . . . to see to it that the raiding officers kept within the limits of the search warrant. No wire-tapping was allowed during his whole regime. If you read some of my opinions with regard to criminal prosecutions, that's where it all comes from.[64]

Moreover, Stimson continued to provide Frankfurter with the recognition from the Yankee establishment that he had begun to receive at Harvard. As each year passed and Stimson introduced him to a widening circle of activities and individuals, Frankfurter's confidence continued to grow. The correspondence between the two during this early period indicates that the relationship was psychologically crucial for Frankfurter. It also reveals that Stimson was one of the first recipients of Frankfurter's flattery.* In dozens of letters to Stimson during this period, Frankfurter expresses his gratitude "for the priceless privilege of your fostering friendship." And Stimson was Frankfurter's hope for liberalism

---

* A typical example is the following:

My dear Mr. Stimson:

Others have given expression to the appreciation universally felt for your public service and professional achievement in securing the conviction of Morse. But no one can testify so appropriately as I to your disinterestedness and tender fairness, but above all, your thoughtfullness, generosity and loyalty towards your subordinates. These stand out all the brighter in the perspective now that the glow and fury of the conflict have passed away.

An experience such as has been my rare fortune during the last few months becomes a life's possession—it is at once humbling and inspiring.

Very gratefuly yours,
Felix Frankfurter [65]

in the Republican party. As they departed together for Washington in 1911, Frankfurter was playing the role of the grateful apprentice. There were no signs as yet of Frankfurter's attempt to become his own man.

. . .

At first, Frankfurter wanted to be an assistant attorney general and asked Stimson to make his case before Attorney General Wickersham.[66] The position, in Stimson's words, "petered out," [67] and Stimson urged Frankfurter to come with him to the War Department. "I think you would find it a broadening experience," Stimson wrote. "If you should accept the position I would rely on you for a good deal more than that work alone, as you doubtless realize from your past experience with me. . . ." [68]

Frankfurter took the job and immediately set off with Stimson on a tour of America's overseas possessions, a trip that included the opening of the Panama canal. They returned to Washington, and Frankfurter took up his role as all-around aide to Stimson.

He wanted me to be his special assistant on all sorts of things. There was a job, somehow or other, into which I could fit called the Law Officer of the Bureau of Insular Affairs which was technically a good job. The Bureau . . . had charge of Puerto Rico . . . the Philippines, San Domingo . . . and the like. That was the nominal shell into which I fitted, but I worked with him mostly on water power because the War Department also had charge of water power on navigable streams. Generally I was his personal assistant.[69]

At the Bureau of Insular Affairs, Frankfurter mingled with high-ranking military men. Again, he calls attention to his self-consciousness about his appearance.

I came to know the bureau chiefs and the Chief of Staff in the War Department. You must remember that I was just a kid. When Mr. Stimson brought me down I was this side of thirty, not only young in years, but not very impressive looking. I was a little fellow—you know, "What is this little civilian doing around here?" [70]

As the law officer of the bureau, Frankfurter represented the government in the insular cases that went before the Supreme

Court. "And of course, that was very exciting for a youngster. That's how I came to know the Justices." [71]

Frankfurter often helped Stimson with speeches. He consistently urged Stimson to use his public appearances "to identify the Republican Party in the public mind as the liberal party, and thereby more immediately further the interests of the Administration as the exponent of liberalism." [72] Progressive thought, Frankfurter said, "demands two active forces. (1) Absolute open-mindedness, and (2) accredited facts as a basis of action." [73] Frankfurter was thinking often about the party system and his place within it; he seems at times in his correspondence to be preoccupied with the relationship of the Republicans to liberalism, a natural enough concern as the debacle of 1912 approached.

He was also exhilarated by life in Washington. In 1911 Frankfurter began keeping a diary; his entries provide a fascinating glimpse into his self-image. The diaries, together with his correspondence from this period, show us a young man buoyed by his popularity and acceptance. They reveal someone extremely concerned with status—both his own and other people's. He was something of a social snob, and yet, at the same time, acutely aware of his own precarious position in the establishment. He meticulously observed the shifting power alliances in Washington and commented often about the nature of power and power relationships. He was still in the process of developing a coherent ideology and image of himself.

He begins to keep a diary, he says, because of the interesting people he meets. "I am fortunate enough," he writes, "to meet men of rare spirit, of vaulting vision and fine deeds. Their talk, my experience in such encounters deserve to be embalmed for I cannot as hopefully as I once assumed rely on a faithful memory." [74] He is well aware of the degree to which Washington is a city in which status translates into power. He is, he says, regarded as a "Stimson man," and thus he

enjoys the pleasantest feelings and relations with the War Department officials—other generals, service chiefs, etc. It makes me smile and at times sad, for it shows the necessity of having a status down here to have full opportunities for effective work and full utilization of the great opportunities of Washington life in the way of rare men worth while and contact with 'the inside.' [75]

To his friend Emory Buckner he writes that "the road to relish here is from contract to status. Stimson has done nicely by me for the wheels are deferentially greased—his press agency has been effective." [76] But despite Stimson's help, Frankfurter remains very much aware of the barrier between Jews and non-Jews.[77]

Frankfurter finds himself holding his own socially with men of power: "Had a delightful call with Senor Crespo, the Mexican Ambassador. . . . I found I could blarney a fact out as straight-facedly as he could—good conversational confetti." [78] And he watches carefully—and admires—the process by which Stimson exerts subtle influence upon President Taft. "President now wrestling with trust problem. Working hard on material and Stimson says 'He is coming to our way of thinking.' Stimson is nursing him along in his present determination to think over the situation. . . ." [79] This phrase—"nursing" men along—is one Frankfurter will soon be using to describe his own style of politicking.

In a crucial diary entry, Frankfurter reveals self-doubt about his intelligence: "Wickersham has a vivid, fresh, agile, prehensile mind, but 'I suspicion' pretty much *as superficial as my own* with considerable ability to mobilize effectively and quickly all his intellectual assets." [80] To his closest friends he would admit similar feelings; in a letter to Emory Buckner, he writes: "Distrust of self, like poverty, will always be with me and occasional confirmations of the soundness of my judgment . . . gives me but a momentary sense of certainty." [81] Frankfurter is not yet the completely self-assured individual he will later become.

.   .   .

In Washington Frankfurter began to develop relationships with two individuals who would be crucial for much of his life and all of his judicial career—Louis D. Brandeis and Oliver Wendell Holmes. Both of these relationships were highly significant emotionally for Frankfurter; both Holmes and Brandeis more or less

adopted him. Both represented the power and influence Frankfurter sought for himself.

While a student at Harvard, Frankfurter had attended Brandeis's lecture at the Harvard Ethical Society entitled "The Opportunity in the Law." It was almost inevitable for Frankfurter to be
attracted to Brandeis—he was the "people's attorney," he was
Jewish, he was interested in the political issues Frankfurter himself was coming to examine. They began corresponding in 1910.
In his 1911 diary, Frankfurter noted:

Lunched today with Brandeis and Denison. . . . Brandeis has depth and
. . . force; he has Lincoln's fundamental sympathies. I wish he had his
patience, his magnanimity, his humor. Brandeis is a very big man, one
of the most penetrating minds I know; I should like to see him Attorney
General of the United States.[82]

If Frankfurter at this early time was finding Brandeis a bit
austere, he delighted in the warmth of Justice Holmes. Throughout his life Frankfurter's friendship with Holmes was his most
cherished possession. It was Holmes who symbolized to Frankfurter the best of everything: the Brahmin establishment, achievement in the law, culture, learning.

Apart from my own chief, Secretary Stimson, the great friendship I
formed with a person of the older generation was Mr. Justice Holmes.
I had a note of introduction to him. . . . We soon became fast friends,
and I became a regular visitor at his house. A regular visitor at his
house meant that you sat in front of the fire when there was a fire, and
sat in his study when there wasn't a fire, and he did practically all of
the talking. He was probably the best talker—not the greatest talking
in volume, but you just didn't think of talking when he talked because
it was such a wonderful stream of exciting flow of ideas in words.[83]

Their correspondence reveals that Frankfurter heaped upon
Holmes the same type of flattery he gave to Stimson, in even
greater volume.

It is, I think, a wise habit of our Puritanism to withhold appreciation
from the living, for thus only the most purified sincerity will break
through the dam of reticence. And so I do not even apologize for
saying that from the time I first came in contact with you, as a fresh-

man in the Law School, through your Common Law, you had *for me*—
the only sure canon of truth—"the gift of imparting ferment." That
this bounty should be enriched by the passion and persuasiveness of the
living fire is a good fortune that makes my indebtedness everlastingly
alive.[84]

Holmes enjoyed Frankfurter's companionship. On one occasion
he wrote Frankfurter:

It will be many years before you have occasion to know the happiness
and encouragement that comes to an old man from the sympathy of
the young. That, perhaps more than anything else, makes one feel as if
one had not lived in vain, and counteracts the eternal gravitation toward
melancholy and doubt. I am quite sincere in saying that you have done
a great deal for me in that way and I send you my gratitude and
thanks.[85]

Theirs was a mutually satisfactory relationship that would grow
in intimacy and intensity as the years progressed.

· · ·

While he was developing relationships with men who were to
figure prominently in his life, Frankfurter was also maturing ideologically during his first years in Washington. He was becoming
mesmerized with the ideas of Herbert Croly, later his close friend
and colleague at the *New Republic*. Croly's *The Promise of
American Life*, published in 1909, was a major source of inspiration for the young Frankfurter, as it was for a generation of
young liberals. In the years before the beginning of World War I,
Frankfurter later wrote, "the rallying cry was Progressivism and
in Herbert Croly it found its philosopher." [86]

The "promise" of American life, for Croly, consisted of three
elements which, he said, needed to be maintained in balance: "an
improving popular economic condition, guaranteed by democratic
political institutions, and resulting in moral and social ameliora-
tion." [87] In Croly's description of how to achieve and maintain
these conditions can be found many of Frankfurter's fundamental
beliefs of this time: an intense patriotism, a Hamiltonian emphasis
upon the national interest, a strong admiration for Lincoln, an

emphasis upon "disinterested" expertise. As he watched Progressive forces organize for the 1912 presidential campaign, Frankfurter was yearning to cement his identification with a cause in which he fervently believed.

The 1912 split in the Republican party was a crucial event in Frankfurter's life. His political position had to this point been determined by his relationship to Stimson—by being identified, in his own words, as a "Stimson man." The Taft-Roosevelt split proved to be a severely difficult event for Stimson; as a member of the cabinet, he felt his loyalty belonged to Taft despite the fact that most of his political sympathies were with Roosevelt. Roosevelt, however, saw things differently, and bitterly denounced Stimson for his loyalty to Taft.

Frankfurter was in near-complete ideological agreement with Roosevelt; he perceived the ex-president as the best hope for Progressive leadership at the national level. Frankfurter's position as a minor official in the Taft Administration—and as a "Stimson man"—thus became, for the first time, a burden. It was difficult for Frankfurter to disagree with Stimson. The episode produced a great deal of anguish for Frankfurter, and can be interpreted as his first attempt at releasing himself from the shadow of his mentor. In an important sense, however, his attempt at release failed; although he strongly desired to leave his job and campaign for Roosevelt, Stimson and others convinced him to remain at his post.

At first Frankfurter urged Stimson to remain as neutral as possible in the Taft-Roosevelt feud. Undoubtedly sensing how difficult his own position would become if Stimson publicly identified himself with Taft, Frankfurter wrote Stimson a long letter in which he urged his chief to remain neutral.[88] Stimson, however, did not take Frankfurter's advice. As the campaign progressed, Frankfurter tentatively decided to leave the administration and join Teddy Roosevelt. He wrote Learned Hand about his tentative decision:

I hope I do not add to your regrets by the news of my not unlikely resignation in the very near future. The last six months here have been one of the big experiences of my life. Its pains are precious. Out of it all has finally come a time-verified determination not to deny my impulses to get out and do my little fighting now in the Progressive ranks.[89]

And he wrote to Stimson:

You know from evidences deeper and more communicable than words what your friendship means to me. I now wish to draw on it to save me from oversight of the slightest loyalty to duty. . . .

I find now the call for active work in the Progressive Party is too insistent, too dominant, not to be heeded if I have fairly considered all the controlling considerations. . . .[90]

But in a postscript, Frankfurter says, "Of course I shall do nothing until I hear from you."

Stimson's reply urged Frankfurter to consider his situation carefully, and clearly indicated Stimson's preference that Frankfurter remain at his job. "There is always a thrill in campaign time which is alluring to the fighting blood of any man, and particularly to the young man," Stimson wrote. "Do not be misled by the hurrah about you, into a misjudgment of the comparative good which you can accomplish in the two paths that lie open before you." [91]

Frankfurter agonized over the decision. He poured out his torment in letters to his friend Emory Buckner.

The air I breath[e] here . . . is fetid, I feel myself cramped, of dubious fitness in the current of things. I chafe that I am not where I long to be, I have the sniff of the fight and find myself—a cog in a bureaucracy. . . . I want to be out of here, even or perhaps because the third party fight is a folly—to me it's real, the odds are challenging, the regenerative power of ideas and ideals as political ammunition too strong a fancy of mine to sit remotely by.[92]

Buckner was sympathetic to the delicacy of Frankfurter's disagreement with Stimson, but chastised Frankfurter for taking himself too seriously. "Your temperament is quite on the side of loss of perspective when things heat up," Buckner chided.[93]

Frankfurter's self-consciousness and self-dramatization during this episode are important psychological evidence, suggesting that he had not yet settled upon a stable political identity. He was a "Stimson man," a member of the Taft administration; at the same

35

time he longed to cement his identification with progressivism. The fact that he even perceived a conflict between his position and his sympathies is significant; Frankfurter was longing to find his proper place in the world, and to dramatize his choice with concrete action.

Eventually, however, Frankfurter decided to remain at his job. Stimson, Brandeis, and Roosevelt himself urged him to do so. Instead of entering the campaign, he attempted to act as a conciliator between Stimson and Roosevelt.[94] When Taft lost the election, Stimson left office and Frankfurter was left politically homeless. He contemplated study abroad.[95] He was entering a period of transition that eventuated in his appointment to the Harvard faculty.

In the spring of 1913, as the Wilson administration took office, Frankfurter was asked to stay at his post under Stimson's successor, Lloyd K. Garrison. A few days after Wilson's inauguration, he wrote Buckner:

A line to tell you that for the present at least I am going to stick here. For all that I can see, Garrison is a real man, and he wants me to help on two or three questions that have become very near to me. I think I can put in a few good licks in the right direction.[96]

Elsewhere Frankfurter reported that his relations with Garrison were "very pleasant." [97] He was working on the water power questions he had handled under Stimson.

Stimson, meanwhile, had returned to private practice in New York, hoping Frankfurter would join him when his transitional work was over.[98] Frankfurter, however, resisted the idea of private practice, as he had always done. It is also probable that he was beginning to chafe a bit under Stimson's tutelage; he was anxious to find his own directions. The tone of Frankfurter's letters to Stimson during the spring of 1913, when Stimson had left Washington and Frankfurter remained, is subtly different from that of his earlier letters; he is less deferential, more assertive. Stimson solicited Frankfurter's advice on speeches, and Frankfurter offered criticisms without the usual flattery.[99] Frankfurter was becoming less pained at minor disagreements with his former chief.

Frankfurter, meanwhile, continued to enjoy the Washington social scene, and his acceptance within it. He had been living in a house that he shared with other bachelors, a place that came to be known as the House of Truth.

It soon became a center of liveliness. How or why I can't recapture, but almost everybody who was interesting in Washington sooner or later passed through the house. The magnet of the house was exciting talk. . . . It started out in the most innocent fashion, but it became a fashionable thing. We didn't make it fashionable, but people would say, "Gee, we had a wonderful time last night at the House of Truth," and so, since most people are copycats, other people would regard it as a wonderful thing to be asked to the House of Truth.[100]

Diplomats, bureaucrats, and Supreme Court justices passed through the house.

I was shaking my cocktails one night when our guest was Mr. Justice Lurton, a Southern gentleman. I had shortly before that argued one or two cases before the Court. As I was pouring out the cocktails to Mr. Justice Lurton, he said to me, "I hope you mix drinks as well as you argue cases."

Well, to be praised by a justice of the Supreme Court for a kid like me was something! Wasn't I proud and happy![101]

Another individual who passed through the House of Truth was a young woman, just graduated from Smith College. Pale and beautiful, Marion Denman held an immediate attraction for Frankfurter. She was bright, irreverent, an agnostic like Frankfurter. And she was as Yankee as Yankee could be—the daughter of a Congregational minister from Longmeadow, Massachusetts, whose family had been in America since before the American Revolution. Frankfurter began his effort to win her, a task which took six years. In his relationship with Marion Denman during these six years—and the conflict that relationship brought with his mother and his culture—Frankfurter would fight out the tormenting battle of his own identity.

.   .   .

37

Frankfurter did not feel he had a future with the Wilson administration. He did not care for Wilson personally; he thought the new president arrogant and a poor politician.[102] He did not wish to join Stimson in private practice. He was at loose ends. During the summer of 1913, however, a new option suddenly appeared.

In early June, Winfred Dennison, one of Frankfurter's closest friends and a roommate at the House of Truth, wrote to Edward H. Warren of the Harvard Law School faculty, a friend of both Dennison's and Frankfurter's. "If you see any reasonable opening in your faculty for Frankfurter," he wrote, "I wish you would let me know about it. . . . He has made a tremendous impression with the Supreme Court. The Chief Justice and two of the other Justices have spoken to me with great enthusiasm of his work and I understand their views are shared by the other members of the court." [103] Warren replied that the faculty was enthusiastic. There was no vacancy, so an endowment was required; on June 24, Dean Ezra Thayer solicited Stimson's aid.

Two days later, Frankfurter wrote Stimson that he had received an inquiry from Harvard.[104] Frankfurter, in this letter, reveals his attitude toward a career as an academic.

If you can possibly snatch a minute I want very much a line from you as to your views. Probably no one knows better than you my potentialities and my aims of usefulness. Yet you may want to know my own attitude toward this proposal. I am not a scholar, *qua* scholar. On the other hand, I do feel very deeply the need of organized scientific thinking in the modern state and, particularly, in a legalistic democracy like ours, the need of a definitely conceived jurisprudence coordinating sociology and economics. In other words, I am struck with the big public aspect of what should be done by our law schools, and the kind of thing that surely is capable of being done with Pound * at Cambridge.[105]

Most of Frankfurter's friends and acquaintances advised against accepting the offer, including Stimson, Holmes, and Learned Hand. Stimson told him that Harvard would not allow him to exercise his dominant talent, the ability to stay in the middle of things politically:

* Roscoe Pound, a leading legal "realist" and one of the founders of modern sociological jurisprudence.

You have the greatest faculty of acquaintance—for keeping in touch with the center of things, for knowing sympathetically men who are doing and thinking, of almost all men—certainly all young men that I know. I query whether that most valuable faculty would not be to a great extent lost at the law school. To me you seem a man whose place is at the center of the great liberal movement which now going on [*sic*] in national and industrial life, and you have already had unusual opportunity for making a circle of acquaintance upon which your future work will be based.[106]

Hand gave similar advice,[107] and Holmes wrote that "academic life is but half-life—it is withdrawal from the fight in order to utter smart things that cost you nothing except the thinking them from a cloister. . . ." [108]

Frankfurter, however, saw the offer as a way out of a difficult choice. He did not wish to remain in Washington, where he was afraid he would become little more than a bureaucrat.[109] He did not want to enter private practice under Stimson. And Harvard appealed to him as a new outpost in the fight for progressivism; above all, Frankfurter felt a need to be at "the center of the liberal movement."

Moreover, he did not look at Harvard as a permanent change or as an abandonment of his political career. He wrote Stimson:

I do not deem it a final choice between public and academic work—even to the extent that it is "academic." I look upon it . . . either as an end or a preparation, say, for five years, as experience will decide. And I feel I'm young enough to let experience decide. This lively item of my youth strikes me as an important factor in the equation. In itself the work *is* public work—our universities increasingly should *be* in politics—with the emphasis on sustained thinking along the very questions of public affairs that have the greatest appeal for me.

The *real* objection is the one you urge—that apparently my equipment is for participation in "the center of things." But, after all, geography may not be a dominating determinant, and if it should turn out that way, after an adequate try, would I be too much on the siding—would not New York be available *then*? [110]

Frankfurter spent the fall and winter of 1913 to 1914 marking time in Washington. He was pursuing Marion Denman, working

on water policy at his job, and generally enjoying life. He realized
that his acceptance of the Harvard offer indicated that he would
soon enter a transitional period in his life. "So much of what I
am, the spirit which I carry into work, the significance I endeavor
to find in life, are things we wrought out together," he wrote
Stimson. "You see all my non-school life has been lived with you
and the wrench has been none too easy." [111] His letters in the spring
of 1914 display buoyant self-confidence; he seems to be consolidating his identity. Within two years of his move to Harvard, however, a series of events will reassert the ambiguity in that identity.

. . .

Frankfurter left Washington in the summer of 1914, and began
preparing for his new career as a professor of law. Spending weeks
in the library going through cases that had been decided since his
graduation from law school, Frankfurter was a bit overwhelmed
and unsure of himself. It is important to note that at this point in
his career he did not think of himself as a scholar, a fact which he
often emphasized to others. To Holmes he wrote: "I'm not a clois-
tered scholar and not even Cambridge, I think, can spoil my zest of
life and my need of steering my boat through the currents of its
rigorous realities." [112] Later, to his friend Morris Cohen, he wrote:

You would have reason to be pleased with my increased enthusiasm for
doing the necessary work of hard-pan study. I have a woeful sense of
my limitations and my ignorances. Sometimes it doesn't quite seem
possible that I should have escaped knowing at least a few more things
than I do. I can't help putting some of the blame on the college as she
was.* . . .

However, I am not wasting energy in crying over what is not. I only
want you to know I am pretty actively alive to the job that is ahead
of me. For the coming year, I am up against the very practical proposi-
tion of giving three courses. I will have to pay my way, as it were, as
I go along.[113]

His attitude toward education as an abstract value was a fundamental part of Frankfurter's ideology. Human nature, he believed,

* Both Frankfurter and Cohen had attended City College in New York.

was amenable to change; change would come first through the scientific study of society and then through the rigorous education to the inexorable truth of these scientific "facts." Enough facts and enough education, and agreement about governmental goals would inevitably follow: "As I see it, there is bound to be less and less difference in *ideals* of government (as knowledge and education and a deeper realization of the social character of society will spread) and more differences as to the methods and means of achieving those ideals." [114] "Human nature" did not exist:

Any suggestion of the fixity of human nature always makes me purr. All too frequently "against human nature" is the pseudo-scientific excuse for the standpatism of a Butler.* To my mind, the fundamental assumption of civilization is the conscious ability to modify and enlarge human nature.[115]

The scientific "expert" thus became the central figure in Frankfurter's plan for government: it was the expert who would study society, accumulate facts, draw conclusions, and educate the public as to the rational necessity of those conclusions. Frankfurter's was thus a philosophy that was both elitist and democratic: elitist in its demand for expert knowledge; democratic in its faith that the public at large was educable.

Frankfurter clearly perceived the link between his philosophy and his move to a new career. He had written to Holmes the previous summer:

I have decided to go to Cambridge if they want me. . . . I would not go up there for a conventional professorship. Academics are neither my aptitude nor the line of my choice—so far as one chooses. The thing is rather different and what challenges me is to bring public life, the elements of reality, in touch with the university, and, conversely, to help harness the law school to the needs of the fight outside. You know better than the rest of us how empirical, how inadequate the foundation of our legislative output, how unthought out much of social reform legislation is. . . . It's up to the Law Schools to deal with the theories of legislation (I know it's a tough job) and in turn help shape the course.[116]

As he sat in the library stacks reading cases in the summer of 1914

---

* Pierce Butler, a conservative Justice of the Supreme Court.

and as he began his career as a teacher of future experts, Frankfurter's Progressive ideology—and his image of his own place and his own contribution to progressivism—was crystallizing.

Also crystallizing at the same time was his admiration for—one is almost tempted to say worship of—the jurisprudence of Holmes. Frankfurter's letters to Holmes are the letters of an apprentice to a master. He unceasingly praised Holmes's judicial output and the philosophy it embodied. "O!" Frankfurter wrote, "If you knew how I praise—whosoever is to be praised, if any—*your* 'magisterial summaries'—particularly these days when I have to read opinions by the wholesale." [117]

To Frankfurter, working in the law meant working out the implications of Holmes. "My dear Justice," he wrote,

I have often ventured to say to my colleagues that all the "modern" tendencies in legal writing—"sociological jurisprudence," "the functional approach" and the rest of the jargonic language—are indicated, if not expressed, in your essays of forty or so years ago. . . . Yes—much of our labor these days is bringing bricks to the building of the structures for which you long ago sketched the blue prints.[118]

"Again and again in studying a particular subject," Frankfurter wrote, "I find that, if you have dealt with it—it's been dealt with." [119]

The approval of Holmes was eagerly sought: "For you to call my work 'really A1' is to be knighted by the King! I'd rather have your 'well done' than anyone else's in all this wide world." [120] Holmes is, Frankfurther tells him, the intellectual head of the Supreme Court; [121] he is the giant of Frankfurter's legal universe:

You know, of course, the great stimulus you are to many of us in our work—for me, none greater. But you are also a source of despair. What can we creeping worms do, and what good is it—when you toss off (I know it isn't quite tossed off) on opinion that illumines so much so brilliantly in a few pages.[122]

What is particularly remarkable about Frankfurter's letters to Holmes is that these compliments are not occasional, but constant. Repeatedly, Frankfurter praises Holmes, thanks Holmes, rejoices in his friendship with Holmes. And Holmes responds and encourages Frankfurter; the justice delights in the flattery and intellectual companionship of the young professor.*

Frankfurter enjoyed teaching. Although at first somewhat lonely in Cambridge after the bright social life of Washington, Frankfurter quickly felt at home at the Law School. His energetic and dynamic personality was well suited to establishing rapport with his classes. "I'm having a happy time of it here," he wrote Stimson. "These youngsters are an inspirational lot." [124] He quickly began attracting the best students in the school. Although he always maintained publicly that he neither sought nor condoned disciples, he did both with great regularity. Indeed, he admitted as much in his private correspondence, where he often spoke of "my boys" or "a pet student of mine." He had relatively little patience for the mediocre student, preferring to concentrate his energies on those of his "young men" who showed the greatest promise as future "experts." As Josephson perceptively commented in 1940:

Frankfurter's attitude toward his students was paternal. In addition to trying to inspire them, he all but adopted his favorite pupils. . . . He became absorbed in their private lives and their ambitions. . . . Having a warm, bubbling, aggressive personality, he tended unconsciously to dominate many of his pupils. At the same time, he enjoyed the companionship of students who fought with him in class.[125]

Frankfurter in these early years enjoyed his relationship with Roscoe Pound. He saw his place in the development of the law as a lieutenant in Pound's army. It was the task of Pound's sociological jurisprudence, Frankfurter thought, to develop systematic principles out of the raw materials of the case system. Frankfurter's friend Morris Cohen had criticized the case system for its failure to produce systematic juristic thought. Frankfurter defended the case system "which has given to us the great storehouse of historical data, now availed of by men like Wigmore, Pound, and others, in gradually stimulating philosophic thinking in the profession and the evolution of a philosophic jurisprudence." [126] Frankfurter's ad-

---

* For example, Holmes wrote on one occasion:

All that I can say in reply is to send you my affectionate thanks—my rather fearful hope that I may never fall from the place you have given me—and my expectation that always while I live, as now, I shall have great cause to be proud of having counted for something in your life. I only wish that as various themes come up I could talk them over with you.[123]

miration for Pound was so intense at this time that Emory Buckner warned him against staying too much in Pound's shadow. "[You] should be very chary in [your] references to Pound," Buckner wrote. "You ought not to give an impression that you are merely his understudy. . . . Strive to erect yourself into an individual state as rapidly as possible." [127] Pound and Frankfurter were close allies in faculty politics during this period. Although they would later become bitter enemies, at this time the relationship was highly satisfactory to both of them.

Along with his developing relationship with Pound, Frankfurter's acquaintance with Brandeis deepened into friendship. In 1913 Brandeis had written of Frankfurter, "He . . . is so intelligent that I consider him a power for the right." [128] Brandeis drew Frankfurter into Zionist affairs; [129] by the time of the controversy over Brandeis's nomination to the Supreme Court, they were intimate. Frankfurter was one of Brandeis's closest allies in the nomination fight.

Brandeis was the last in Frankfurter's trio of elder mentors. In many ways, however, Frankfurter acted as more of an equal to Brandeis than to either Stimson or Holmes. Their friendship began in earnest later than Frankfurter's association with Stimson or Holmes, at a time when Frankfurter had assumed his position at Harvard and was in the process of removing himself from Stimson's shadow. Their work together on Progressive and Zionist matters made their relationship more comradely than Frankfurter's earlier work with Stimson or his friendship with Holmes. And, of course, they were both Jews; Frankfurter was not receiving from Brandeis the recognition of the Brahmin establishment, but the recognition of one of his own.

Still, the Frankfurter-Brandeis relationship was not one of complete equals; Brandeis was very much an authority figure in Frankfurter's life. In 1916 Brandeis began sending Frankfurter money to cover his "expenses in public matters undertaken at my request or following up my suggestion," [130] an unusual arrangement that lasted for a number of years. Their relationship was extremely close. Brandeis wrote to Frankfurter's mother in 1916: "Your son has won so large a place in our hearts and brought so much of joy and interest in our lives that we feel very near to you who are nearest to him." [131] And Frankfurter heaped upon Brandeis the flattery and praise he was using more and more upon people whose support meant a great deal to him. After Brandeis's Court confirmation, Frankfurter wrote:

And now that it is dear Justice Brandeis—"O, the difference to me"! Effort finds new zest, and hope new validity, all one's powers a deeper source of strength. Of course from the citizen's ranks to office has for you been only a change in forum of public service. . . . Both as to the end and as to the means of life you have been a steady, convincing guide. Building not on miracles, except the miracles of intelligent, disinterested effort, the ground you have sown is bound to fructify, as you go on to sow seeds of large, free-spirited living in the quiet great field on which you are to labor.[132]

. . .

During these first three years at Harvard, Frankfurter made good his intention to remain active in liberal enterprises outside the Law School. He was a trustee of the *New Republic* and a close advisor to its staff in its early years of publication; he also wrote numerous pieces for the magazine. He became intimately involved with Florence Kelley's National Consumer's League. He maintained a voluminous correspondence with lawyers and government officials, and at the same time was constantly commuting to New York and Washington, sometimes two or three times in a single week.

The *New Republic* nicely fit Frankfurter's Progressive faith in education; the magazine was to be a means of educating the elite who would then educate the mass public. Urging Stimson to write an article, Frankfurter wrote:

It takes extraordinary occasions to drive truths home to the public. What seems to me particularly important is to inform thinking people, those who in varying degrees exercise intellectual leadership in the country. Without being smug about it, I suppose one can say that a goodly percentage of those who read the New Republic are people who think and whose thoughts have influence beyond themselves.[133]

Frankfurter and Herbert Croly, the guiding light of the magazine, were very close at this time. In his reminiscences, Frankfurter said of Croly: "I suppose I was as close to him as anybody. We became more and more intimate and he, I think, found more and more comfort in my responses, perhaps because I was more expressive than others, and conveyed my feeling, my warmth of feeling, more articulately."[134]

Frankfurter's involvement with the National Consumer's League gave him an opportunity to argue several landmark cases before the Supreme Court. He took over from Brandeis, after Brandeis's appointment to the Court, the reargument of the Oregon labor cases.* Frankfurter had performed an extraordinary feat of behind-the-scenes maneuvering to get these cases put down for oral argument; the incident was the first instance of what would soon become the central tactic of his political and personal style. Although he was counsel for the cases, the attorney of record was the Attorney General of Oregon, who had agreed with the opposing side to submit written briefs without oral argument. Frankfurter was convinced that the cases required oral argument and decided to call on Chief Justice White, an altogether extraordinary move.

He was a massive man, a charming gentleman and a devout Catholic. . . . As he said, "My son, what brings you here?" the happy thought struck me to say, "Mr. Chief Justice, I am not at all sure that I have a right to be here. I am not at all clear that I should put to you the matter that I'm about to put to you, but I come to you as though in the confessional." Well, that was a master stroke. I felt at once as though the whole church were enfolding me.[137]

Frankfurter persuaded the Chief Justice that the Court should deny the motion for leave to submit briefs without oral argument. "I always regard that as my single most successful professional achievement. That's what is called *ex parte* practice."[138]

Frankfurter's oral argument was impressive. Arguing the ten-hour case, he engaged in a heated exchange with Mr. Justice McReynolds, the most conservative member of the Court.

During the course of the argument McReynolds said to me, "Ten hours! Ten hours! Ten! Why not four?" . . . in his snarling sneering

* These cases provided one of the first and most important tests of Progressive labor legislation before the New Deal. Oregon had passed a statute providing maximum hours for men, which the Court upheld;[135] it also passed a minimum-wage statute for women, on which the Court divided four-to-four.[136]

way. I paused, synthetically, self-consciously, dramatically, just said nothing. Then I moved down towards him and said, "Your Honor, if by chance I may make such a hypothesis, if your physician should find that you're eating too much meat, it isn't necessary for him to urge you to become a vegetarian." Holmes said, "Good for you!" very embarrassingly right from the bench.[139]

During these early years at Harvard Frankfurter came close to consolidating his identity. He had removed himself from Stimson's shadow and was taking on roles of his own choosing—professor of law, Progressive reformer. He was entering new and rewarding relationships—with Brandeis, with Pound, with his students. He was still pursuing his romance with Marion Denman. He was active, he was happy. And he had received recognition from and found a place within the single institution that represented most strongly for him the American establishment—the Harvard Law School. "I no more thought of myself," he later recalled, "as a member of the Harvard Law School faculty than I would have felt myself a member of the House of Lords—in fact, more easily, probably, considering the people who are in the House of Lords." [140]

In 1916, however, a series of events shattered Frankfurter's fragile, all-but-consolidated sense of self. The death of his father, tensions with his mother, and the beginning of serious problems with Marion ushered in a period of difficulty and strain. The ambiguity in Frankfurter's identity reasserted itself, and he struggled to create himself anew. He would emerge three years later triumphant; but in the process of reasserting and reassembling himself Frankfurter developed some aspects of his personality that had serious consequences for his character structure and future behavior.

.   .   .

The spring of 1916—Frankfurter was 33 [141]—was the turning point. Two events served to destroy Frankfurter's almost complete sense of well-being: the death of his father and the controversy surrounding the Brandeis appointment to the Supreme Court.

The loss of his father was the most traumatic event Frankfurter had yet experienced. He remembered his father as representing "joy"; Frankfurter was now left to deal with his mother, the representative of "duty." Frankfurter wrote to Stimson:

Pneumonia in its ravage carried my father off leaving all the wrench and void that the first intimate grief brings one. It wasn't only the wrench of habitual affections—divergent as our details of life were cast Father and I were in fundamental interests and temperament. [*Sic*] You will know the rest. There is nothing but time and work and the sense of the greater need of mother.[142]

Throughout his correspondence in 1916 and 1917, one can feel Frankfurter's pain of loss. Writing Marion, he recalls his father's love of the joyous Passover holiday. "All that is gone—irrevocably," he tells her. "The kind of critter that I am, there are much less than a handful to whom I'll speak of my loneliness, to say that on the eve of the feast [Passover] it is with me deeply." [143] Many years later, when comforting Harold Laski on the death of his father, Frankfurter remarked, "I know what happens when that parental tie is severed—the face of the world is never the same." [144]

At precisely the time of his father's death, Frankfurter was engaged in the controversy over Brandeis's nomination to the Supreme Court. In the letter to Stimson quoted above, Frankfurter says of the furor over the appointment, "the bitterness and passion round here is unbelievable." The controversy surrounding the appointment could not help but raise important moral and personal issues for Frankfurter. He wrote Stimson, who had expressed hesitation about Brandeis, a blunt letter.

I'm rather saddened to think that you . . . should have reservations about Brandeis because I feel sure if you had time to study the case you would not entertain them. I have had time to think clearly about it and I have studied it all much and hard. The upshot is a deep conviction of cruel wrong to Brandeis, above all to the court and country in depriving them of his services. Of course I feel, ordinarily under restraint in talking about Brandeis because it's so easy to attribute my views to racial particularity. But I need have no such hesitation with you. I'm sure you know I can discriminate, and do decide not on such easy lines of bias, that, in fact, I feel even more strongly against Jewish self-seekers . . . than their Gentile analogues. I feel deeply about the Brandeis matter because it raises deep moral issues.[145]

Along with his concern over the Brandeis affair, Frankfurter's concern for his mother moves clearly into his correspondence as the spring of 1916 progresses. He was, he later said, his mother's "especial hope and comfort" at this time.[146] At the close of the school year he goes home to visit her; references to her in his letters increase. Frankfurter's knowledge that his mother would almost certainly disapprove of his relationship with Marion Denman became, at this time, a fundamental source of strain in his life. This strain affected his relationship with Marion; during the summer of 1916, tension builds between them. Marion tells him that her "confidence is gone"; he is, she tells him, "as remote as the Alps." [147]

Frankfurter had always been sensitive to the issue of romantic relationships between Jews and non-Jews, as he once explained to Holmes about a Jewish woman married to a Gentile: "You know how deeply rooted the feeling against intermarriage is in us Jews —she has felt herself isolated from some of her old associations, the old traditions grip her with a new tenacity. . . ." [148]

The evidence indicates that Frankfurter did not reveal his deep feelings for Marion to his mother until February 1917, a year after his father's death.[149] At that point, his mother's opposition helped to precipitate a break in their relationship. It seems clear that in the spring and summer of 1916, before informing his mother, Frankfurter is forced to deal not with her explicit disapproval but with what he assumes her reaction will be. It may be that he delayed telling her about the relationship because he did not wish to upset her so soon after the shock of his father's death. What is clear, however, is that Frankfurter's concern for his mother's feelings about the matter increased dramatically during this period.

These two simultaneous events—one public, one private—the furor over the Brandeis appointment and the difficulties connected with his relationship with Marion—served to unsettle Frankfurter and to shake his self-confidence. He was confronted with the fact that he was not a complete insider; that the Yankee establishment could work itself into a frenzy over the appointment of a Jew to an important post; that a romantic relationship between an immigrant Jew and the daughter of a Congregational minister was not typical, not likely to be easily accepted by either side. Frankfurter, who had so recently moved in fashionable Washington circles and had been appointed to the Harvard faculty, was jarred back to the very real ambiguity and fragility of his status and position. His religion and his culture—"his father and his face"—which he had come to regard as little more than accidents, suddenly loomed once again as powerful forces in his life.

There were, moreover, difficulties in his relationship with Marion that had nothing to do with their relative social positions but rather with the clash of their personalities. Marion was a fragile person, tense, often ill or tired, delicate, high-strung. During this period she was unsure of herself, searching for a career and a place in the world, and she began to chafe under Frankfurter's dominant, aggressive personality. Their correspondence reveals a prolonged psychological tug-of-war that often breaks into explicit accusations. On one occasion, Marion wrote:

Because of what you are, and have been, You, and yet not you but the whole experience of you, has a tremendous bearing on my directions. You threaten the securities of a person whose securities are only in the making, and will never be better than slow and [illegible] and painful. I must establish and maintain myself not only against my own nature, but against that experience, which is itself more destructive than [illegible]. I must make my own life after my own pattern, even if it is less than it would be if I let myself follow you.[150]

Frankfurter attempted, as best he could, to calm Marion and to provide her with a source of strength. What he failed to realize was that by attempting to provide direction to her life he only intensified her lack of self-assurance. He wrote:

It's very difficult indeed to meet your "hopes and fears" because in the very nature of things, my perception of them (were I even less insensitive than I am) are at least different, if not less, than yours. But the difficulty is the best of all reasons for not running away from the difficulty, the best of reasons for trying to meet you as best I can. . . . I am resolutely determined—and if humans have any power of conscious direction we must not fail in this—not to be other than health of life for you, by affirmation or by abstention. Less than that would impair my sense of the rightness of things. . . . My friendship must be capable of being that much good. . . . It must come out right.[151]

Like his conviction that the proper study of enough "facts" would produce inevitable conclusions about societal goals, Frankfurter was convinced that good motives and diligent care would inevitably produce happy human relationships. But the tension between Felix and Marion continued, even after their marriage.

· · ·

In the fall of 1916, the presidential election brought Frankfurter another conflict with Stimson. Frankfurter, after much soul searching, decided to vote for Woodrow Wilson, while Stimson supported Charles Evans Hughes. "I'm afraid I am disappointing you severely in my decision to vote for Wilson," Frankfurter wrote in late October. "I'm sorry—but Hughes' whole campaign leaves me no alternative." [152] Frankfurter was so intent on justifying his decision that he prepared a sixteen-page memorandum on his reasons for supporting Wilson, in which he called Stimson "the strongest personal attachment to the aspirations of the Republican Party," and said that "to part with him involves the strongest emotional wrench in the whole process of decision." [153]

In his memorandum Frankfurter for the first time identifies the Republican party as the party of big business. "The wealth and culture of the country undoubtedly until recently has been Republican. . . . But the last ten years have brought an increasing unsettling in American parties." His support of Wilson can be taken as the symbol of his movement away from the Roosevelt-Stimson wing of progressivism toward the Brandeisian condemnation of economic concentration. The Democratic party is now his hope for the future: "One may reasonably hope . . . that the Democratic party will absorb the national ferment that will come from a frank facing of the labor problems, from a frank avowal of the essential rightness of the labor union movement." In his correspondence with Stimson, Frankfurter once again assumes that reasonable men cannot disagree about goals, but only about means to their goals; and thus the disagreement between them "is not, after all, as to the analysis of the issues, or the nature of the problems, or the general line of development we must take, but a difference in choice as to which is the most promising immediate instrumentality to accomplish our desires." [154]

In the spring of 1917, a year after his father's death, Frankfurter was called to Washington by Secretary of War Newton Baker. When he had left Washington in 1914, it was with the idea of trying the academic life for five years or so. He had never given up the idea of a public career, never fully taken on the identity of a scholar. Now, in 1917, as he re-entered the public world, Frankfurter once again grappled with the question of his career; he seriously considered not returning to Cambridge.

By his own admission, Frankfurter was now entering the most trying season of his life. He will later describe this period as a time when he "carried anxiety locked and secreted with a wasteful helplessness." [155] In both his public and private lives he was faced with fundamental uncertainty and ambiguity. He was troubled about his relationship with Marion and his mother's attitude toward that relationship, uncertain about his career and his place in the world. He had cut himself off not only from the tutelage of Henry Stimson but also from his protection. He did not know where he belonged—Washington, Cambridge, New York. He was once again in search of a firm identity.

But this time, unlike the period of his earlier public career in New York and Washington, the search for an identity was more desperate, more difficult, more intense. Frankfurter was in his mid-thirties, not his twenties, and time seemed to be running out; moreover, the fact that his life seemed to lack an inner core of coherence and certainty contrasted sharply with the sense of well-being he had enjoyed so recently. He is a man searching for control, for mastery, for an end to ambiguity. He eventually finds it; he creates a new identity, a new self. It is a self that is more strident, more consciously sure of itself, more outwardly confident, more aggressive and dominating, and, in some important ways, more neurotic.

．　．　．

"When the war broke out for us in 1917," Frankfurter later recalled, "I had a wire from Secretary Newton D. Baker asking me to come down for the weekend, if I could. I packed my suitcase, and the weekend didn't terminate until the fall of 1919." [156]

One of Frankfurter's first assignments took him to Europe on the bizarre Morgenthau mission. The purpose of the mission was to attempt to detach Turkey from the central powers; the public announcement, however, said the purpose of the mission was to "ameliorate the condition of the Jewish communities in Palestine." [157]

Before sailing for Turkey, in June of 1917, there was a serious break between Frankfurter and Marion, culminating the year of difficulty that had begun with the death of Frankfurter's father. It is evident from his letters that a chief cause of the break-up was Frankfurter's perception that he had to choose between Marion and his mother. Aboard ship, he writes Marion:

Yes—I aspired to share life with you, as Fate should permit sharing. And yet you were right. "Friendship" was to remain the seeming symbol for us. . . . Why did it remain the symbol? I suppose it resolved itself into a choice between you and mother. I hope you will not view it as such. To understand you will remember all that clusters around the traditions of thousands of years. Mother loved the only sight she had of you—she wanted that picture of you in the house. But alas! you in yourself were also a symbol—the symbol of differences in "race" and "faith" and all the other separating institutions born of the past. The thing goes deep, down to the very source of life, if it goes as it goes in those elders. I could not destroy what was left of zest and strength in her—most was expected of me, and there you are. For your understanding I know I've said more than was necessary. For your swiftness of mind and heart a hint suffices to reveal depths. Well—thus it was not to have been, but I think of the glory that was.[158]

But in the months following this break, in a series of new positions and successful activities culminating at the Paris Peace Conference, Frankfurter rebuilds his confidence to the point where he can, finally, throw off the burden of his doubt and propose marriage.

The first step in this process of rebuilding his self-esteem was Frankfurter's trip to Turkey. Frankfurter had not wanted to go; President Wilson, however, insisted. In all probability the State Department felt that the presence of a Jewish professor would give credence to the announced public function of the trip.

Frankfurter did not care for Henry Morgenthau. He found the former ambassador to Turkey pompous, foolish, and arrogant. "By the time we got aboard [ship] I knew more about Turkey than Morgenthau had acquired in all his years there because my knowledge was critical and analytical, and his was just general, hot-air impressions."[159] Frankfurter found that dealing with the egotistical Morgenthau "was a great lesson of the insinuating influence of flattery and massaging the ego. After the ego begins to be massaged and it feels good, then you're perfectly reconciled to having it massaged and gradually you have to have it massaged."[160] Frankfurter is learning to flatter—and he will continue to flatter the men around him for the rest of his life.

The trip, moreover, was an exercise in behind-the-scenes power: not only was the entire mission a secret operation, but Frankfurter perceived his own role as a behind-the-scenes manipulator of Morgenthau, the figurehead.

After a while I realized that the real purpose in having me go with Morgenthau, the thought behind the insistence on sending me, was that they thought that I could control him. I had a nurse's function, to prevent the wilful, but imperious, child from being any more foolish than could possibly be avoided.[161]

This trip abroad was Frankfurter's first real contact with European aristocracy; he carried with him letters of introduction to various people from his friend Eustace Percy, an assistant to the British foreign secretary. He was beginning to enjoy mingling with the European social elite, as he would long continue to do. He felt a renewed sense of self-confidence and discovered new talents and abilities. A few months later he wrote his close friend Walter Lippmann:

I gather some little satisfaction out of the soundness of my observations and deductions in my trip abroad. It isn't a personal satisfaction but just an encouragement of the correctness of my judgment, for I did feel that I was talking about things that I knew very little about, except most everybody else knew even less.[162]

Frankfurter returned to the War Department in the late summer. In the fall, however, he assumed a new position, as secretary and counsel to the President's Mediation Commission. Wilson had established the commission to control the growing number of strikes in industries crucial to the war effort, most of them in the West. In the fall of 1917, Frankfurter traveled around the country on business for the commission. The trips and his success at work fed his growing confidence. He was beginning to come out of his period of turmoil; he was beginning to think of himself as a skillful administrator who knew how to get things done.

Frankfurter traveled to Arizona, southern California, San Francisco, Chicago. In each labor dispute he and the commission were more or less successful in bringing about a settlement. Often Frankfurter was able to rely upon his ties in the legal world to achieve results. In a mining dispute in Arizona, he discovered that the absentee owners of the mine were British; he sent a cable to Eustace Percy and got results. Sometimes he relied upon Harvard ties with the attorneys representing the industries.[163]

Two incidents investigated by the commission were especially crucial to Frankfurter: the deportation of strikers from Bisbee, Arizona, and the trial of Tom Mooney. Both fed Frankfurter's growing concern for proper legal procedure; both helped to paint a false public picture of Frankfurter as a radical. And both forced him to do public battle against loud and powerful opponents, a process crucial to his developing sense of self.

The Bisbee case involved vigilante action against the I.W.W. A thousand union miners in Arizona were rounded up, shipped by train to New Mexico, and left in a desert town without food or water. The vigilantes were led by Jack Greenway, a former rough rider, who appealed to Teddy Roosevelt when his actions were criticized by Frankfurter's commission.

Frankfurter's indignation at the incident was tremendous. In recalling the case, he remembered that his friend and assistant, Max Lowenthal, had become ill after the Bisbee investigation. "This made a great impression on me," Frankfurter recalled, "because that was a just verdict on, a just response to, the cruelty, ruthlessness and callousness that was involved in what was done in

Bisbee. . . ." [164] The incident was, for Frankfurter, a clear contest between "reason" and "passion."

> This was done by otherwise perfectly nice, decent people. Jack Greenway was a very nice man. I knew his widow. . . . He was doubtless a good man in all relations of life in which passion didn't supplant his fairness and reason, and it left a deep impression on me as to what cruelty means and how cruel conduct affects those who are immediately the victims of it.[165]

The Mooney case was even more dramatic; in Frankfurter's words, "the dramatically most enduring episode of the task that was committed to the . . . Commission." [166] Mooney, a labor organizer, had been sentenced to death for planting a bomb that killed several people in San Francisco in the summer of 1916. The mediation commission was persuaded that he had been convicted on the basis of perjured testimony. In its report—written by Frankfurter—the commission urged President Wilson to intercede with the governor of California and obtain a new trial. The case aroused a great deal of publicity and public pressure, and the governor, bowing to public sentiment, merely commuted Mooney's sentence to life imprisonment. He remained in jail until 1939.

The Mooney case was perhaps the most crucial incident in Frankfurter's public life before the New Deal. The publicity aroused turned him into a public defender of unpopular causes, a role he enjoyed and continued to play for many years to come. Moreover, the case created a public controversy between Frankfurter and his hero, Teddy Roosevelt.*

Roosevelt's reaction to the Mooney case as well as to the Bisbee deportations was illiberal and unthinking; he began making statements decrying "Bolshevik influences" in the labor movement. Frankfurter was at first horrified by Roosevelt's statements, and assumed that "the Colonel," as he called Roosevelt, was being misled.[167]

Roosevelt, however, continued to make statements critical of

---

* Although many commentators identify the Sacco-Vanzetti case as the most crucial event in Frankfurter's life before the thirties, I interpret it as an experience *confirming* many parts of Frankfurter's already completed identity. See chapter 3. The Mooney case, on the other hand, was a *transforming* event, in which a part of Frankfurter's identity was created. Thus, I have interpreted the Mooney case as a signally important event.

Frankfurter's commission, and Frankfurter was reluctantly forced to admit that he was not simply being misled. They engaged in a correspondence that became public. A letter from Roosevelt to Frankfurter was published in the *Boston Herald* that accused Frankfurter of "taking, on behalf of the Administration an attitude which seems to be fundamentally that of Trotsky and the other Bolsheviki leaders in Russia; an attitude which may be fraught with mischief to this country." [168]

A month later, Frankfurter responded with a long letter to Roosevelt. Of the Mooney case, Frankfurter wrote: "I think if you knew all the facts, I think if you inquired of those who see fairly, and without blind passion, in San Francisco you would find that I pursued the inquiry in a thorough-going, judicial, and if I may say so, sensible way. . . ."

And about the situation in Bisbee, Frankfurter wrote the ex-president:

I submit it is not fair to your own standards of impartial justice, to your characteristic of being open-minded to facts, for you, some three thousand miles away from the scene of action, away from an intimate study of the facts—the circumstances, the personnel, the industrial conflict. . . . I say it is not fair for you to pass judgment upon the deportations just on Jack Greenway's say-so, to brush aside the conclusions of a trained and impartial investigator whose desire and ability to obtain the truth, you have heretofore had many occasions never to find wanting.[169]

Frankfurter gained a reputation for radicalism in these cases that he never quite shook off. It was a completely undeserved label; Frankfurter was in both cases concerned with due process of law rather than the specific merits of the I.W.W. or Tom Mooney's politics.

But the incidents were highly significant for a number of reasons other than their effect on Frankfurter's reputation. They provided him with concrete evidence for his conviction that "reason" and "passion" were contradictory values, and gave him support for his assumption that "reason" would always lead to fairness; they fed Frankfurter's conviction that fair procedure was the essence of justice; and, most importantly, they presented him with his first opportunity to publicly defend a righteous cause against powerful opposition. In these cases we see the birth of the Felix Frankfurter who would, in the years to come, take an unpopular stand for tolerance at Harvard and defend Sacco and Vanzetti.

These cases thus nurtured Frankfurter's growing self-confidence and provided him with new elements for his identity—here was Frankfurter the defender of the downtrodden, Frankfurter the fearless fighter against misinformed opinion and "passion." He was convinced that he was right, and willing to take a public stand on the basis of that conviction. " 'The Education of Mr. Felix' is certainly what my historian will call this year," Frankfurter wrote Walter Lippmann in October 1917.[170] A year later, Frankfurter would remember his western trips as a crucial time of triumph over difficulty and pain. To Marion he wrote revealingly about this period:

Those three months went deeper in my "public" life, and my private, than probably any other three months. I lived more reflectively, more inwardly. . . . No wonder those three brooding months left their traces, no wonder you found me different in January. I suspect I was deeper, truer. I was fair to all the forces—you cannot know, but of course you do, through what layers I was breaking. . . .[171]

In January he returned to Washington, and, as this letter indicates, his relationship with Marion began to improve dramatically. He carried on his battle with Theodore Roosevelt. In March, he was sent abroad by Colonel House, President Wilson's closest advisor, on a special mission to investigate labor conditions in the Allied nations.

In May of 1918, Frankfurter's intertwined public and private successes leapt forward; he was made the chairman of the newly created War Labor Policies Board in the Labor Department; his proposal of marriage was accepted by Marion. By the late spring and summer of 1918, Frankfurter's confidence was solidifying and his energies becoming almost boundless.

His correspondence with Marion during this period of success is remarkably candid. He was happy and felt secure in both his work and his private life; the old doubts about his place in the world had been buried under fast accumulating successes. The effect of these work-related successes had brought his self-esteem to the point where he could ignore the problem of religion and propose to Marion. "I awoke as one set free, who has burst through fetters of cobwebs," he wrote her on the day she accepted his proposal.[172] A few months after the proposal he wrote her:

It took me years to get over . . . the strong feeling that the substratum of my nature was too sad for you, that I had no right to ask your radiance and spirit of life to take the risks of me. I'm over that restraint, as I've come over other deep restraints. . . .[173]

He realized that he had broken through barriers, and he was exhilarated by this triumph. "It would not be wholly surprising if I *did* attain manhood the last four months," he wrote to Marion in August. Significantly, he said this after writing that he felt his mother would be able to accept his marriage.[174]

His happiness and energy spilled over into his work, just as his success at his work fed his personal self-confidence. His new position in the Labor Department gave him a higher status and more authority than he had in the War Department.[175] He was, he happily proclaimed to Marion, becoming a new man:

Here I am—trying to build up a new organization and putting sixes and sevens together. . . . I'm becoming a new man—early rising, sharp, short interviews, accessible to men social callers, giving orders and seeing to their enforcement. . . . I'm changing the habits and temperaments of a lifetime, turning the confetti of conversation into commands and social talents into drastic administrative competence. And there is zest and strength and a peace to me. . . .[176]

He wrote that he was enjoying "the miracle of intensified effort"; he reveled in "the inevitable rightness of things." He saw the intermarriage issue as a problem that could be rationally handled.[177]

In August, Frankfurter wrote Marion of the likelihood of his mother's adjustment to their relationship:

I must have seemed filled with joy over my visit with mother. Well—I am. I do not want to exaggerate, to minimize the tenacity of terrific traditional barriers, but I *am* ever so much more cheerful, than, somehow, I had dared to be. I know her, and I know you (both would protest my "knowledge") and so I know how you will hit her. And while it is a grim job still, the accommadation that will have to be made I now know will, because of you, be much more attainable. There are big forces clashing—and the bigger ones, the overcoming ones are with you. Mother has a talent for endurance much sharpened by experience. . . . I am so cheered today—and therefore pounce over to you—because I feel her powers of adjustment will be greater than I had thought. . . .[178]

Despite Frankfurter's happiness, undercurrents of doubt about the relationship persisted in Marion's mind. Repeatedly, Frankfurter sent her reassuring letters. "That was a somber letter," he wrote, "it seemed written far away and in doubtful days. . . . If another could gauge one's feelings, if you knew what such glimpses of your own griefs, your sense of my inadequacy, do to me—well you might believe that I'm learning some things. . . ." [179] When Frankfurter described the past, it was with sadness; whenever he spoke of the future, he stressed its unlimited possibilities, and how much he required a "sense of freedom":

Since almost boyhood I knew not what I *would* to be but the kind of things I would to do. It therefore became irrelevant whether I was a "professor" or a practitioner, an ambassador or a man without a title. I had a ferment within me, certain discontents—pain and guilt on the whole—With much that was and that so obviously should be otherwise. I had a curious and questioning and alive mind and it would play. The clue to doing the kind of things I wanted and want to do was—and is—freedom.[180]

Frankfurter was now satisfied that he had solved the problems of his past and confident about his abilities to handle the future.

·　·　·

In his new government position, Frankfurter was faced with sustained and tough opposition; his response was to equate opposition to stupidity or self-seeking, and to seek vindication over his opponents. It was the response to opponents he would give for the rest of his life.

His first opponent was a man named Walsh, who opposed his policies on the eight-hour day. He wrote Marion that "the incongruities of the world have a new chapter when Walsh seeks to undermine me as the enemy of—the eight hour day!" In the same letter, Frankfurter said, "all my past work (almost) seems like child's play compared to this for heretofore there was little of opposition on the part of selfish or suspicious men and now there is much." [181] Elsewhere, Frankfurter described doing a "nifty job" with Walsh. He wrote:

The winter will be plenty tough for us both. . . . For my job is becoming more and more engrossing, the difficulties of opposition are revealing more and more intensely (I'm pained, at times, in my constant surprise at ignorance and pettiness and self-seeking) the problems will be even acuter should peace come. The upshot is that I must keep myself, at all times, fit as a race horse. . . .[182]

Throughout the fall of 1918, Frankfurter cheerfully reported his triumphs to Marion; his delight in vanquishing those who oppose him is evident throughout. Another of Frankfurter's opponents at this time was Judge Gary of United States Steel, one of the most powerful men in American industry. Frankfurter had decided that the steel industry was the key to achieving the eight-hour day; after Gary ignored several of his letters, Frankfurter threatened to make the dispute public. Gary responded, offering to meet with Frankfurter in his hotel suite in New York; Frankfurter insisted on Washington. Frankfurter's office was small, so he had all of the furniture cleared out for Gary's party. In his reminiscences Frankfurter said:

Well, that was quite an experience, a striking illustration of arrogance, the sense that they are really more important than government, and, of course, the importance of standing your ground . . . he had to be put in his place.[183]

Frankfurter described himself to Marion as being "keyed up" over his "masterly performance" with Gary. It was a "very masterly stunt—really and truly masterly and therefore artistic." [184] Frankfurter won his battle; Gary announced that the Steel Corporation would adopt the eight-hour day. It was, Frankfurter told Marion, "a really big achievement."

The Frankfurter that is emerging from this period of success is becoming self-righteous. He bristles at opposition; he demands that the rest of the world live up to his expectations and standards. He is becoming sure of himself to the point of arrogance. He comes to regard himself as a symbol of righteousness fighting against stupidity and prejudice. He enjoys battling against enemies. He feels he is in command—of himself, of events, of the people around him.

What Frankfurter had created for himself in these years in Washington was, in the language of Karen Horney, an *idealized* self-image. Although an idealized self-image is based upon characteristics rooted in reality, it is "idealized" because it greatly exaggerates skills and virtues and ignores deficiencies; it thus can function psychologically to solve the pressing problems of creating and maintaining an identity that is, at its base, shaky and ambiguous. From the near total dejection and uncertainty of the previous period of his life—the period of his father's death and his difficulties with his mother and with Marion—Frankfurter had gone to a period he perceived as being a complete success. He had discovered new talents and made them the essence of his self-image; he had buried his doubts and fears under a compulsive search for success and triumph. The achievement of his ends and the imposition of his goals upon others had become important to his sense of well-being; opponents had to be "put in their place." The key to his success was his perception of his ability to handle men—in his own words, "personalia."

. . .

The Paris Peace Conference was the culmination of this period of Frankfurter's life. Here, all the elements of his self-image were reinforced and brought together into a coherent whole.

Paris was a vastly exciting and stimulating experience for Frankfurter; he was acting on a larger stage than he had ever occupied before. Sent as a representative of the American Zionist organization headed by Brandeis, hoping to work out the terms of the mandate for a Jewish state in Palestine, Frankfurter felt himself to be a pivotal figure. Soon after arriving in Paris he wrote Marion:

I've surveyed the situation and know what lies ahead of us—and the work that falls to me to do. The propoganda stage is over and intensive detail is the need—it was needed long ago, unfortunately there was no one here either with the understanding or the will to organize, or rather both. But I'm taking hold, the recalcitrant elements . . . are yielding and we ought to be well under way before long. It's a bit strange that circumstances are forcing me to be an organizer—I who am supposed to be so unsystematic. . . .

In a word it's the old story of carrying into effect "principles" and that means work, work, by technically equipped people.

That's the difficulty of the position of the U.S.—lack of adequate, liberal-minded experts.[185]

Frankfurter thought of himself as an organizer, as one who smoothed over differences, as a conduit of information and influence. Above all, he was a handler of men:

Weizmann is no easy man to handle. I've done my "nursing" of men in my day and of all kinds of temperments—Stimson and Morganthau and Pound and Wilson, but Weizmann is the most difficult. He is a burning temperment. I'm very fond of him, have a deep affection. And that creates the toughest part of the job . . . he's an irresistable cuss— he can be irresistable but he must be resisted constantly. . . . I systematically hold him off, create barriers to the coercion of his affection. And I know I must be on the alert against him. . . .

L.D.B. [Brandeis] is equally hard to resist, has equally to be guarded against. . . . Weizmann reflects by himself and then tells you "it is decided" and that's where my job comes in—to undecide him, to prevent him from deciding and doing a thousand and one reckless things. I have to "interpret" him all the time. He is an Arab steed—ardent, fiery, and I must ride him. We are a good pair and I handle him (at least no one else can). How? You see he is deeply fond of me.

And that's only part of the job—Weizmann—there are lots of others to manage.[186]

Frankfurter considered himself—and was considered by others— an expert on several matters, particularly those related to labor: "I wasn't here 48 hours when the technical advisor of the British section of the Labor Commission came to me with his troubles. . . ."[187]

At the request of the State Department, Frankfurter took part in the drafting of the charter of the International Labor Organization. He thought of himself as a detached, disinterested, scientific expert; he felt he had much to contribute. And in his voluminous correspondence with Marion, he repeatedly returned to his role as a mediator between men, and the "ceaseless necessity of guiding the clash of personalities." [188] "What a lot of prima donnas I have to keep in time," he lamented.[189]

Frankfurter's sense of self-importance grew. In a letter to President Wilson pleading for American approval of the Balfour Declaration for Palestine, he said:

You will forgive me for writing, but circumstances have made me the trustee of a situation that affects the hopes and the very life of a whole people. Therefore I can not forebear to say that not a little of the peace of the world depends upon the disposal, before your return to America, of the destiny of [Palestine].[190]

Frankfurter found it pleasant to be needed, to have important people depend on him; he wrote Marion of "this touching reliance of people." [191]

Frankfurter had the time of his life in Paris. More than once, he wrote Marion that he had caught glimpses of himself in the mirror and that, much to his surprise, he found himself attractive. His old uneasiness about his physical appearance was gone. He put his sparkling charm to work on everyone with whom he came in contact. Many of his friends were there—Walter Lippmann, Eustace Percy, "all sorts of Harvard people." "I never felt better in my life," he told Marion. He was recognized for his charm and wit, for his intelligence and expertise. He was secure in his relationship with Marion, whom he would marry upon his return to the United States. He felt that he was a new, powerful, important man. By acquiring this image of himself, he had buried all of his old doubts and fears about who he really was under an avalanche of success.

CHAPTER 3

1919–1929: The Decade of Triumph

FRANKFURTER had emerged from his period of turmoil when he returned to Cambridge in the fall of 1919. He had finally consolidated his identity; he had created out of the materials of his experience a self-image and a style. During the next twenty years, until his appointment to the Supreme Court in 1939, he would repeatedly apply that successful style; he would perceive himself as dominating every personal and professional situation in which he found himself. The next two chapters will explore his behavior during these two decades of accumulating success.

The self-image Frankfurter had created for himself during his early years in Washington and Cambridge was a product of psychological necessity; it grew out of an intense need for self-confidence and certainty. The result was an exaggerated self-image, resting upon an arrogant self-importance. In the decades to come, before his appointment to the Court, this self-image would be constantly reinforced by its successful application to different situations. Frankfurter's well-being would thus come to depend to a greater and greater extent upon this self-image and its success.

On his return from Paris, the outlines of this self-image and style were clearly visible. Frankfurter thought of himself as a disinterested expert, as an educator of men and public opinion, as a fighter against passion, stupidity, and intolerance, as a defender of the wronged, and as an expert at "personalia." He was sure of his abilities to the point of regarding himself as a symbol of reason and fairness.

Above all, Frankfurter's consolidation of his self-image had depended upon ever-increasing success and upon receiving recognition for his success. He felt, in every circumstance, that he was right and capable of achieving his goals, that he could take command of a situation, that he could overcome opposition. His ability to defeat opponents was, in fact, crucial to his psychological functioning. Only by constantly "winning" could Frankfurter prove to himself that he measured up to his own self-image. The only point of ambiguity in this self-image—at least consciously—concerned his relationship to the establishment: Frankfurter continually hovered between considering himself an insider and an outsider.

His political style, which he had applied with great success in Washington and Paris, included the generous application of flattery (as with Henry Morgenthau), behind-the-scenes maneuvering (as with Chief Justice White and with his Harvard contacts during his western trips), and a willingness to do forthright battle against "the enemy" (as in the Labor Department). During the twenties and thirties, Frankfurter would apply this style to a series of situations—to his relationships at Harvard, to public events, to the New Deal. Each time, it would work.

.   .   .

Frankfurter had not been sure he would return to Cambridge from his wartime service, and seriously considered joining the faculty of the just-established New School for Social Research in New York. Herbert Croly, by now a close friend, was urging him to make the change. "I have wrestled with the angels and it has not been easy," Frankfurter wrote Croly. "You have been the hardest factor in the situation, for by this time you must know the tenacity of the personal tie between us and the great pull that is exercised over my judgment by your view of the problems that are the deepest common concern, and my reaction to them." [1]

Frankfurter, however, eventually decided against the New School offer. One reason for his decision was that he thought of his role at Harvard as symbolic; his appointment symbolized, he later wrote, "recognition by the School of the part to be played by law schools and the law in the solution of pressing public problems." [2] Moreover, he did not like the fact that there were risks involved with a new university; such risks, he felt, would deny him the "sense of freedom" he required to work. At the same time, he told Croly, "there are very strong affirmative reasons for taking me back to Cambridge." He listed three such reasons:

1. The opportunity of influencing year by year the dominant minds in the legal profession in a country which necessarily to such a large degree is governed by the legal profession.

2. The [Law] School is the best place for a lawyer's influence.

3. I could not help feeling that I would be deserting Pound at a crucial period in a struggle which is part and parcel of a liberal movement. . . . I should have only six hours of teaching with the expectation of being very active in public affairs in my field of interest.[3]

As this letter hints, Frankfurter at this time was beginning to pay attention to faculty politics at Harvard. While Frankfurter was away in Washington and Paris, trouble had been brewing in Cambridge over his alleged "radicalism." When the trouble surfaced, Frankfurter was positively delighted at the thought of plunging into a good fight. Roscoe Pound was his ally, A. Lawrence Lowell, the president of the university, was his enemy, and liberalism and tolerance were his standards. From Paris, he wrote Marion a phenomenal letter in which he divulged that he saw the trouble to come at Harvard as "great fun":

I'm more excited today than I've been for an age! "And if you ask the reason why"—it's Pound's letter. . . . It's great fun ahead—and all because of that Mooney report, a tame legal document that no self-respecting lawyer could have failed to write. But of course, that's not all! Back of it . . . the lines are being drawn between those who are scared stiff less the world with which they are familiar (and in which, on the whole, they find themselves very comfortable) is going to be touched by these "foreign ideas" and those who want changes other than violence—sooner or later. . . .

And so—you'd find me out of bounds today. The poor things, Lowell and the Corporation* have got me on their backs now. Never in Kingdom come would I get by them now if I were up for a new appointment. . . . I don't know how people feel who get an unexpected fortune from an unknown ancestor—but I know they never felt as happy as this letter of Pound makes me feel. It's a real fight—and a fight that matters. . . . I'm so bucked up and eager for the fray ahead. . . .[4]

"Gee but I feel happy!" Frankfurter wrote Marion a bit later. "Think not only of having something to fight for, but something to fight against. It's just sheer joy. . . ."[5] In his reminiscences Frankfurter later said:

I was the spearhead in the [Bisbee Report], and then the Mooney report, and these were deemed to be manifestations that the Bolshevik Revolution was coming to America. Here was this professor of law at the Harvard Law School on behalf of the government of the United States lending himself to a sympathetic attitude towards these dangerous people! That's what stirred up the animals![6]

In the early twenties, Frankfurter was clearly in a fighting mood, and loving every minute of the fight. At Harvard, in his outside activities, in politics generally, he took on the role of the militant crusader. He vocally defended his own actions as well as the actions of others. He tangled with old friends; he demanded that they live up to his own high ideals. He trounced enemies.

Perhaps his most prominent enemy was Harvard's president. Early in 1922, Frankfurter and Lowell, in the first of many skirmishes in a long war, disagreed over the question of faculty teaching time. Lowell wrote to Judge Julian Mack, a member of the Harvard Board of Overseers and a close friend of Frankfurter, that "a professor ought not to undertake work, even of a desirable public character, which has an unfortunate effect upon the School, either by diminishing the energy which he puts into his teaching or by tending to bring undo criticism upon the School. . . . I have sometimes felt that Professor Frankfurter was doing more outside work than was wholly wise."[7]

* The Harvard Corporation—comprised of the president and fellows of Harvard College—is the governing body with ultimate authority in matters concerning faculty appointments.

Lowell, a descendent of two of the most prominent of Boston's first families, was the archetypical Brahmin. More than anyone else, he represented to Frankfurter the snobbery of the Boston aristocracy—an aristocracy to which Frankfurter knew he could never really belong. Lowell was in fact an anti-Semite; he had opposed Brandeis's nomination to the Supreme Court in 1916, and in the spring of 1922 attempted to impose a quota on the number of Jewish students at Harvard. Frankfurter and Judge Mack found the idea of the quota abhorrent; Mack attempted to have Frankfurter appointed to the Committee on Admissions to oppose Lowell. Lowell sent Mack a curt note in which he said that "I do not myself feel—and I find that the vast majority of the people with whom I have spoken do not feel—that Professor Frankfurter has the quality of solid judgement that would make him a good member of the committee." [8] Frankfurter responded to Lowell:

I am told that you regard my views on a policy limiting the proportion of Jewish students at Harvard as "violent" and "extreme." I cannot believe that you have so expressed yourself. For we have never discussed this subject; and, of course, I assume that you do not depend on second-hand reports for your knowledge of a man's attitude on such a complicated issue.[9]

Frankfurter was not appointed to the Committee; Lowell was not successful in achieving the imposition of a quota.[10] But despite the fact that no formal quota was established, a policy was adopted lowering admissions standards for students "outside of the East and North," which had the same effect. Thus, although Lowell was rebuffed publicly, the admissions policy was changed to accomplish his purpose.[11] The animosity between Frankfurter and Lowell, so well captured in this incident, would surface repeatedly during the decade in a series of escalating battles.

. . .

The year following the controversy over the admissions quota brought an intense battle at Harvard over the behavior of one of

Frankfurter's liberal allies on the faculty, Zechariah Chafec. Chafee had written an article on the *Abrams* case, a wartime sedition case,* which, some people claimed, contained factual errors. Chafee, Frankfurter, and some of their colleagues in the Law School had signed a petition asking the president to commute the sentences of the defendants in the case. "That was our great offense," Frankfurter later said indignantly, "that we thought these people shouldn't be getting these heavy sentences which Holmes in his dissenting opinion so strongly condemned, though he couldn't do anything about it." [12]

The Harvard Board of Overseers appointed a committee to look into the conduct of Chafee and his colleagues. At the meeting of the committee, Lowell defended the members of the faculty, but, as Frankfurter was always careful to point out, not because he agreed with them but because he had always felt that the overseers had no right to meddle in faculty affairs. For Frankfurter, it was a matter of principle; for Lowell, it was a question of bureaucratic prerogative.

Frankfurter was Chafee's most ardent champion,[13] and the Chafee "trial" was a memorable occasion for him.

Chafee gave a calm, detailed, factual account of the Abrams case, stated the grounds why he thought the result was unfair. . . . When Chafee got through he said very quietly what I always thought was one of the most impressive sentences I ever heard in my life. He said, "I come of a family that have been in America from the beginning of time. My people have been business people for generations. My people have been people of substance. They have made money. My family is a family that has money. I believe in property and I believe in making money, but I want my crowd to fight fair."

Then he sat down, and I tell you that really was a wonderful avowal of faith.[14]

Soon after the Chafee incident, Frankfurter turned to another cause; he began a defense effort for Alexander Meiklejohn, the president of Amherst College, who had been dismissed, many people claimed, because of his outspoken liberalism. He first

---

* The Court divided seven to two, Holmes and Brandeis dissenting. Holmes, in a famous dissent, strengthened his concept of "clear-and-present-danger." See chapter 5, p. 133.

wrote Meiklejohn a sympathetic letter [15] and then urged the *New Republic* to devote a great deal of attention to the controversy. In a letter addressed to "My dear New Republicans," Frankfurter said that the journal's failure to devote sufficient space to Meiklejohn's cause was "the most disheartening attitude during all my knowledge of the Paper's affairs. . . ." [16]

－　·　·　·

The defense of liberal academic colleagues was only one of Frankfurter's causes during the early twenties. He had decided to return to Cambridge in part because Pound promised him free time; he used that free time for a large number of activities.

He was involved with national labor negotiations, including the 1920 strike of the Amalgamated Clothing Workers in Rochester, New York.* Sidney Hillman, whom Frankfurter had known from the Labor Department, asked him to take charge of the union's defense. Frankfurter spent several weeks in Rochester. He brought with him Leo Wolman, later an economist for the union. He regarded his use of an economist as an important step for the American labor movement as a whole: "I believe that was the beginning of unions' realizing that union efforts aren't merely parading with placards and such like, but unionism, both as a force and a quality, depended on intelligent direction." [17]

Frankfurter continued his association with the National Consumer's League; in 1923 he argued the *Adkins* case before the Supreme Court.† He also advised the NAACP and the ACLU. Roger Baldwin, the founder of the ACLU, has said that Frankfurter was "our constant advisor and critic, from whom we re-

---

* The Union had been enjoined from picketing and charged with being illegally organized.

† *Adkins* v. *Children's Hospital,* a 1923 case in which Congress had passed a minimum wage law for women in the District of Columbia. The law was upheld in the lower court but overturned by the District of Columbia Court of Appeals. Since the 1917 minimum wage decision (see p. 46), four of the justices had been replaced: White by Taft; Day by Butler; Clark by Sutherland; Pitney by Sanford. The 1923 Court voted five to three against the law in *Adkins* (Brandeis not participating). Frankfurter had assembled a lengthy factual brief for his argument. The *Adkins* argument took a great deal of Frankfurter's time in the spring of 1923. To Emory Buckner he wrote: "I have been driven lately (as a result of Minimum Wage Cases, briefs and arguments at Washington, etc., etc.) hence my silence."

ceived endless useful suggestions for lawyers, law points and tactics." [18] He kept up his ties with lawyers in New York and Washington, often supplying recent Harvard Law School graduates for his friends' law offices. He was constantly busy, constantly moving. "I live mostly on trains," he wrote Morris Cohen.

He was often highly and publicly critical of men in power; he signed a report critical of the Department of Justice and Attorney General Palmer. He was well aware that this public criticism of the government, as well as his other activities, had an effect upon his public image.

I do not speak by the book, but my recollection is that that [the report on the Justice Department] had a good press. Nevertheless there it was, another matter to worry the timid and conventional-minded—Bisbee, Mooney, Hillman and the Amalgamated, and now worrying about being a little rough with people who were a menace to this country. [19]

Frankfurter recognized the delicacy of his position; as a Jewish professor at Harvard, his outspoken liberalism was an easy target. One incident demonstrates his recognition—and relish—of this public image. Asked to chair a meeting in Boston concerning the recognition of the Russian government by the United States, Frankfurter at first refused.

I did not want to preside. I told the Committee who were arranging the meeting—they were all old Americans, Shurtletts, Codmans, Brooks, etc.—I told the committee they should get some leader with a good Back Bay name, that in the present ferment they should avoid having a Jew of alien origin preside at a meeting concerned with Russia. [20]

No one else would preside, however, and Frankfurter reluctantly accepted. He was careful not to appear too radical.

I wasn't born yesterday. I'd acquired a good deal of experience by this time, and I very carefully prepared my chairman's speech simply by stringing together quotations from Asquith, Smuts, Lord Milner, Bob Cecil—you know, people like that, three hundred percent kosher, and that was my speech. [21]

Frankfurter during this period continued to be active in Zionist affairs. Although he devoted a great deal of energy to his Zionist activities, he did not wish to take on any formal or full-time association with the organization. To Brandeis he wrote of his never-ending need for "a sense of freedom" and his desire not to become dependent upon any single organization. "The feeling, perhaps even more than the fact, of independence is my most sensitive spot," Frankfurter wrote, "and I just would be a deadened and ineffective paid employee of the organization. My value would be killed—and no matter what form my salary would take." [22] During the summer of 1920 Frankfurter traveled with Brandeis and other Zionist leaders to London to try to heal the widening gap between Zionist factions. The convention of the Zionist movement in the spring of 1921 was the climax of a breach between Brandeis and Weizmann that had been developing for some time.[23] Frankfurter, the American closest to Weizmann, saw the disagreement and at first tried to paper it over.[24] At the convention, Frankfurter was a floor leader of the Brandeis forces and gave a rousing four-hour speech to the delegates. Despite his efforts, the Weizmann forces won and took over the organization. Brandeis and Frankfurter resigned from the movement.[25]

. . .

Frankfurter was often forced to defend his many militant actions, both publicly and privately. The most dramatic case of public defense involved charges made against him by James M. Beck, the Solicitor General, about the Mooney case. In a letter to the *New Republic*—Frankfurter's home ground—Beck criticized Frankfurter for questioning the judgment of the California authorities and the jury in the case.[26] The staff of the *New Republic* asked Frankfurter to answer the letter, and Frankfurter, for the first time, publicly defended the Mooney report. Frankfurter's reply was long, detailed, and cutting. "So experienced a lawyer as Mr. Beck," Frankfurter wrote, "will I am sure readily assent to the importance of defining the issues of the discussion instead of squirting ink at large, like a cuttle-fish." [27] Frankfurter effectively demolished Beck's arguments. It is clear that in his reply Frankfurter was answering not only Beck but all those members of the establishment who had been critical of the Mooney report.

73

The facts of the case, Frankfurter reiterated again and again, spoke for themselves. "I am convinced," Frankfurter wrote, "that any fair-minded reader who carefully compares the 'facts' as set out by Mr. Beck with the full record, is bound to reach the inevitable conclusion, however reluctantly, that the document to which the name of the Solicitor General is signed, is an incredible combination of confusion, suppression, mutilation, and fabrication."[28] The publication of his reply was a public triumph for Frankfurter; he received many letters of congratulation.[29]

Privately, Frankfurter was forced to defend himself to Henry Stimson. In March of 1921, Stimson, in their most serious disagreement to date, accused Frankfurter of not paying adequate attention to his reputation and the reputation of the Harvard Law School. A friend of Stimson's, a professor at Yale, had shown him some "Bolshevist propaganda" he had received in the mail with Frankfurter's name on it. Stimson wrote his former protégé a stinging rebuke:

I defended you, as I have several times had occasion to do the past year or two. . . . I do not think that any good American should be circulating this stuff in America indiscriminately among people whom he does not know. . . . I should like to know how your name comes to be used in such manner. . . .

I think you should pay a little more attention to being on your guard not against evil but of the appearance of it. . . . I think that actions that you have taken have, to a certain extent, damaged your own power among your fellow-citizens, and have, to a certain extent, hurt the school. I think that in future you should be more cautious. . . .[30]

Frankfurter's reply was lengthy; his tone was that of a martyr to the cause of free inquiry and free expression.

I know absolutely nothing about the transmission of the Russian Press Review to the Yale Professor. . . . But surely, Mr. Stimson, you must get a good deal of "literature" of causes with which you are wholly out of sympathy. Surely it is an astonishing suggestion that the receivers of propaganda thereby even presumptively associates himself with its support.

He defended his record at Harvard:

As to the quality of my class-room work you have in your own office enough men who passed through my classes to bear witness. . . . I leave it to them to say whether the temper of my mind in class and out of class is strictly scientific, whether I seek painstakingly to convey the exact state of the law, to interpret even decisions and views with which I disagree in a fair and scientific attitude, and to be critical only in the spirit of truth-seeking which is the established tradition of Thayer and Gray and Ames. Further I must be judged by my legal writings, by my briefs, and by my arguments in court,—all of them in cases of a public nature without a retainer, using the courts as a laboratory for my ideas as a teacher. This is the material on which, I submit, I am to be judged. This is the material—and I say it in all humility—upon which I am ready to be judged.

Frankfurter defended his right to engage in activities outside the law school; he listed his recent ones.

Tell me if in all these instances I "Have not been solicitous of the good name of the great school" which I represent. I know that for the passing moment these were not popular causes, but I also know that law is something deeper than passing popular passion. And if a professor at the Harvard Law School should refuse to associate himself with causes that seek the vindication of the law, simply because for the moment such vindication runs counter to popular opinion, how much respect would you really have for the character of such a teacher? [31]

What is most striking about Frankfurter's political stance in the early twenties, so well represented by this reply to Stimson, is his militancy. During his earlier period of teaching at Harvard, before the war, he had been cautious and concerned not to damage his reputation in any way; now, Frankfurter was proud to be a marked man. These were the years of his crusading liberalism. He saw himself as a symbol and exponent of reason, as a courageous fighter against the hysteria of the times. This was his image of himself; his militancy and the frenetic pace of his activity were a function, at least in part, of his need to constantly prove to himself the validity of his self-image.

Frankfurter knew that he was a symbol of the outsider to many in the establishment, that he was, as he called himself, "a Jew of alien origin." He continued during this period to be sensitive to the place of Jews in the legal world. To his friend Emory Buckner, whose law firm was filling up with Frankfurter protégés, he wrote of a particularly promising student: "I assume that you have all the Jews that the traffic can bear but you're letting a rare thing go by in Birnbaum." [32] He was defensive about his religion; to Stimson he wrote of his Zionist activities: "I am deeply interested in Zionism which I suppose I am entitled to be interested in, and to give as much time to as though I were a prominant Mason, or an important lay member of a church." [33] Frankfurter knew that he was different. He was not, during the twenties, trying so much to be an insider, as he was before the war. Instead, he was the critic, the person who reminded the insiders of what they really stood for, the Jew who understood the Yankee values of "reasonableness" and "fairness" better than the Yankees themselves.

. . .

1924 was a watershed year for Frankfurter's politics. The presidential election, in which he supported the third-party candidacy of Robert LaFollette, together with his involvement in Justice Department investigations, occupied his public activities for much of the year. The behavior of the American bar became one of his central concerns. Two men in particular represented to Frankfurter the faults of the bar: John W. Davis, the Democratic presidential candidate, and Harlan Fiske Stone, the attorney general and soon-to-be-appointed Supreme Court justice. Frankfurter became almost obsessed with the behavior of these two men—as he would later become obsessed with the behavior of some of his judicial colleagues.

Frankfurter had voted for Wilson in 1916 and for Cox and Roosevelt in 1920, but by 1924 was dissatisfied with the Democratic party. He was, in fact, dissatisfied with the entire tenor of public life.

"Prosperity" was in the saddle. People were more or less prosperous, and there was fantastic money-making on the exchange through gambling in securities. . . . This was brought home to me in very concrete ways; namely, through the bright students, the best men intellectually speaking, the top men at the Harvard Law School. They were sons of ministers, farmers, mechanics and small shopkeepers, and the whole drive, the whole propulsion, or compulsion almost, for their future were the attractions of New York. . . .

The bar was indifferent. They were too busy themselves shoring up rickety structures, being in on cuts.[34]

Frankfurter despised Davis. In Frankfurter's eyes, Davis was being falsely hailed as a liberal; he especially disapproved of Davis's Wall Street connections. The firm of which Davis was a partner represented J. P. Morgan, and—unlike Frankfurter himself—Davis had not spoken out against the illiberalism of the day. Frankfurter attended the Democratic convention in New York that nominated Davis on the 103rd ballot; after the nomination he wrote Marion: "This nomination ought to accelerate a clarification of American politics by furthering a realignment. . . . We now have something to fight for and build for: here is the great chance and necessity for a permanent realignment and a new party." [35]

Throughout his correspondence, Frankfurter stresses the choice Davis made upon returning from Great Britain in 1921,* a choice Frankfurter thought dishonorable: "He was urged by close advisors to go into practice in New York by himself, because it was certain as anything can be that as an advocate he would command all the practice he wanted. He refused. He preferred to accept what is said to be a minimum guarantee of $100,000 per year as a member of the Stetson firm." [36]

In addition to his dislike of Davis, there were positive factors drawing Frankfurter to the third-party movement. In a piece for the *New Republic* entitled "Why I Shall Vote for LaFollette," Frankfurter wrote that "neither of the two parties . . . faces the issues," the most important of which was "great inequality of property." [37] And Frankfurter admired LaFollette personally. "I'm reading LaFollette's autobiography," he wrote Marion. "There is an integrated, incorruptible personality. . . ." [38] Frankfurter wanted to become active in the campaign, but did not have the time.[39] Although he did not expect LaFollette to win, he did not feel he was throwing his vote away: "If you think of an election not merely as a discrete, isolated episode, but as part of

---

* Davis had been the American Ambassador to the Court of St. James.

a process of the unfolding of American life, then you don't throw your vote away." [40]

Together with the presidential election, Frankfurter's other preoccupation in 1924 was with the Department of Justice and the behavior of the attorney general, Harlan Fiske Stone. Stone had been appointed to succeed Harry M. Daugherty, Harding's attorney general, who had resigned in disgrace after the threat of a Senate investigation headed by Burton K. Wheeler of Montana. Wheeler, a Progressive, was LaFollette's vice-presidential running mate. Daugherty, before leaving office, took revenge on Wheeler by having him indicted for dubious business dealings which allegedly took place after he had been elected to the Senate.

Stone thus inherited the messy Wheeler case. Despite great pressure to drop the case, he appointed Assistant Attorney General William J. Donovan to study the case; Donovan's report convinced Stone to allow the case to go to a federal grand jury. [41]

A good deal of the pressure on Stone to drop the case came from Frankfurter. Frankfurter was a member of the Wheeler Defense Committee, which also included among its members William Allen White, H. L. Mencken, Harold Ickes, Sidney Hillman, Herbert Croly, and Norman Thomas. [42] In lengthy correspondence with Stone, Frankfurter combined flattery and gentle persuasion to make Stone change his mind. Stone stood firm; Frankfurter grew more persistent. [43]

Privately, Frankfurter was furious with Stone. His correspondence with his friends is full of comments highly critical of Stone's behavior and his entire career. Stone's nomination to the Supreme Court was pending, and Frankfurter felt Stone's ambition for the Court was determining his behavior in the Wheeler case. "The plain fact is that Stone is . . . now playing the game like the rest of them," Frankfurter wrote Judge Mack, "strongly motivated, at least unconsciously, by his desire to get on the Supreme Court." [44] Frankfurter was highly critical of Stone's delegation of authority to others; he felt Stone had not done enough to clean the Daugherty men out of the Justice Department. Writing to Walter Lippmann, Frankfurter praises one of his articles in the *New York World* with which he agrees. In this letter, Frankfurter predicts that Stone will become a conservative on the Supreme Court—a supreme irony in the face of the eventual reputations of both Stone and Frankfurter himself.

Today's piece reveals, if I may [say] so, an appreciation of what is at stake—the ineptitude of Stone . . . that Stone has had since April within which to go to the bottom of that case *himself*, that the Daugherty forces are largely still ruling in the Department. . . . The details are managed by others and he seems to be acting largely on the say-so of others, whose say-so is, to say the least, doubtful. . . .

As a Senator, I should vote for Stone's confirmation—but with my eyes open as to what we are getting. The one thing we can be sure of is that apparently he will NOT be a great judge! No one who knows his writings and his mind on matters affecting constitutional law (the essence of the S[upreme] C[ourt]'s business) can have any doubt about that. Several of my colleagues here know him intimately and like him. Not one think he has any approach to "greatness." And being a man of obstinate self-righteousness his Washington experience will harden him and in ten years he will be one of the most conservative Justices of the Court.[45]

Frankfurter, with Roscoe Pound, prepared a nine-page memorandum for Lippmann after the *World* suggested the need for limitations on Congressional powers during investigations. The memo praised highly the accomplishments of the Senate investigators, which "are beyond question." As for the "alleged abuses" of the Congressional investigating power, they quickly dismissed their significance. Frankfurter and Pound wrote that

It must be remembered that our rules of evidence are but tools for ascertaining the truth, and that these tools vary with the nature of the issues and the nature of the tribunal seeking facts. Specifically, the system of rules of evidence used in trials before juries . . . [is] not applicable to inquiries by Congressional committees. Of course the essential decencies must be observed, namely the opportunity for cross examination to those who are investigated or those representing issues under investigation. . . .

They concluded that

There is no substantial basis for criticism of the investigations conducted by Senator Walsh and Senator Wheeler. Whatever inconveniences may have resulted are inseparable incidents of an essential exertion of Governmental power, and to talk about these incidents is to deflect attention from the essential to the irrelevant.[46]

When it suited his purposes, Frankfurter willingly abandoned his commitment to squeaky-clean legal procedures.

Frankfurter sent copies of his correspondence with Stone to his closest friends—Brandeis, Buckner, Judge Mack, Learned Hand. He grew testy when Buckner disagreed with him: "I am greatly disappointed by your comments on the A.G.-F.F. correspondence— as I have been, of course, by the whole attitude of the 'leaders of the Bar' towards the course of the Washington investigations. . . . The plain English is that Stone is ducking responsibility." [47]

In another letter to Buckner, Frankfurter revealed what he considered the wider significance of the Wheeler case:

What bothers me about the attitude of lawyers like yourself is how little you seem to care about these Washington disclosures, and how casually you have taken it all. . . . Not one lawyer of importance spoke out during all those years that the Daugherty administration was widely suspected in private, not one lawyer of importance spoke out after the dogged persistence of Wheeler forced the issue. . . . The public talk by men like Hughes,* to his everlasting disgrace, has been solely disingenuous stuff. . . .

You will be right to infer that I feel very deeply about this whole business because, for me, it was the acid test of our profession and the full weight of the profession was thrown against those who sought to clean the temple and kick out the money changers.

Frankfurter concluded with another attack on Stone:

Consider one other fact, which I do not want you to quote, that in private conversation Stone said that the size of the fee which Wheeler's firm was to get, to wit, ten thousand dollars for handling some nineteen cases in the courts and attending to the office work that was involved in addition, was suspiciously large—this from a man who resigned the deanship of Columbia Law School to go to Sullivan and Cromwell at a guaranteed income of one hundred thousand dollars! [48]

* Charles Evans Hughes, Republican presidential candidate in 1916, associate justice of the Supreme Court (1910–1916), and, eventually, chief justice (1930– 1941). By the time of his own appointment to the Court, Frankfurter's assessment of Hughes would change dramatically.

In 1924, Frankfurter was in a frenzied fury at the bar. He deplored the bar's complacence and the materialistic orientation of most lawyers. He was furious at John W. Davis and at Stone because they did not live up to his conception of the proper behavior of a lawyer. He was preoccupied with the idea that a lawyer faces a personal choice—he can either sell himself to the highest bidder, as Davis and Stone did, or he can shun money-making and devote himself to good causes, as he himself did. Identifying opposites—men like Davis and Stone—helped Frankfurter justify his own choice to himself. "As I wrote Stone," Frankfurter told Buckner, "Wheeler means nothing to me. . . . But the courageous and disinterested administration of the law means, outside of my personal life, pretty much everything to me." [49] On a trip to New York during which he saw many lawyers, Frankfurter wrote Marion, "how true it is of these 'trained minds' . . . that their stocks determine their views." [50]

As Frankfurter watched men like Davis and Stone receive high office and honor—Davis as the nominee of the Democratic Party, Stone as a member of the Supreme Court—he refined and reinforced his sense of his own worth. He clung to the value of the choices he made—the choice to shun Wall Street, to devote himself to educating lawyers, to speak out on public issues. The behavior of others who made different choices was used by Frankfurter to reinforce his own self-image; men like Davis and Stone became negative reference points. To serve that function, they had to be perceived in the worst possible light. [51]

·   ·   ·

For Frankfurter, 1924 was a year of personal difficulty as well as a year of intense political involvements. Marion had been showing signs of emotional strain for some time; it was the beginning of a long and difficult period for her. For much of her life she would suffer from nervous and emotional tension; her psychological difficulties were particularly acute during the twenties.

There had been tensions between Marion and Frankfurter during their courtship which foreshadowed their later difficulties. Frankfurter recognized that Marion was frail and began taking charge of her activities. He dominated her; she resisted. Soon after their marriage in the fall of 1919, the strain of their pull-and-tug took its toll. In September 1921, Frankfurter wrote Stimson that "all our summer plans had to change, for the early summer heat and a year's fatigue brought on a case of nervous exhaustion in Marion, so we spent the summer on Cape Cod. . . ." [52] A year later, Frankfurter wrote Stimson, "Marion is fast coming out of the woods—tho these subtle 'nervous' difficulties are stubborn mysteries." [53]

Marion did not, however, quickly come out of the woods; in 1923 she had a serious breakdown. She began seeing T. W. Salmon, a well-known psychiatrist in New York.* Marion was exhilarated by her therapy.

I spent from 4 o'clock till eight in Dr. Salmon's office this afternoon. . . . I'm worn and also too exhilarated to be able to talk about the experience. . . . Exhilarated not because I think he will be successful in "solving" the problem because I don't know as to that and I have no optimism ready for the occasion—but because I do believe he has been successful in finding out why there is a problem and it has been perfectly staggering to see him do it. . . .[54]

Marion continued seeing Dr. Salmon during 1924; he recommended travel for her. In January, she vacationed in Florida; in the summer of 1924, while Frankfurter was preoccupied with the Democratic convention, she traveled to California to visit her family. In late fall, 1924, she felt she was done with her therapy, and wrote Frankfurter one of many revealing letters.

My bottom impression was that Dr. Salmon considered me "done"— at least he gave me the very definite feeling that I'd gone too far for him to be able to "help" me—and as on fundamental things we entirely agreed as to what was what. . . .

He gave me no advice beyond such things as plenty of exercise outdoors, a full program, new people, an occasional trip away from home, etc. He also advised me, with a great deal of humor, to fight somebody or something, exercise my pugnacious spirit, but when I told him the third party was my outlet he said it was a poor one—

* Because Marion would periodically travel to New York for treatment while Frankfurter remained in Cambridge, the course of her illness is quite well documented in her letters.

danger of becoming a martyr which was the very worst thing in the world for the inferior feeling.[55]

By the spring of 1925, however, Marion's difficulties surfaced once again; she was institutionalized for rest and treatment. "So you just settle back and stop worrying about me," she wrote Frankfurter, "just knowing that I'm in the best hands in the world and that a hard time is turning into a better time." [56] During her hospitalization, which lasted several months, Marion stopped referring to "my" problem and began referring to "our" problem.

You understand I know why I am apparently so unresponsive. Partly I have to learn to be less given over to emotion that isn't practical and pragmatic—But I appreciate what a triumph it is for you to discipline yourself to being calm and matter-of-fact for my sake. . . . That it's our problem instead of mine alone brings us only closer together.[57]

When she was about to leave the hospital, she considered a trip abroad, but decided against it: "I thought in view of the fact that so much of our problem was still unsolved, in practice, it would be risky to go so far away from help." [58] Marion continued to see Dr. Salmon periodically until his death in October 1927.

There is no question that Frankfurter's dominating personality had a negative impact upon his wife's psychological condition; several individuals who knew them have testified to this effect. Citing interviews with, among others, the late Alexander Bickel, Joseph Lash writes that "there were friends who thought that the neurasthenia that put [Marion] intermittently under psychiatric care in the Twenties was rooted in some inner resistance to her marriage, as if she were never able to resolve her problems of living with a dynamo—a Jewish one at that. . . ." [59] Gardner Jackson, a member of the Sacco-Vanzetti Defense Committee, made a similar assessment in his Oral History reminiscences.

Somewhere in the winter, January or February of '28, Felix Frankfurter came to me and said that he understood I was collecting . . . the letters of Sacco and Vanzetti and was planning to have a book of them published. He told me that I knew the condition of his wife, Marion. . . . She had had problems of emotional adjustment to her life with Felix and was, all during that period, under the care of a very well known psychiatrist in New York. Felix told me that he was very much worried about her and said that if I would only agree to have her take on the co-editorship of this book of letters with me, he thought, and the psychiatrist thought, that it would be a very great therapeutic value in her situation.

I should say that in the course of the case, after I became completely immersed in it, I, of course, saw a great deal of Felix and Marion. In the course of these intimacies, I did become the confidant of Marion and received from her expressions of the difficulties she had encountered in having married a Jew, and the social pressure to which she was subjected, and her inner struggle against this complex of circumstances. More than that, of course, Felix, being the kind of human being he is, or was and still is pretty much, made for difficulties. He is such a vital, dynamic, aggressive personality that that in itself was a difficulty, let alone the fact of being Jewish.[60]

The correspondence between Frankfurter and Marion amply supports this interpretation of their friends. Frankfurter dominated Marion; psychoanalysis gave her the strength to stand up to him. Marion herself accused Frankfurter of being insensitive to her problems. "You curly captains of action," she wrote on one occasion, "know nothing about these dark hesitations, doubts, justifications which to us are the very essence of life. If we only had the time to tell you what life really is for us, you'd be amazed."[61] But Frankfurter often bristled when Marion called attention to his tendency to dominate her and ignore her problems. Referring to a recent letter of hers, he wrote on one occasion: "I don't like [its] assumption of intolerance or exactitude that it implies to me."[62] Still, Frankfurter cared deeply for his wife and attempted as best he could to help her. During periods of difficulty he flattered her, as he had done while trying to win her during their long courtship. Frankfurter's excessive flattery hurt rather than helped, however. "I don't even like to have your favorable comments," Marion scolded him on one occasion, "since they all tend to self consciousness."[63] Frankfurter was only dimly aware that he inhibited his wife. At one point he wrote her: "I have been thinking very hard to what extent and why, if at all, your mind is more inhibited, or less continuously (almost) eager when I'm about. . . ."[64] This, however, is one of the very few comments in their correspondence in which Frankfurter accepts any responsibility for his wife's condition.

Frankfurter's attitude toward women in general was quite condescending. In his diaries and reminiscences he expressed admiration for women who are content to live through their husbands.[65] "How deeply women sink themselves in others," he had written in his 1911 diary. "Someone must be the object of their devotion. . . ."[66] Speaking of the women he meets at the 1924 Democratic convention, Frankfurter writes, "I met all the women who 'do things' before the resolutions committee, all of them. Heaven help us, what mush heads they are, almost all of them, even the very nice ones, whom I like as women. . . ."[67] Frankfurter expected Marion to live through him; he did not treat her as an equal. On one occasion, he wrote her: "You know that I refer to your judgment on taste and style and effectiveness of argument where it doesn't involve the center of my thinking on matters about which I feel you haven't all the background that seems to me, on further reflection, important on evaluation."[68] Throughout their courtship and marriage, Marion struggled against the subordinate role Frankfurter had cast for her.

· · ·

While his relationship with Marion was sometimes troubled, Frankfurter's relationships with Holmes and Brandeis provided nearly conflict-free gratification during the early twenties. The correspondence between Frankfurter and Brandeis grew during this period; the tone of that correspondence suggests there was also a deepening of intimacy between the two men. It was natural for Brandeis and Holmes to move more centrally into Frankfurter's vision as his relationship with Henry Stimson came under heavy strain. Brandeis continued to support Frankfurter financially; when Marion's psychiatric treatment became a financial burden, Frankfurter turned to Brandeis for help.[69]

Brandeis enjoyed the companionship of Frankfurter. When he learned of Frankfurter's plans for marriage in 1919, Brandeis wrote to Marion: "You know how much Felix has been to us; half son, half brother; a bringer of joy, an enricher of life."[70]

Frankfurter supplied both Brandeis and Holmes with their law clerks; these clerks, in turn, supplied Frankfurter with information about Brandeis and Holmes.

Frankfurter also received inside information about the Court directly from Brandeis. Frankfurter would often migrate to Chatham, where Brandeis kept a summer home on Cape Cod. He sometimes stayed there for weeks at a time, as he did during the summer of 1924 while Marion was in California.

Hello, Dearest, from quiet Chatham to quiet Claremont. It's so quiet here. . . . And I shall promptly settle down to the "daily stint" on the U.S. Reports—with ample talks with L.D.B. on work of the Court (the inside details there tell everything.) He feels as one continually bottled up and as he puts it "When I talk to you I feel I'm talking to myself"— so out come the innermost judicial secrets. . . . LDB and I have the best kind of professional time together, even better than Holmesy would be these days, for L.D.B. nowadays tells me more. You see how much on the make I am professionally.[71]

During that month of July, 1924, Frankfurter spent many long hours gathering information from Brandeis: "L.D.B. . . . is giving me simply inestimable material from the inner most secrets of the Court. I shall have wonderful material for future work in School and, I hope, rich matter for professional literary output." [72]

Frankfurter bore constant witness to the influence of Brandeis upon Holmes; he began to regard Holmes as the innocent being awakened to reality by Brandeis, the teacher.

Isn't Holmsey's letter sweet and much more. What a complete life his is—what complete integrity and beauty—tho you are dead right about its shelteredness. And *he* is an innocent, beyond compare, about some things—as I gather from LDB's Court talk. Their friendship is a rarely beautiful thing—they *are* so different.[73]

As for Holmes himself, Frankfurter continued to worship him.

The awing majesty and wonder of him. . . . He and I had one of the very best talks we ever had—and he took me with both his hands, his eyes all afire as we looked, not said, "good by" to each other. . . . "Young fella—you do cheer me up with all you bring." It was a lasting meeting.[74]

Frankfurter's letters to Holmes during the twenties continue to heap praise and flattery on the elderly Justice; these letters almost have the tone of love letters.

To know you is to have life authenticated not through you but in my own rich increase of life. The abundant measure of life being at once proof of its worth, I count it as one of my ultimately precious benedictions to have you be—for so I feel—be part of me.

When I saw you from the very first I knew it was *there*—the answer to life that needeth no "answer," that accepts without fatalism, that questions without humorous arrogance. Above all *there* is the beauty and the gay valor of you, for me forever. You give me the exhilaration, the life-intoxicated ferment that no other man does—and with you I feel the overtones and undertones which need no speech and have none.[75]

And Frankfurter delighted in the recognition he received from Holmes and Brandeis. He wrote Marion:

I know what Holmes means by saying the ultimate reward of a professional job is the opinion of a few masters. . . . Of course L.D.B. has the bias which you have pointed out, at least on one (!) occasion. But even so—he is not wholly poisoned and so I'm a bit startled to have him say that our new paper . . . is "thrilling." Or is he—senile! [76]

And he felt he was part of their community of thought. Writing to Walter Lippmann about a paper he has drafted concerning reform of the federal court system, Frankfurter said: "I ought now to say that on some of the questions B.* and I disagree. As to the specific items of disagreement with B, I take comfort in the fact that I happen to be on the side of Holmes and Brandeis." [77] Repeatedly in his correspondence, Frankfurter emphasized the degree to which he, Holmes, and Brandeis agree on fundamentals.

.   .   .

In his other personal relationships during this period, Frankfurter displayed some characteristics less appealing than those he exhibited in his relationships with Holmes and Brandeis. He often domi-

* "B" refers to Learned Hand.

nated and used people, particularly young people who were attracted to him. The reminiscences of Gardner Jackson demonstrate how this aspect of Frankfurter's personality could operate when he was courted by an unknown supplicant.

When we came to Boston to live, I made a conscious effort to go and see Professor Frankfurter and introduce myself. I was unknown to him, but was just a young admirer of what I had seen of his mind. . . . I was not received cordially by Frankfurter. By this I mean that it seemed to me, and in retrospect and in talking this over with my wife it still seems to me, that he felt I was not on his intellectual level, so that there wasn't an immediate cordiality. In fact, I had to, every time we got together, force myself to get his attention. In fact, the relationship between Felix and myself in those early years was such that my wife was very condemning of me in an almost serious vein. At one point she said, "I refuse to be married to a guy who becomes a messenger and slave of a fellow he wants to know," which really was the relationship for quite a period.[78]

Frankfurter got to know Jackson from his efforts on behalf of Sacco and Vanzetti. On the day the two anarchists were sentenced, Frankfurter asked Jackson to introduce him to the famous journalist Heywood Broun, whom Jackson knew and Frankfurter wanted to meet. "I think I'm not unfair when I say that there was a notable change in his regard for me from that point on," Jackson said. "This a pretty harsh description, but I don't believe it's unfair." [79]

Many others have testified to Frankfurter's paternalistic domination of his disciples. Mrs. Mark Howe, the wife of the man Frankfurter chose to write Holmes's biography, has been quoted as saying that despite his affection for his protégés, Frankfurter was overly paternalistic and authoritarian toward them, sometimes ignoring their best interests.[80] Howe, for example, was instructed to undertake the Holmes biography, which was, according to his wife, not good for him.[81] Even Marion recognized that Frankfurter's relationships were not always good for the recipient; Frankfurter's loyalty, she once said, "is sometimes a curse." [82]

Frankfurter tended to dominate his peers as well as his subordinates; he was often arrogant and dogmatic in his correspondence. "Once in a while, as in your [last] letter," Walter Lippmann wrote him, "there is an unconscious dogmatism which gives me a sense of being rushed and pushed, not unlike that of being physically jostled." [83] Frankfurter often grew indignant when his friends disagreed with him. "What I think about the court issues," he told Learned Hand after a squabble, "is set forth in a letter in the N.R.* for October 1st, which I wish you would do me the kindness to read." [84]

Frankfurter was often quite pushy. According to Harold Laski he would issue commands as if he were a despot.[85] He often pushed disagreements upon his friends. "I know how unpleasant it is for you to discuss differences of opinion," he once wrote Herbert Croly, "but I think it's much better for us to discuss than to suppress them." [86] "I'll run the risk of annoying you," he wrote Emory Buckner during one of their disagreements, "and having you think I'm losing that precious thing, a sense of perspective. . . ." [87] And Frankfurter occasionally displayed flashes of paranoia; he sometimes felt that his friends enjoyed seeing him suffer. When Henry Stimson was appointed as Secretary of State under Herbert Hoover, he wrote Harold Laski that "several of my friends take keen satisfaction in what they regard as my discomfiture over Stimson's appointment, believing as they do that it will 'cramp my style', as they put it, as a critic of the Hoover administration." [88]

But despite such instances of paranoia, Frankfurter held on to the feeling that he could control the men around him. For example, of his Harvard colleague Thomas Reed Powell he said: "I don't suppose I ever had a friend about whom I occupied myself more to enhance his ego and to stimulate him to creative work, by suggesting this and that outlet, by getting publishers after him. . . . Powell was very susceptible to flattery, you know." [89]

Frankfurter generously applied flattery to everyone in his field of vision, no matter how vitriolic his private remarks about the individual.[90] Yet Frankfurter was well aware that flattery was a technique of ingratiation:

The only secretary that I ever fired was one that I had when I came here who was generally too officious. My gut bust when she told me

* *New Republic.*

one day what a fine opinion I wrote. I couldn't stand that—to have my secretary tell me. She was thoroughly incompetent to know whether it was a fine opinion or not. Whether she was incompetent or not, I didn't want a member of my staff to tell me that I was a good man.[91]

Despite this sensitivity to flattery, Frankfurter loved praise he thought genuine. The account of Lloyd Garrison—a long-time associate—is quite revealing of this side of Frankfurter's character. A dinner was given in Frankfurter's honor at which many of his friends and protégés praised him effusively; according to Garrison, Frankfurter loved every minute of it.[92]

But whatever his attitude toward giving or getting praise, Frankfurter was, above all, a snob. The Harvard Law School was the best law school; his friends were the wisest men, the best lawyers, the most charming people. If a man measured up to Frankfurter's standards, he could be warm, charming, and helpful to him.

Perhaps the most important characteristic of Frankfurter's relationships was their intensity. Frankfurter's energy level was astounding; one could, in Dean Acheson's words, "feel the intensity of his nervous energy."[93] The result of his energy was an almost "charismatic impact on those around him";[94] he was always the center of attention.[95] He often raised his voice and seemed quite agitated to those around him.[96] He never stopped talking.[97]

. . .

The event during the late twenties to which Frankfurter devoted a great deal of this intense energy was the defense of Sacco and Vanzetti. Frankfurter had been abroad when the murders that resulted in the arrest of the two anarchists took place. He did not pay much attention to the case at first; he made it a habit not to read newspaper accounts of trials, which he thought were always inaccurate.

I paid no attention to it, but one day I saw that William G. Thompson had become counsel for Sacco-Vanzetti and that interested me. William G. Thompson was one of the most conspicuous lawyers in Boston and particularly conspicuous as a trial lawyer and an appellate lawyer. So far as we have any he was a barrister, not a corporate adviser, but a court man. I knew him, greatly respected him, admired him. I knew him somewhat because he was a great friend of Mr. Stimson.[98]

Sacco and Vanzetti had already been convicted; Thompson was making a motion for a new trial. Based on the testimony of the ballistics expert who had examined the bullet taken from the body of one of the victims of the sensational murder, Thompson concluded that the district attorney in the case had acted dishonorably. Although the expert had said repeatedly that he had "no opinion" as to whether the bullet had passed through Sacco's pistol, the district attorney asked the question in such a way as to enable the expert to say that "it is consistent with being fired from that pistol."

When I read that in the paper, something happened. . . . When I read about that motion something happened to my insides. What reading it triggered was the experience I'd acquired under Mr. Stimson's guidance and rules, the standards he represented which had become habits of mind as to how a district attorney should conduct himself. If what [the ballistics expert] said was true, it was reprehensible beyond words, and it undermined any confidence in the conduct of the case, that a district attorney should try to get an expert to swear to something that he repeatedly said that he couldn't swear to.[99]

Frankfurter then got the stenographic minutes of the case.

If I hadn't been the kind of fellow I am, if I hadn't had my experience with Mr. Stimson in the United States Attorney's Office, if I didn't care passionately about the clean administration of justice in the United States, if I didn't feel as strongly as I do about law, it wouldn't have had that affect on me, but taking the total of me for granted, what moved me into action was not a nice, quiet determination, but the triggering of my convictions, my impulses to action, the triggering of my total being by the kind of disclosure that was made. . . .[100]

Frankfurter directed one of his young protégés, Sylvester Gates, to write the first draft of an article about the case;[101] Frankfurter edited the article, and it was published in the *Atlantic Monthly*, and later as a small book.

The article stirred intense feelings; once again, as with the Mooney case, Frankfurter was cast into the role of a public de-

fender of an unpopular cause.[102] His article was attacked in the
Boston Transcript by John H. Wigmore, dean of Northwestern's
Law School and the author of the basic law school text on evidence.
Wigmore wrote, he said, "to vindicate Massachusetts justice."
Frankfurter replied in the *Boston Herald*, edited by his friend
Frank Buxton. "They held the presses. There it was, a front-page
story, and it really atomized Wigmore. Mr. Lowell said . . . 'Wig-
more is a fool! Wigmore is a fool! He should have known that
Frankfurter would be shrewd enough to be accurate.'" [103]
Lowell had been appointed by Governor Fuller of Massachusetts
to head a commission investigating the case. The commission found
that the two men had had a fair trial, and the governor, based on
their finding, refused clemency.

Frankfurter's opposition in the case was thus personified in a
figure with whom he had already tangled earlier in the decade.
When asked to summarize the significance of the Sacco-Vanzetti
case, Frankfurter cited not the substance of the case but the involvement of himself and President Lowell. He quoted John F.
Moors, "a Yankee of Yankees, a Bostonian of Bostonians, an intimate, close personal friend; indeed a Harvard classmate of President
Lowell and a member of the Harvard Corporation." Moors had
reportedly said,

it was characteristic of Harvard and in a way to the glory of Harvard
that two Harvard men were the leaders of the opposing forces in the
Sacco-Vanzetti affair. . . . Lawrence Lowell was incapable of seeing
that two wops could be right and the Yankee judiciary could be
wrong.[104]

Lowell symbolized for Frankfurter the worst prejudices of the
Brahmin establishment. To Roscoe Pound, Frankfurter wrote:

My mind is wholly absorbed by the Sacco-Vanzetti case and I just
haven't a thought for anything else. To have seven years of systematic
perversion of the machinery of justice validated by the authority of the
President of Harvard University, when in fact he himself unwittingly
is part and parcel of the social forces which help to explain the conviction and forthcoming execution of two innocent men, does too far-
reaching violence to my notions of law and justice to enable me to rid
myself of a sense of personal responsibility for such a wrong.[105]

Lowell, Frankfurter felt, was unable to perform the act most important for a disinterested scholar—he was unable to transcend his own attachments:

His crowd, the Yankees, were right, and the alien immigrants were what they were—pacifists and draft dodgers. He was incapable of doing what men have done, namely, say their crowd was wrong. You have to transcend the warm feeling of familiarity and reject that warm feeling in a spontaneous loyalty that transcends to greater loyalties, abstract virtues, truth and justice.[106]

Sacco-Vanzetti was a key episode in Frankfurter's life. It functioned as a test case for his most cherished beliefs; it powerfully affirmed his image of himself.[107] The case confirmed Frankfurter's courageousness: "A very important factor, and one that gnaws at my curiosity all the time, is the fact that men who know do not speak out." [108] It fed his conviction that facts speak for themselves: "It is to me simply incredible how an open mind can escape the conviction that Judge Thayer was not a fit person to preside in this trial. . . ." [109] It confirmed his sense of his own objectivity; he was a "disinterested student" of the case, a "disinterested student of the administration of criminal justice." [110] It confirmed his sense of himself as an expert; he spoke of the case as one "as to which, in view of my experience and professional pre-occupation, I was presumably as well qualified to speak as anybody in Boston." [111]

The case was a test case for the centrality of legal procedure. Various aspects of the case violated "all my notions of Anglo-American procedure"; [112] "the more I know about things, the more I study the ways of decisions, the more I realize the part played by procedure." [113] "Suffice it to say," he wrote Learned Hand, "that since I have come to manhood there has never been a matter which seems to me to put so much to the test our pretension about law as the instrument of justice." [114] And, above all, it was a test case against the intolerance of the establishment: "I know of no better issue on which to meet the forces of intolerance, suppression and materialism than the Sacco-Vanzetti case." [115] His own position vis-à-vis that establishment was constantly on his mind during his involvement in the case: "Criticism of me in the conservative circles in Boston . . . is compounded of the fact that I am supposed to be a 'radical' . . . and that it so happens I am not only an outsider in this community, but also a Jew." [116] Brahmin Boston, represented by Lowell, was the enemy.

If they want to fight, they may have more fight than they want. Just remember that any move on their part will tear wide open the whole issue and they will find themselves on the defensive. The Lowell report simply will not wash. We must not forget that the pertinacity of passionate prejudice which lies at the bottom of the Sacco-Vanzetti case has no such hold outside Massachusetts. When people ask me, "Do you plan to resign?" I say to them, "Why should I? Let Mr. Lowell resign." [117]

Above all, Sacco-Vanzetti confirmed to Frankfurter the general sense that he was in the right. "I am ready to go to the stake for the accuracy of my reflection," he wrote Judge Mack about his recollection of a particular incident; the attitude was one he felt toward the entire case.

.   .   .

Frankfurter's involvement with the Sacco-Vanzetti case had an inevitable effect upon his position at Harvard. The affair was at its height during a Law School endowment campaign; "as usual," the historian of the Law School has written, "talk went round that Frankfurter's activities had diminished gifts." [118] Frankfurter was aware of this talk; his response was that his activity had in fact profited the school.[119]

Sacco-Vanzetti put a further strain on Frankfurter's relationship with Roscoe Pound, a relationship that had been souring as the decade progressed. At the time of Frankfurter's return from Paris, Pound had been his intimate friend and ally; their correspondence during the period of 1919 to 1921, and Frankfurter's comments to his friends, reveal their high regard for each other. They both saw themselves as liberal victims of reactionary times and commiserated with each other about the difficulty of their position at Harvard. They worked together on the Cleveland Survey of Criminal Justice.

As Frankfurter's militancy during the twenties grew, however, he came to regard Pound as timid. By mid-decade there were numerous uncomplimentary comments about Pound in Frankfurter's correspondence with his closest friends. By 1925 Frankfurter was telling Marion that he had to "put up" with Pound, but that he could handle him: "By the way, Roscoe in a long letter writes like a well-behaved civilized human being and climbs down from his tantrum—which he almost always does when you pull up the reins (to mix my figure). He is like some small boys, who, some educationists say, occasionally have to be 'panked.' " [120]

Frankfurter told Marion—in a remarkable example of psychological projection—that Pound had an "inferiority complex vis-à-vis the blue bloods." [121] Frankfurter felt that Pound had not yet liberated himself from his attachments to the establishment, as Frankfurter himself had done. Frankfurter often spoke of Pound's needing or achieving liberation—to Holmes, Frankfurter writes that Pound needed "liberating" from his learning; to Herbert Croly, that Pound's liberalism was being liberated.[122] Pound became a symbol of the timidity Frankfurter had himself rejected; he was thus another negative identity figure for Frankfurter, like John W. Davis and Harlan Fiske Stone.

Pound at first objected to the publication of Frankfurter's Sacco-Vanzetti article. Frankfurter wrote to Brandeis:

For once I'm stumped . . . with R[oscoe] P[ound]—he has told widely, and particularly Massachusetts Supreme Judicial Court Justices that I published "against his remonstrances" before their decision was out, which is wholly false.* After it was out he said he wished I had waited and when I began to argue with him, he said "I know you think other wise and are entitled so to think" and two days thereafter he came to me and said "I have thought a great deal about our last talk re S-V. I'm glad you published your book—it was in the interest of justice that you should have done so." But having been questioned he, as so often, lied out of fear and timidity and then came to me [illegible] the judges, but suppressing what happened.[123]

Frankfurter and Pound also tangled over faculty appointments. In the mid-twenties, as he became increasingly identified with his

---

* Frankfurter's article was published while an appeal was pending before the Massachusetts court. Some members of the Harvard Board of Overseers were outraged by Frankfurter's timing, but President Lowell defended Frankfurter's right to publish when he did. This took place several weeks before Lowell was appointed to the commission by Governor Fuller.

public crusades, Frankfurter's correspondence with Roscoe Pound was full of discussions concerning various law school jobs.[124] Frankfurter felt that the quality of the man, rather than his area of speciality, was the most important fact to consider: "Courses are important only if important men give them," he said.[125]

In 1926, Frankfurter pushed for the appointment of Nathan Margold, a Jew, to the faculty. The appointment was to Frankfurter a test case for religious tolerance. "The issue I wish to raise in the Margold case," Frankfurter wrote Pound, "is whether or not he is to be considered on his merits—in the light of his professional equipment, his character and qualities—or whether the fact that he is a Jew is also to be taken into account. He isn't the first case who raises the question, but he happens to be a particularly good case. . . ." [126]

Margold was appointed as an instructor for a year, with the understanding that he would be re-evaluated based upon his performance. Despite the fact that he did well as a teacher, the religious issue once again was raised. Frankfurter now was furious at Pound. "The objection that is now raised against Margold is that he is a Jew," Frankfurter wrote. "It is inconceivable to me that the Law School of James Barr Ames should now turn down Margold because he is a Jew, although he has satisfied the test as a teacher." Frankfurter continued:

You are reported to have stated to at least four of our colleagues that Margold cannot be added to the Faculty because Bettman, Friendly and Glueck are possibilities, and that would make too many Jews on the Faculty! So far as I am able to ascertain, there has been no enunciation or indication of policy that would lead one to know how many Jews would make too many on the faculty! [127]

Another faculty appointment leading to friction between Frankfurter and Pound was that of James M. Landis, one of Frankfurter's closest friends. In the academic year of 1924–25, Landis worked for his doctorate under Frankfurter; [128] in 1926, he was appointed assistant professor. In 1927, he published, with Frankfurter, *The Business of the Supreme Court.* A year later he was considered for a full professorship.

Frankfurter's 1928 diary documents the controversy surrounding the Landis matter.[129] Landis's promotion had been agreed upon by the faculty; the administration, however, made an offer to Henry L. Shattuck, a prominent Boston attorney and a member of the Massachusetts legislature. Frankfurter considered Pound too timid in his dealing with the administration over this matter. To Pound's plea for restraint, Frankfurter replied that "about some things there can be no compromise—they involve too deeply respect and confidence. In the light of all the circumstances, the Landis affair is such an issue." [130] Frankfurter objected to Shattuck, in part, because he was too partisan; in his diary he wrote of the dangers of "introducing a partisan public man into research field where above all, freedom from partisan entanglements is essential." [131] Landis was eventually appointed to the position.

Frankfurter's relationship with Pound never recovered from the cumulative weight of their controversies during the late twenties. By the time of Frankfurter's involvement in the New Deal, their relationship had deteriorated to the point where their disagreement over Frankfurter's absences from Cambridge to be in Washington could generate a full-scale war.

· · ·

Frankfurter's strident liberalism in political matters was matched by his image of himself as a courageous, forthright, "disinterested" scholar. Contrasting himself with Henry Stimson, he wrote that "the point of view of the disinterested scholar of legal history may be as relevant as that of a man of action immediately involved, however scholarly his general professional outlook may be." [132] Frankfurter perceived his role to be the study of the relationship between law and public problems. At the height of his involvement with Sacco-Vanzetti he wrote:

It is important to remember that the only significance I had when I was called to the School, and the basic reason which led to my call to the School, was that I had shown competence in the application of law to modern problems. . . . Ezra Thayer * . . . told me that he would rely on me considerably to represent the School to the public and so symbolize recognition by the School of the part to be played by law schools and the law in the solutions of pressing public problems.[133]

* Dean of the Law School at the time of Frankfurter's first appointment in 1914.

Frankfurter took part in several long-range studies of the legal process. In the early twenties, he and Pound were invited to survey criminal justice in Cleveland; in the late twenties, he took part in a massive study of crime in Boston.

In his teaching, Frankfurter continued to devote most of his attention to the brightest students—men like James Landis, Alger Hiss, Charles Wyzanski, and Thomas Corcoran—whom he would soon be sending to Washington to staff the New Deal. He loved students who could perform for him: "I get pleasure out of a performance, strangely enough, even when it isn't mine." [134] Despite his militant stance against the narrow-mindedness of the Yankee establishment, and despite his attitude toward religion as an "accident of birth," Frankfurter was harder on Jewish students than on non-Jewish students. "I know that I exacted higher standards from Jews than from other people," he admitted in his reminiscences. "Perhaps, it was on the whole a good thing for Jews who have any capacity." [135] Frankfurter was never able to shake his resentment at the degree to which he was excluded because he was a Jew, never able to overcome his ambivalence concerning his religion.

On the eve of the thirties, Frankfurter had not yet become a truly national political figure. In his activities to date, however, he had displayed many of the characteristics he would reveal during the New Deal and his tenure as a Supreme Court justice. The style he had evolved—and the self-image from which that style derived—would now have profound national consequences. As his friendship with Franklin Roosevelt brought him into the White House and eventually onto the Supreme Court, Frankfurter crossed the invisible line, becoming an insider once again. During the twenties—a decade Frankfurter perceived as one of repeated triumphs and vindications—Frankfurter had further developed the self-righteousness and the desire to vanquish his opponents that would now be played out upon the stage of national politics.

CHAPTER 4

1932–1939:
The Cambridge-to-
Washington Shuttle

T HE THIRTIES found Felix Frankfurter center stage in New
Deal Washington. Both as a personal advisor to FDR and as the
man who would supply scores of Harvard men for the growing
federal bureaucracy, Frankfurter's behavior had a profound impact upon the shape and substance of national policy. Although it
took a bit of time for the Frankfurter-Roosevelt relationship to
warm to the point where Frankfurter could play the part of a
palace intimate, by the middle of the decade he was perhaps the
single most important nonelected official in national government.

Frankfurter's personality—his combativeness, his militancy, his
self-righteousness—fit perfectly the infighting that characterized
the chaos of the New Deal. Although during the twenties Frankfurter's energies had been scattered among scores of different activities, his intensity would now be focused upon a single target:
the president of the United States.

·   ·   ·

Frankfurter had first come to know Franklin Roosevelt when both were middle-level functionaries in Washington during World War I.* Roosevelt, then assistant secretary of the navy, often discussed labor matters with Frankfurter, who was chairman of the War Labor Policies Board. Frankfurter later said—perhaps with a touch of exaggeration—that they saw or spoke to each other nearly every day in 1917 and 1918.[2]

During the twenties, they were casual acquaintances. In 1924, Frankfurter wrote Marion about Roosevelt's "Happy Warrior" speech nominating Al Smith for president, which he heard in person at the Democratic convention of 1924. It was, he said, "one of the most thrilling experiences of my life. . . . Complete simplicity and sincerity—I never heard such proof of incorruptibility." [3] Frankfurter was happy to see his friend elected governor of New York in 1928. Roosevelt began to seek Frankfurter's counsel on several matters, particularly those related to public utilities, one of Frankfurter's specialties at the Law School. In 1931, Roosevelt persuaded Frankfurter to serve as chairman of a commission charged with reforming New York's judicial system. Frankfurter agreed, but then quickly changed his mind, telling Roosevelt that he had too many other things to do. He telegrammed the governor that he was "CONFIDENT I CAN CONTRIBUTE WHATEVER HELP I CAN BE THROUGH CONSULTATIVE WAYS ALTHOUGH NOT MEMBER OF THE COMMISSION." [4] As he had done throughout his life and as he would continue to do in the thirties, Frankfurter shunned formal attachments and offices, preferring to serve as a behind-the-scenes advisor.

Early in the contest for the Democratic presidential nomination in 1932, Frankfurter backed Al Smith. He had enthusiastically supported Smith in 1928, and he had, at this point, more than passing doubts about Roosevelt's capacity for national leadership. In 1930, however, Frankfurter had written Walter Lippmann that he would support Roosevelt:

Despite all, I should vote for Roosevelt. I know his limitations. Most of them derive, I believe, from lack of incisive intellect and a kind of

* They had met briefly earlier, at a luncheon in 1906. They spoke of books, and Frankfurter advised Roosevelt not to underline books but to mark a significant passage by drawing a line in the margin.[1]

optimism that sometimes makes him timid, as well as an ambition that leads to compromises with which we were familiar in Theodore Roosevelt and Wilson. But on the whole he has been a very good governor. . . .[5]

Along with his doubts about Roosevelt's leadership capacities, there was a personal edge to Frankfurter's coolness to the future President: he was somewhat hurt that he was not invited to join Roosevelt's Brain Trust in the period before the presidential nomination. He continued to express reservations about Roosevelt during the summer of 1932 and immediately after the election. Just before the convention, Frankfurter wrote C. C. Burlingham: "I am wondering what will come out of Chicago. . . . If F.D.R. is nominated, it will certainly prove there is no limit to the amount of fumbling one can do and still win a game." [6] To Learned Hand, immediately after Roosevelt's election, Frankfurter was even more blunt: "I did not during the campaign nor do I now expect the milleneum from Roosevelt." [7]

When Roosevelt began campaigning, he found Frankfurter useful in bridging the gap that separated him from the Smith forces in the party. On his way to Chicago to accept the Democratic nomination, Roosevelt spoke to Frankfurter at great length over the telephone. Frankfurter insisted that Roosevelt see Governor Ely of Massachusetts, a Smith backer. Roosevelt refused; Frankfurter persisted. Roosevelt finally suggested that Ely speak to his son Jimmy, then living in Boston. Frankfurter, in the same conversation, said that he wanted to speak to Roosevelt about economic matters. In the memorandum he made of their conversation, Frankfurter reported the following exchange, in which he adopted the tone he would continue to use with Roosevelt—that of the teacher, the specialist, the expert. "Remember this in your speeches about a balanced budget," Frankfurter quotes himself as saying. "When you are in the White House you'll be confronted with a deficit next year probably as big as this year's. . . . It's very important to remember that in what you say and don't say. That's what they'll leave for you. There are some specific things I want to talk to you about later." [8]

In the same conversation, the two men discussed Frankfurter's nomination by Governor Ely to the Supreme Judicial Court of

Massachusetts. Several of Frankfurter's friends had thought the way to counter Frankfurter's label as a "radical" was to engineer an appointment for him to the Massachusetts court.[9] Frankfurter did consider the offer carefully; he sought the advice of his close friends.[10] The possibility that the Massachusetts court could lead to eventual appointment to the Supreme Court was very much on his mind, but, once again, Frankfurter chafed at the idea of assuming any formal office. He told his friends that it was not his nature "to take one place because it will lead to another":

Apart from life's contingencies and the special uncertainties that enter into appointments to the Supreme Court, it is constitutionally impossible for me to take an office not because it is intrinsically the wise thing to do but because of the hope thereby of advancing my chance for some other place.[11]

Moreover, Frankfurter undoubtedly had another political arena on his mind; the chance that Roosevelt would soon become president undoubtedly suggested the possibility of future influence in Washington.

. . .

During the campaign, Frankfurter's role was subdued. He continued to serve as a conciliator of Smith forces; he advised Roosevelt on the Walker investigations.* Roosevelt invited Frankfurter to help the Brain Trust, but there was too much animosity between him and its members for any effective cooperation. Raymond Moley disagreed with Frankfurter often, although they respected each other; A. A. Berle, however, not only disagreed with Frankfurter but disliked him personally.[13] Here, in these pre-election difficulties between Frankfurter and Roosevelt's other advisors, is the origin of the factions that would separate the first and second New Deals. "The Professor," in the words of Joseph Lash, "was no innocent when it came to palace politics. He knew how to bide his time." [14]

* The Seabury Commission in New York brought serious charges of corruption against New York City's mayor Jimmy Walker. Frankfurter advised Roosevelt to deal firmly with Walker; Roosevelt sought Frankfurter's advice on "the ethics and the law involved." [12]

During the campaign, Frankfurter saw a bit of Roosevelt. He wrote to Brandeis in August:

F.D.R. invited Marion and me, and I persuaded Marion to go to see what the whirl is like under which a Presidential candidate is supposed to live and think. . . . Marion says I talked to him as tho he might be one of my students. . . . I put to him many things and he listened and took notes. . . .

Altogether—while Marion says he agrees too readily, is too optimistic— it was a very fruitful visit; certainly solid attention to business and very attentive on his part to details and considerable grasp of facts once they are put to him.[15]

In October, Frankfurter wrote Marion: "Politics you say have claimed your scholar-husband, and I'm afraid that's not half un-true. That too will pass—very soon."[16]

During the period of transition between the November election and the March inauguration, Frankfurter began fulfilling what was to become a crucial function: the supplying of men to staff the New Deal. In time, scores of his former students and protégés would find their way to Washington, creating a network of influence for Frankfurter that extended into virtually every crevice of the growing bureaucracy.

Frankfurter began at the top, by arranging meetings between Roosevelt and Henry Stimson, who had been serving as Hoover's secretary of state.* Slowly but surely, Frankfurter began making personnel suggestions; before long, he was a one-man employment agency.

Soon after the March inauguration FDR invited Frankfurter to become solicitor general. Once again, Frankfurter spurned formal office, telling Roosevelt that he preferred to remain a general advisor. Moreover, he said, he did not wish to devote the long hours of technical legal work required of the solicitor general. Roosevelt persisted, telling Frankfurter that he wanted to put him on the Supreme Court. But Frankfurter insisted that he wished to decline the post.[17]

---

* As a result of the meeting, Roosevelt endorsed the Stimson-Hoover far-eastern policy, to the dismay of the Brain Trust. Later, Frankfurter was instrumental in the appointment of Stimson as Roosevelt's secretary of war.

Frankfurter's desire to remain free to function as a general advisor and not assume a formal role in the administration is consistent with the pattern of behavior he exhibited throughout his life. Then, too, he had just turned down the Supreme Judicial Court of Massachusetts, which some considered a higher honor than the solicitor generalship. Holmes, for example, thought it would be "queer" to turn down the Massachusetts court but accept the Washington post.[18] Also weighing into Frankfurter's calculations was the fact that he had been invited to Oxford for the academic year of 1933 to 1934, a great honor for him, a lifelong Anglophile.

Frankfurter was in fact seeking general influence with FDR at this time rather than any specific post or policy goals. In the period of 1933 to 1935, Frankfurter wanted to pull the administration, in whatever way possible, toward the ideology of Brandeisian liberalism. The aging Brandeis—referred to as "Isaiah" by his intimates in the administration—held an almost mystical aura for Frankfurter and, especially, for Frankfurter's protégés. He was their oracle, their inspiration, their tactician, and their critic. They perceived the New Deal as a chance to finally bring about some of the reforms for which they had all struggled since the turn of the century. Although as the decade progressed, inevitable fissures would open up within the Brandeisian camp—indeed, by the end of the decade Brandeis and Frankfurter would be close to a quarrel—in these early years, at least, they were united by common purpose.

The ideological core of Brandeisian liberalism was its emphasis on smallness. As many of the advisors of Roosevelt's first New Deal —Tugwell, Berle, Moley—struggled to create a planned and centralized economy, the Brandeisians sought to restore the simple and decentralized market economy of the nineteenth century. Their key program was trust busting—breaking up the large banks, the large corporations, the large utility companies. To the first New Dealers, business was to be a partner; to the Brandeisians, business was the enemy. A memo prepared in 1933 by Harry Shulman— one of Brandeis's lieutenants—quotes the justice as setting forth his program in clear and stark terms.

The object is to make men free. The Government is to impose limitations in order to achieve that object. . . . First, I would take the Government out of the hands of the bankers. . . . By appropriate federal taxation, I would split up the banking business into its separate parts and prohibit any bank from doing any more than one kind of banking business. . . .

Second, by appropriate federal taxation I would limit the amount of property which any person could acquire or pass down upon death. . . . Thirdly, by appropriate federal excise taxes I would limit the size of corporations. I would do it not only with respect to corporations to be formed in the future, but also for existing corporations. . . . I would leave a lot of power to the States . . . and have the federal government help and direct the States by appropriate taxation. The federal government must not become too big just as corporations should not be permitted to become too big. You must remember that it is the littleness of man that limits the size of things we can undertake.

Fourthly, I would establish a system of unemployment compensation. . . . The system should be operated by the states but the federal government by appropriate taxation and exemption from taxation should furnish the force which would compel the establishment of such systems. . . .

The author of the memorandum suggested to Brandeis that his program "was attempting to do the impossible—to turn the clock back." Brandeis's reaction "was immediate and spirited: why shouldn't we turn the clock back? . . . At any rate whether the program can be executed or not is a separate question. . . . First, we just determine what is desirable to do and then we can find ways and means to do it." [19]

Frankfurter realized that this ideology of smallness flew in the face of the first New Deal; nevertheless, he prodded the president wherever he could. And increasingly, Roosevelt was finding Frankfurter a congenial and stimulating advisor. "Felix has more ideas per minute than any man of my acquaintance," Roosevelt is quoted as saying. "He has a brilliant mind but it clicks so fast it makes my head fairly spin. I find him tremendously interesting and stimulating." [20] For his part, Frankfurter was having the time of his life. "To have an aristocrat of the nation as a personal friend," Albert Sacks has written, "who would also deliver the United States from economic disaster and war and give him the opportunity for service at the highest level made Frankfurter's cup run over, and provoked his ardent patriotism and personal loyalty." [21]

That loyalty manifested itself in part through the generous application of flattery, by now a familiar Frankfurter trademark. In their 772 pages of published correspondence, there is an almost unbelievable amount of flattery heaped upon the president by Frankfurter. After speeches, he would send telegrams, comparing FDR to Lincoln. After a difficult decision, Frankfurter would praise the president's statesmanship and courage. In a difficult period of stress, he would strive to bolster his friend's ego. Even Max Freedman, the most ardent of Frankfurter's admirers and the editor of the Frankfurter-Roosevelt correspondence, was forced to admit: "It may . . . be said that [Frankfurter] was an artist in adulation; and sometimes, forgetting the artistry, he laid on flattery with a trowel. Sometimes the flattery, it must be admitted, may seem excessive and repugnant." [22] Although Frankfurter would often criticize FDR in his letters to Brandeis,[23] not one word of criticism was made directly to the President.

FDR warmed to the treatment. "That was a particularly nice message you sent me about the address," he would write.[24] "The thoughtful message you sent me made me exceedingly happy." [25] "As always, you say things that hearten." [26] Frankfurter perceived the president as lonely and proud and in need of attention. Henry Stimson, in a revealing fragment, wrote in his diary:

[Frankfurter] gave me a very nice little message as to my relations with the President and begged me to see more of him and seek out more opportunities for more talks with him. He said that the President cherished it and would not take offense. I told him that I had been keeping away because I did not like to bother him. He said that was wrong—that he was a very lonely man and that he was rather proud and didn't like to ask people to come to him but that he was sure that he would welcome my approaches if I would make them.[27]

Frankfurter flattered whoever was closest to the throne as well as Roosevelt himself. In the early thirties, he subjected Moley, Harold Ickes,* and Hugh Johnson† to the treatment; in the forties, it was Harry Hopkins.‡ It is difficult to avoid the conclusion that Frankfurter flattered those he felt would be useful to his cause.

---

* Ickes served as secretary of the interior from 1933 to 1946.

† Johnson served as administrator of the NRA from 1933 to 1934.

‡ Hopkins held several different jobs in the administration before becoming secretary of commerce in 1938; during the forties, he was one of Roosevelt's closest advisors.

Frankfurter was positively thrilled by his closeness to the center of things. During his trips to Washington he would write Marion letters in which his exhilaration jumps off the page. Soon after the inauguration he wrote:

These are crazy, hectic hours for me—on the go all the time, with demands on me to settle the universe, world ills, railroads, Indian affairs, public works etc. etc. It's all very funny and sad—to think the way the world is run. But Frankee has created a hopeful atmosphere—if only he can act on it wisely while it counts.

Everyone has been after me—as though I could move mountains. Everyone, including poor Steinway & tenacious George Rublee & handsome, tousled Herbert F[eis] and the very competent Francis P[erkins] & & & & & &

But—of course there are also . . . "marooned colored" talk and really good beer and other stuff and lunch with Holmsey and lots all else—so called "life."

But—I'm glad we're not in office—it would be awful and distracting beyond measure and truly not satisfying.[28]

Frankfurter clearly thought of himself as the teacher of the president. In letters to Brandeis, he would report on the progress of his influence; together, they would plan strategy for the future.

I was alone with him [FDR], Wed. night, from 9:30 to 1 a.m. and yesterday from 9:45 to 11. We covered much ground. . . . He is in fine form—his old self, it seemed to me. When I turned in at 1, I told Marion F.D. has, of course, intellectual limitations, but did not show any defect of character that I wished the Pres't of the U.S. did not have. . . .

He seems keenly aware of intentions of Big Business and Finance and so when I told him, very frankly, your views re/"irrepressible conflict" he said "he's put his finger on the crux of the situation." . . . From that I went on to housing situation and large public works program. He agrees that present housing [program] will be failure—I told him why. Explained material costs and labor, that dealing with latter presupposes reduction of former etc. etc. . . . I put it to him hard—and he took careful notes.

We talked personal ties—Jim Farley and Tugwell, and he is troubled about their talk and writing and will shut them up. . . . He sends you his warmest regards.[29]

The New Deal strengthened Frankfurter's sense of himself as an expert, as a man of knowledge. Political leadership, after all, was merely education, and he was an expert at that. "Since leading people is essentially a task of education done on a vast scale," he wrote the President, "I venture to draw on the experience of twenty-five years of teaching."[30] His correspondence with FDR and with others is dotted with references to himself as an expert on this or that subject, and on government in general:

I have known more or less intimately the official ways and methods of five Presidents. And I have spent the whole of my life as a rather close student of the contemporary political affairs not only of our own country but of Great Britain.[31]

It has been my business to study closely for more than twenty years the work of regulatory bodies both national and state, and perhaps you will forgive me some general observations.[32]

HOPE IT WILL NOT BE NECESSARY TO MAKE FINAL DE-CISION REGARDING FORM AND PROCEDURE FOR SYSTEM-ATIC PUBLICATION OF EXECUTIVE ORDERS UNTIL I HAVE HAD OPPORTUNITY FOR TALK WITH YOU. IT HAPPENS TO BE A PARTICULAR SUBJECT OF MINE AND I AM BRINGING A DETAILED SCHEME AND DRAFT FOR NECESSARY LEGISLATION.[33]

Even libraries were a "special" subject of his.[34] And, of course, he was an expert on the Supreme Court: "I merely know intimately the history of the Court, and especially during the last few years."[35]

His greatest specialty was human relations—"personalia." As he had done throughout his life, Frankfurter in the New Deal played the role of the counselor, the conciliator; he was the person who brought people together, who knew how to fit an individual into just the right niche in the bureaucracy. His correspondence contains literally hundreds of letters dealing with personnel matters—letters to and from department heads and White House advisors, to and from his "boys." "Everyone thought Frankfurter was the voice of Jove," according to Jerome Frank, at this time a member of the agriculture department.[36] When Frank and Frankfurter began to disagree about various New Deal policies, Frank chided him about his proprietary interests in his "disciples." Frankfurter reacted strongly.

As to your vague hints about some of my friends, I will say only that you quite misconceive the relation of those friends to me. A teacher who has disciples is a teacher who fails in the essential task of his office. Whatever action any of my former students in Washington may have pursued, follows, I hope, from convictions of inner propulsion and not in response to any wishes or orders. This is too ridiculous a conception for you to entertain.[37]

Frankfurter always denied that he had any form of control over his protégés, particularly after his role and his influence became public knowledge.[38] Yet his correspondence reveals that he was constantly in touch with these individuals, making suggestions, commenting on pending legislation, criticizing those who deviated from the party line. If an individual crossed over to the enemy's camp, he was mercilessly ostracized. When Jerome Frank quite early began to show signs of affinity with the economic planners of the first New Deal, he was cut off; Frankfurter would often write Brandeis about "crossing off" individuals who disagreed with them.[39] Frankfurter's correspondence also reveals that his advice was often eagerly sought—and given a great deal of weight—by the people he had placed in the administration.

Frankfurter considered the public service his specialty, and his proprietary interest in his young men as a simple manifestation of that interest. "You know that there is no single aspect of public affairs with which I have been more deeply concerned," he wrote FDR from Cambridge, "than the promotion of public service as a permanent career for the nation's best abilities. That, in a way, has been my predominant interest in the School here." [40] He had no doubt at all that he knew the right man for the right job, from the Cabinet down to the most obscure bureaucrat of the Labor Department. Scores of people ended up in Washington through Frankfurter's influence or with his help—Dean Acheson, Alger and Donald Hiss, Charles Wyzanski, James Landis, Paul Freund.

They were dubbed his "happy hot dogs" and he was immensely proud of them; his ability to place people in Washington was a source of deep satisfaction to him. These men served, in Frankfurter's own highly revealing words, to "insulate" his "intervention." [41]

Frankfurter's most spectacular "hot dog" was Tommy Corcoran. A student at Harvard in the mid-twenties, Corcoran was awarded by Frankfurter with his most cherished gift—a clerkship with Holmes. "I'm perfectly delighted that Corcoran is giving satisfaction," Frankfurter wrote Holmes. "I'm not surprised—he is one of the most delightful and sweetest lads I've ever had." [42]

Although he was on the staff of the Reconstruction Finance Corporation, Corcoran by 1934 was, in the words of Arthur Schlesinger, Jr., "operating all over Washington. Soon introduced into the White House circles, he made an instant impression." [43] In many ways, Corcoran was similar to Frankfurter: he was a flatterer; he loved to work behind the scenes and pull the strings. "Whenever a crucial law had to be drafted or crucial brief written, Corcoran conjured up a task force from his young men around the government. . . ." [44]

Frankfurter loved Corcoran. "Tom is of course good fun," he wrote Marion, "and he gets joy out of my quick perceptions of his humor." [45] On another occasion he wrote from the White House:

Tom is full of a thousand strategems and devices—but he can throw them off and just go in for giving pleasure without turning a hair. He played and sang . . . and damned good he was, too. The more I see of him, the more extraordinary he is—the kind of vitality, versatility, devotion that O.W.H. and L.D.B. (differently) and you and I (still differently) "get" and enjoy, but many folk neither understand—like T.R.P[owell]—nor relish, because they fear such exuberance, such skill and such subtlty.[46]

Through Corcoran, Frankfurter was able to keep himself completely aware of Washington gossip despite his absence from the scene. A network of individuals rapidly developed throughout the Capitol, many of them reporting to Corcoran who would, in turn, report back to Frankfurter. To many observers on the scene, the Frankfurter-Corcoran crowd was a disciplined machine, especially in contrast to the economic planners of the first New Deal, who were notorious for their inability to agree with each other. "This," an observer has said, "was in marked contrast to the unity and discipline of the Little Hot Dogs, who knew only one play but had plenty of substitutes and a will to win." [47]

. . .

The major concrete task Frankfurter undertook during the early New Deal was the drafting of the Securities Bill of 1933.* Roosevelt had promised securities reform during the campaign; the revelations of the Senate's Pecora committee concerning Wall Street shenanigans made swift action imperative. Sam Rayburn, at this time chairman of the House Commerce Committee, asked Raymond Moley to find him someone who could write a securities bill. In April, Moley turned to Frankfurter.[50]

Wall Street was the devil of Frankfurter's universe, and he relished the chance to tame the money-changers and teach Wall Street lawyers a lesson. When summoned by Moley he brought with him Benjamin V. Cohen and James M. Landis; they would do the actual drafting of the bill, he told Moley, while he, Frankfurter, would remain in Cambridge and direct things as closely as he could. "Felix was bursting with enthusiasm for the job," Moley later wrote.[51] The Landis-Cohen bill eventually became the Securities Act, signed by Roosevelt in late May.[52] It was a harsh and controversial bill which soon had to be amended; Frankfurter, however, defended it vigorously.

---

* Frankfurter's frequent absences from Cambridge to attend to New Deal business did not endear him to Roscoe Pound. Pound disliked FDR intensely, and Pound and Frankfurter openly feuded over the latter's involvement in Washington. Frankfurter often postponed and missed classes, although he claimed never to have done so. The feud between Frankfurter and Pound split the Law School faculty. In his reminiscences, James Landis comments that "there was a very distinct cleavage between [Pound] and Frankfurter. . . . I think both of them had a little desire for power, you know, and Frankfurter had his clique and Pound had his." [48] Frankfurter's proximity to the President while maintaining his faculty position also helped create a break with Walter Lippmann. Lippmann published a column in 1936 critical of academics engaging in partisan politics. Although not mentioning Frankfurter by name, Frankfurter assumed it was meant for him. In Max Freedman's words, "He never forgot and never forgave what Lippmann had written." [49]

The controversy surrounding the securities bill was a symbolic and highly personal fight for Frankfurter. He broke with old friends who criticized the bill; he attributed opposition to base motives, as he usually did when criticized on an important matter. The Wall Street lawyer had been responsible for the securities mess, he felt, and had to be taught a lesson. All of those lawyers who had rejected his path—public service—and had instead devoted themselves to money-making were now to be punished.[53] Wall Street, Frankfurter said, thought of him as the "Red Terror."[54] He could not accept the possibility that there might be real defects in the bill; criticism of it was a function of self-interest. "It would surprise neither you or me," he wrote FDR's confidant, Louis Howe,

that the real culprit of the drive against the Securities Act are some of the leading law firms who make such a fat killing out of the abuses which brought the Securities Act into existence. They really want to do business at the old stand. And some of the powerful newspapers are also enlisted in the attack because the Securities Act is cutting into and will cut into their profitable but socially illicit financial advertising. . . . Between lawyers and newspaper owners they are finding no difficulty in arousing the timidity and cupidity of some of the bankers to regain profitable immunities which they never should have had.[55]

To his friend Eustace Seligman, who criticized portions of the bill, Frankfurter wrote sarcastically:

I am amused by your naivete and still more saddened by your complacent dogmatism. To differ with you, especially on matters as to which you have had the partial experience of representing special interests is, apparently, proof positive of ignorance born of exclusion from the great world in which you have so fortunately moved.[56]

Even Henry Stimson criticized portions of the bill. Stimson wrote that Frankfurter's response to his criticisms "gave me the impression that for the first time in my years of experience with you there had entered into your mind an element of personal feeling which swung you from the balance of fairness which I have always grown to expect."[57]

•   •   •

The hostility to business that Frankfurter manifested in the drafting of the Securities Act was a key ideological component of the Brandeisian ideology, an ideology that was coming into increasing conflict with the program of the first New Deal. As the number of Frankfurter's placements in Washington increased, and as events made the ideological divisions between the economic planners and the Brandeisians more clear-cut, Washington began increasingly to divide into two hostile camps. By 1934, the economic planners—particularly Tugwell—felt that Brandeis was "declaring war." [58]

Frankfurter spent the academic year of 1933 to 1934 as the George Eastman professor at Oxford. He continued to map out general strategy with Brandeis through the mails; he received a never-ending stream of information about the growing conflict in the administration from some of his "boys," particularly Cohen and Corcoran.[59] Frankfurter, in turn, sent a constant stream of letters with suggestions and instructions to Corcoran, Cohen, Wyzanski, and others.

In England, Frankfurter came to know John Maynard Keynes, and began his effort to introduce Keynes onto the Washington scene.[60] Although in the early thirties Frankfurter was a budget balancer, by the mid-thirties he had been converted to the philosophy of deficit spending. The evolution of his economic thinking paralleled the general trend of economic thought. The administration had taken office promising a balanced budget, but as heavy welfare spending contributed to larger deficits and a mounting debt, it became more and more difficult to regard government spending as a temporary expedient.[61] What we needed was an economic theory to justify the permanent stimulation of the economy by government spending.

Frankfurter quickly recognized that Keynesian theory provided such a justification. In December of 1933, Frankfurter urged Keynes to write Roosevelt in support of heavy increases in public works appropriations.[62] In the spring of 1934, Keynes traveled to America to receive an honorary degree at Columbia; Frankfurter did his best to introduce him to all the right people, including the president. To Corcoran, Frankfurter wrote:

A little item of business. Keynes is to be in Washington in two or three weeks, and I gave him a note to you, which I hope he will make use of. I want you to give a small dinner, including Jim and Ben, perhaps Rayburn and Matthews, but in any event a small dinner, so as to secure a thorough discussion of Securities Act and Stock Exchange control. Keynes will come to Washington after a week or so of New York, during which I am sure a lot of his Wall Street friends will pump him full of poison which they will call facts. He is as keen as a lynx, but even he . . . has hardly an idea, though I have tried to instill a few illustrative examples into his mind, of the piracies and greed of American finance or the huggermuggery and abuses of the Stock Exchange.[63]

In late May, Keynes took tea at the White House with FDR. "The meeting," Schlesinger comments dryly, "does not seem to have been a great success." [64] Roosevelt found Keynes arrogant; Keynes found Roosevelt somewhat illiterate in economic theory. Beyond their personal difficulties, however, Roosevelt's well-known intellectual style—his desire to combine and fuse competing ideologies—made the full-scale acceptance of Keynesian theory impossible.[65] Frankfurter and his lieutenants, particularly Cohen, continued to push Keynesianism wherever they could, but it was not until after the Supreme Court's *Schechter* decision in 1935, killing the NRA, and the recession of 1937 that the administration became more fully committed to Keynesian theory.

As Frankfurter prepared to leave Oxford and return to America, he received a combat brief from Corcoran and Cohen. In this letter, Frankfurter's two protégés reported that the ideological divisions within the administration were coming to a head and suggested that Frankfurter would need extensive de-briefing just to understand what was happening.[66] To Brandeis, Frankfurter wrote that he would delay his return as long as possible. "I see no purpose in getting involved in Washington matters during the summer," he said. "F.D.R. will in any event be away and I don't want to be torn to shreds by the thousand and one inpingements to which I shall be subjected immediately on my return." [67]

.   .   .

The year following his return from Oxford—from September 1934 to September 1935—was a turning point both for Frankfurter and for the New Deal. The death of the NRA in the *Schechter* decision created a climax to the palace struggle that had been building for some time. In shifting gears to the second New Deal, Roosevelt came to lean more heavily on Frankfurter and Frankfurter's protégés.

The first New Deal ultimately depended upon the viability of the all-class coalition of the 1932 election and, particularly, upon the cooperation and support of the business and industrial sectors.[68] To the Brandeisians and particularly to Frankfurter, this reliance on business was anathema. Frankfurter continually pushed Roosevelt to "dump" business. In May of 1935, as the *Schechter* decision neared, Frankfurter wrote Brandeis: "If only Business could become still more articulate in its true feelings toward F.D.R. so that even his genial habits would see the futility of hoping any thing from Business in '36, so that he would act more on 'irrepressible conflict.' " [69]

The NRA hierarchy had for some time wanted to test their program in the Supreme Court.[70] Although Frankfurter was ideologically opposed to the NRA and never enthusiastic about its program, he was loyal to Roosevelt and devoted to the administration's success; he did not want to see a key administration program defeated in court if it could be helped.

On April 1, in the *Schechter* case, the second Circuit Court of Appeals upheld most of the provisions of the NRA in a case dealing with the live poultry industry—the famous "sick chicken" case. NRA administrator Donald Richberg wanted to carry the case to the Supreme Court and was able to convince Attorney General Cummings and Solicitor General Stanley Reed to use *Schechter* as a test case. Frankfurter was alarmed. Corcoran wired Roosevelt, who was away from Washington on a fishing trip, that Frankfurter thought it unwise to test the NRA in court; [71] Roosevelt wired Cummings not to announce the appeal, but the telegram arrived too late.[72]

On Monday, May 27—"Black Monday" to the members of the administration—the Supreme Court handed down its decision in *Schechter* and two other New Deal cases. The Court declared the NRA unconstitutional in *Schechter*; it also found the Frazier-Lemke Act for the relief of farm mortgages unconstitutional, and declared that FDR's removal of Federal Trade Commissioner William Humphreys had been unconstitutional.

Cohen and Corcoran were in the courtroom; they were called to the robing room by Brandeis. The next day, Cohen typed up a memo describing what had occurred and gave a copy to Frankfurter. Brandeis, according to the memo, excitedly said that the Court's decisions required a complete change of the administration's programs—away from federal centralization—and that Cohen and Corcoran were to have Frankfurter speak to Roosevelt immediately.[73]

The fate of the first New Deal at the hands of the Supreme Court did, in fact, make a fundamental shift of policy necessary. Here, finally, was Frankfurter's opportunity.* The result of Frankfurter's proddings and Roosevelt's turn of mind was the second hundred days, during which the administration pushed for five major pieces of legislation: the social securities bill, the Wagner labor bill, a banking bill, a holding companies measure, and a tax plan. All had been in the works before *Schechter*, but Roosevelt's decision to push these measures was crucial for their success. After a few weeks of indecision in June, Roosevelt energized himself and the administration.

Frankfurter had a hand in several of these new measures during the long summer of 1935 when Roosevelt kept Congress in Washington. "F.D. seems to want me around on odds and ends," Frankfurter wrote Brandeis, "and there are diverse matters of policy—Conference Committee on Holding Companies Bill . . . vacancies for different commissions, tax programs etc. etc.—On which I do what I can." [75]

While Marion visited her family in California, Frankfurter spent

---

*William Leuchtenberg has written:

As Roosevelt surveyed the wreckage left by the *Schechter* decision, and pondered which fork in the road to take next, Frankfurter was always by his side, sometimes arguing alone with the President before turning in for the night as a guest at the White House. The Harvard professor insisted that the attempt at business-government cooperation had failed, and urged Roosevelt to declare war on business. Once the President understood that business was the enemy, he would be free to undertake the Brandeisian program to cut the giants down to size: by dwarfing the power of holding companies, by launching antitrust suits, and by taxing large corporations more stiffly than small business.[74]

much of the summer of 1935 living at the White House. It was the high point of his relationship with FDR.[76]

I'm right here in the House, exercising judgment and turning out memos for F.D. as to state of various bills in Conference and recommendations for F.D.'s action, with leaders, when he returns on Sunday. . . . It would be funny were it not tragic when I reflect on the extent to which just a handful of us (that's the truth) just now are thinking beyond the next three minutes, and do the kind of things that the best type of British Civil servant eg. Maynard Keynes and Salter are doing. . . .[77]

Once again, Frankfurter saw himself as an expert at "personalia"; he was "holding people's hands," he told Marion, and he "told the skipper that when he leaves here, he and I could go in psychiatric business." [78]

I *am* of all sorts of uses here—and not merely "human relations," though human relations are 9/10 of public affairs, well—8/10. We may get a holding company bill that will be a real achievement. At present I'm engaged in what Tom calls throwing a pontoon bridge over a roaring torrent. In less picturesque language, to reconcile the vague and partial ideas, and the jostling and conflicting wishes of divers personalities. F.D. calls me "John" or "John Davis" because of the "conservative" compromise I'm urging on him—I, the arch destroyer of Property—and the Constitution.[79]

As the summer moved on, Frankfurter's influence grew. "F.D. wants me really around—so that I've not dined out of the White House once." [80] Frankfurter loved the White House, loved his position and his relationship with FDR.

He—F.D.—has been sweet and even caressing through all these days (for instance the other evening he said warmly "and how is Felicia tonight" as I walked in for the pre-dinner cocktails).

Last night we had a truly gay small dinner, in the great state dining room—F.D., the girls, Hall Roosevelt, the pagan brother of the righteous Eleanor . . . Joe Kennedy and myself. A good time—truly— was had. . . .[81]

As he prepared to leave the White House on September 1, he

wrote: "And thus endeth a rather strange chapter—almost 3 months in the White House. . . . I liked F.D.'s leave-taking of me—he said nothing, but gave me a really warm hand-clasp and a strange, grateful look of the eye and 'I'll see you soon in Hyde Park.' " [82]

The ideological tone of the legislation Frankfurter helped produce during the summer of 1935 was different from that of the first New Deal, although it is easy to overstate the division between the first and second New Deals.[83] Roosevelt did not commit himself fully to Brandeisian ideology, but rather leaned more heavily in that direction, largely because his other advisors had failed him. Not until the recession of 1937, moreover, did Roosevelt more fully commit himself to the antimonopoly elements of the second New Deal legislation and to Keynesian fiscal policy.[84]

But whether there was in fact a sharp dividing line in 1935, Frankfurter clearly perceived one; he saw the summer of 1935 as his time of triumph over his enemies. Public life was warfare, and opponents were self-seeking and ignorant. To Jerome Frank, by now an enemy because of his affiliation with the first New Dealers, Frankfurter wrote: "The administration plainly has reached a new stage. From now on it must be to a large extent trench warfare. I don't think your temperament and your interests are peculiarly suited to participation in that kind of enterprise, as such." [85] A year later, Frankfurter wrote Frank on the same theme:

What you, and a number of people in Washington had not realized from the beginning, is that public life is warfare, that it is always permeated by people who are in Holmes' phrase, fired with a zeal to pervert, that the luxury of letting one's mind roam through one's tongue is a luxury that can't be indulged in, and that there are lots of things that can be and should be done but shouldn't be talked about.[86]

Frankfurter's correspondence is full of military imagery. "Washington air makes me sniff the old air of battle. . . ." he tells Marion.[87] To Brandeis, Frankfurter writes that "Landis . . . must be made to realize that the first engagement is the beginning and not the end of the war." [88] He derides the various groups surrounding the administration: the "Progressives," the "liberals," the "planners," the "conservatives"—all are to be watched warily.

To Marion he writes that he is engaged in "defeating evil ends"; [89] there is always "bad advice to short-circuit or to counter-act head-on." [90] He alone is disinterested; his opponents are not: "Apart from the intrinsic limitations of bad judgment, the lack of prophetic powers, too many people give bad advice because obstructed by self-interest. That is so rare in itself—disinterestedness, and to find disinterestedness and insight is damn rare." [91] "Men, men, men—that's our need, men of competence, devotion, non-egocentrism, tact and driving force. How [our] miserable shallow educational systems, and the traditions of easy money-making and business blah have left us bleak and derided of really effective men. . . ." [92] When he has influence on a policy, Frankfurter refers to it as an "opportunity for the good." [93]

Frankfurter took very personally much of the business opposition to the New Deal, and the anti-Semitism which, he felt, resulted from that opposition.

The drive against Jewish influences in the Administration has its real source in and derives its powerful sustenance from those vested interests which are directing the attack against the economic program of the Administration. . . . It's Wall Street that is using the Jewish stick precisely as it has used and will use any other stick. . . . That is the crucial and never-to-be-forgotten fact, that the lines are drawn fundamentally according to interests. . . . The lines are drawn . . . not between Jew and non-Jew, but between right democratic national purposes and the maintenance of selfish interests.[94]

As he had done repeatedly, Frankfurter took political opposition personally and ascribed base motives to his opponents. His success in 1935 was persuading the president to make his opponents the opponents of the administration.

.   .   .

Between the coming of the second New Deal and his appointment to the Supreme Court in 1939, the major event with which Frankfurter was concerned was Roosevelt's Court-packing scheme in 1937.

Roosevelt's hostility to the Court had been building steadily during the decade. After the *Schechter* decision, the president held a news conference in which he attacked the Court for a full hour and twenty-five minutes, accusing it of trying to return the country to the "horse-and-buggy" days of a self-sufficient economy. The Frankfurters were staying overnight at the White House; a few minutes before the press conference, the president "casually suggested . . . that they might enjoy attending the conference." [95] Frankfurter, who was seeking more and more to hide his influence from the public eye, declined; Marion sat next to Mrs. Roosevelt. Frankfurter had no idea that the president was planning to attack the Court. To Brandeis he wrote:

F.D. gave me no intimation whatever that he was going to do the press conference talk. I knew nothing of it until Marion told me just as we were coming to lunch with you. I assume that F.D. purposely did not consult me or tell me why—why I know not, except perhaps that he had political purposes and so naturally would not consult me.[96]

Two years later, when Roosevelt announced his Court-packing plan, he once again did not take Frankfurter into his confidence until after he had publicly announced the scheme.[97] Just before the announcement, FDR wrote Frankfurter: "Very confidentially, I may give you an awful shock in about two weeks. Even if you do not agree, suspend final judgment and I will tell you the story." [98] Frankfurter responded:

Are you trying to find out how well I can sit on top of a Vesuvius by giving me notice that "an awful shock" is in store for me "in about two weeks"? Well, I shall try to hold my patience and fortify my capacity to withstand "an awful shock," but you certainly tease my curiosity when you threaten me with something with which I may not agree. That, certainly, would be a great surprise.[99]

The fact that he was excluded from the deliberations over the plan must have upset Frankfurter, who thought that he enjoyed the president's complete confidence.[100]

Once the plan was announced, FDR asked Frankfurter for help; Frankfurter gave it willingly, becoming a chief architect of the campaign for passage of the president's plan.*

*Max Freedman writes:

He had given the most solemn oath of silence and public neutrality to the President. After the plan was announced, Roosevelt phoned Frankfurter at Cambridge and exacted the pledge. He told Frankfurter that he intended

Frankfurter remained absolutely silent to the public about the plan, while counseling FDR and his advisors whenever he could. Although he disagreed with the substance of the plan, his loyalty was such that he was willing to overlook his objections and take part in the campaign. "Frankfurter could have elected to sit the struggle out," Lash comments, "but he was an intensely loyal man. He had come to love Roosevelt—and the influence that went with that love." [102]

His friends—and his wife—were shocked by his behavior. Marion, once again in California, wrote:

I gather from your letters that you have kept mum about all the Court business. How you *can*, I don't see. I know all the arguments against you making a public statement, but why you must martyrize yourself to the extent of keeping even Alfred Cohn in the dark as to [your] relation to the bill? I hate the whole bill so thoroughly, think it so cheap and dishonest, and I can't bear to have you accused of being in any way responsible for it. I'm a bit fed up with this silence business.[103]

Marion felt that FDR had "dropped" Frankfurter:

I feel a mounting distrust and dislike of him myself. It is plain that when he found you wouldn't "go along" and also that your connection with him entailed a certain amount of publicity of a kind he doesn't like, he decided to drop you quietly over the side of the boat. . . . He has all the faults of a woman of the scheming kind. Bah! [104]

In response to Marion, Frankfurter expressed what became his standard refrain: the plan had to be understood against a background of the Court's behavior "for thirty years."

Yes—we should be living the Court furor through together, but—keep your chemise on—emulate my calm, for I really have it. And I suppose I have it because I know all around this subject as I do about none other in the world. That enables all the factors to find their place and the emotions of displeasure at all that is phrase or tactics to be properly chilled and calm [*sic*] by the realization of the forces that led to this

---

one day to put him on the Supreme Court, and he did not want him entangled in this particular controversy. Would Frankfurter help him to get out of this mess even though he strenuously disliked many parts of the Court-packing plan? [101]

explosion—a sense of choices and risks and losses and gains all around. *The* central fact, as I wrote you, is that a few, very few obstinate and blind men impervious to rational, disinterested argument have written their narrow prejudices into the Fundamental Law of the land—for 30 years. Holmes admonished them against it—and during the last 15 years they have been more and more inaccessible to reason. And so it could be as justly said that this was a of [*sic*] unpacking the Court as packing it.[105]

To many of his closest friends, who criticized him for his silence, Frankfurter strained to come up with an explanation. C. C. Burlingham suggested that professors of law have a special obligation to the public; Frankfurter replied:

Professors of Bills and Notes, and Roman Law, and Perpetuities, and Criminal Law, *et al, et al,* as such, are not equipped with that basis of specialized knowledge regarding the work of the Court during the last 20 years, on which alone judgement on the President's proposal can presume to speak with expert knowledge.[106]

"To entangle the law schools in something as to which law schools have no special competence to speak," he says flatly, ". . . is doing a great disservice to the community and to law schools." [107]

Frankfurter told his close friend Grenville Clark that he would not speak out because he was perceived as an outsider by the public.

Through circumstances in the making of which I have had no share, I have become a myth, a symbol and promoter not of reason but of passion. I am the symbol of the Jew, the "red," the "alien." In that murky and passionate atmosphere anything that I say becomes enveloped. I would be heard and interpreted by what you call the average man—the reader of the Hearst papers, the Chicago Tribune, the Legion, the D.A.R.'s, the chambers of commerce, I am sorry to say the "leading" members of the bar all over the place, the readers of Time, the Saturday Evening Post, etc., etc.—not as the man who by virtue of his long years of service in the government and his special attention to problems of constitutional law and the work of the Court spoke with the authority of scholarship, but as the Jew, the "red," and the "alien".[108]

Frankfurter advised FDR to accept no compromise even when the Court began upholding New Deal legislation and VanDevan-

ter's resignation gave Roosevelt a chance to appoint a new justice.[109] He criticized Hughes and Roberts mercilessly for their
"switch." * The Court, he said, was playing politics just as much
as the president, which was inexcusable.

What I am concerned about is the vitality of the court in the country's
confidence. Robert's behavior in the Washington *Minimum Wage*
case . . . made me feel as though something very dear had died—my
faith that the Court's processes had integrity. . . . As a teacher I have a
nearly priest-like office towards the young men whom I teach. I wish
you would come up here and subject yourself to their cross-examina-
tion on the *Parrish* case and [other] decisions, in the light of the
circumstances under which they were rendered, and the opinions
that were delivered, including Hughes', during the last two or three
years.[110]

When Brandeis signed the letter sent by Hughes to the Senate
Judiciary Committee, claiming that the Court was fully caught up
in its work—thus denying one of Roosevelt's supposed justifications for enlarging the Court—Frankfurter and Brandeis came
close to a break. Frankfurter composed a long and angry letter to
Brandeis.[111]

I know that some subjects are not to be canvassed. But I should stifle
my conscience if I withheld comment on the C. J.'s statement. . . . For
one who has watched the Supreme Court for now thirty years as
closely as a mother watches a sick child it has been none too easy to
keep quiet while this debate has been raging. The C.J.'s statement
does not make it easier. I suspect it looks different to one outside the
Court and not so deeply tied up with the institution itself. . . .

Of course the President dished up phoney arguments with which
somebody—I know not who—supplied him. . . . Disingenuousness on
the part of the Chief Executive hardly excuses disingenuousness on
the part of the Chief Justice—not only disingenuousness in professing
not to deal with issues of policy and yet powerfully seeking to affect
them, but disingenuousness in the calm that there was no time to
consult the other justices. That is too ridiculous. . . . I resent the
C.J.'s putting you in the front line even with your approval. . . .

*Soon after the announcement of the Court packing plan, the Court handed
down decisions in which both Chief Justice Hughes and Owen Roberts voted
to uphold New Deal legislation—the famous "switch in time that saved nine."
In later years, Frankfurter would drastically revise his opinion of the behavior
of Hughes and Roberts in these decisions. See pp. 142ff and 183f.

Tampering with the Court is very serious business. Like any other major operation it is justified only by the most compelling consider-ations. But no student of the Court can be blind to its long course of misbehavior. I do not relish some of the implications of the President's proposal, but neither do I relish victory for the subtler but ultimately deeper evils inevitable in a victory for the Hugheses and the Butlers and their successors.[112]

Frankfurter, however, did not send this letter; his friendship with Brandeis was too precious.[113] He did, however, criticize Bran-deis to others,[114] and other members of the administration were less careful about hurting the old justice's feelings. Tommy Corcoran, in particular, never forgave Brandeis for what he considered his betrayal. A few months after the controversy, Ben Cohen wrote Frankfurter about a visit to Brandeis, and Brandeis's disappoint-ment that Corcoran was not there also. In this intriguing letter, Cohen said that Corcoran was especially upset that Brandeis would not consider resigning from the Court—an act, Cohen said, that might have guaranteed Frankfurter's own appointment to fill the vacant seat.[115]

The Court-packing fight was supremely difficult for Frankfurt-er. Driven by loyalty to defend a policy he had no hand in formu-lating and with which he ultimately disagreed, enduring strained relations with close friends, his wife, and with the revered Brandeis, the emotional toll affected his health. Frankfurter had had peri-odic back trouble which returned in the spring and summer of 1937, "giving him such pain . . . that he could scarely either sleep or sit up." [116]

·   ·   ·

Frankfurter's appointment to the Supreme Court was, in a sense, a reward for his loyalty during the Court-packing fight. Roosevelt had promised Benjamin Cardozo's seat to the West, and Frank-furter was helping him canvass the qualifications of men from that region. Members of the administration, however, pleaded with him to appoint Frankfurter; there was, Roosevelt later said, a con-spiracy to secure his appointment.[117] Roosevelt had told Harry Hopkins that he would appoint Frankfurter to Brandeis's seat when Brandeis resigned,[118] but many members of the administration pleaded with Roosevelt not to delay Frankfurter's appointment. "If you appoint Frankfurter," Harold Ickes said to Roosevelt, "his ability and learning are such that he will dominate the Supreme Court for fifteen or twenty years to come. The result will be that probably after you are dead, it will still be your Supreme Court." [119]

Robert Jackson * stressed to Roosevelt the degree to which Frankfurter could hold his own with Chief Justice Hughes, as did Associate Justice Harlan Fiske Stone, who also saw the president to discuss the vacancy.[120] Stone, like Jackson, stressed Frankfurter's ability to compete intellectually with the chief justice.[121]

Although he always claimed to have been completely surprised by his nomination, Frankfurter was well aware of the machinations on his behalf. Corcoran, in particular, wanted to see Frankfurter on the Court, and wanted Brandeis to resign to make it possible. As early as August 1938, one month after Cardozo's death, Frankfurter received the following letter from Henry Stimson, vacationing in Switzerland:

A few days ago George Rublee wrote me to say that some friend of both you and of the President was anxious to have me write the President recommending you for the Supreme Court. This friend was unwilling to have his name known even by me. This request gave me much anxiety, for I have been so outraged . . . by the president's attempt to control the Supreme Court . . . that I did not feel as if I could address him on that subject at all. . . . But I have felt very sorrowful ever since that I could not render this assistance to you at this crisis in your life.[122]

For public consumption, Frankfurter claimed to have had no knowledge of his appointment until the night of January 4, 1939, when, standing in his underwear at his home in Cambridge, the president called. "All I can say," he supposedly told the president, "is that I wish my mother were alive." The next day, when his name was sent to the Senate, Harold Ickes held a party in his office; Harry Hopkins, William O. Douglas,† Frank Murphy,‡ Missy LeHand, and Tommy Corcoran were there.[123]

---

*Jackson had recently been named solicitor general after serving as assistant attorney general.

† Douglas served as chairman of the Securities and Exchange Commission from 1936 to 1939.

‡ Murphy was at this time attorney general.

Frankfurter sailed through the Senate confirmation hearings with Dean Acheson representing him at his side. After his confirmation, Frankfurter thanked Ickes for his help. Ickes wrote in his diary: "He was plainly delighted with his appointment, but I really think that this pleasure was not altogether personal. He feels that he is a symbol and that his appointment means much to the liberal cause." [124]

His close friend, Alfred Cohn, was present at the swearing-in ceremony, as were many members of the White House circle. Cohn later wrote Frankfurter that the ceremony had gone well, "except, Mr. Justice, your hand shook when you were taking the oath, as only the initiated could see. . . . I should not mention it but for the fact that *for several weeks* past it has been doing the same thing. . . ." [125]

CHAPTER 5

1939–1943:
The Unexpected Challenge

FELIX FRANKFURTER had every reason to believe that his tenure as a justice of the Supreme Court would be a smashing and enjoyable success. He had devoted his life to the study of the law; he had had intimate personal relationships with Holmes and Brandeis, whose jurisprudence would dominate the now-liberal Court; he had carefully cultivated friendships with men who were now or soon to be his colleagues. He had been successful in every role he had thus far chosen in his life—academic, liberal spokesman and activist, advisor to the president. The Supreme Court was an arena in which he felt himself superbly qualified to triumph once again.

But something went wrong. For the first time in his life, and much to his surprise, Frankfurter was faced with a situation in which he could not triumph, in which he could not overcome opposition to his policies and goals. For the first time, he was faced with strong-willed colleagues who resented his attempts to influence and lead them. The Supreme Court was a political arena fundamentally different from those to which Frankfurter was accustomed. He shared power—equally—with eight other men; he could not function in his usual capacity of free-lance advisor. Although he did his best to translate his style of behind-the-scenes maneuvering to the Court, by constantly flattering his brethren and deluging them with suggestions and criticisms, he had, finally, only one vote in nine. He could not pick and choose the cases on which to fight out his battles; he could not withdraw into the shadows and bide his time, as he did during the New Deal. Moreover, his constant use of flattery and professorial instruction were often counterproductive with men who perceived themselves to be his equal and in no need of his help. Frankfurter's style backfired; his initial years on the Court represented Frankfurter's first confrontation with a sustained challenge to his self-image in a field he considered his own.

.   .   .

Frankfurter had always been convinced that he held the key to the world of constitutional jurisprudence; that key was the thought of Harvard professor James Bradley Thayer as interpreted by Oliver Wendell Holmes. Frankfurter never tired of citing Thayer as the ultimate authority in constitutional law; he readily and repeatedly called Thayer the man "who through his writings has influenced me most as to public law." [1] "It is one of the tragedies of my life," he often said, "that [Thayer] was gone by the time I entered the Law School." [2]

The essential assumption of Thayer's theory was the necessity of judicial self-restraint in the face of "reasonable" policy decisions by popularly elected legislatures. The crucial—but unarticulated —premise of this assumption is that the United States is in fact an open polity, in which the political process accurately and fairly reflects all citizen preferences.[3] Thayer's doctrine of self-restraint had always appealed to Frankfurter. It coincided with his intense patriotism—and his belief in the possibilities of popular education —to hold that necessary social change could in fact be achieved through elections, given an adequately led and educated populace. When the pre-1937 Court was actively invalidating progressive social legislation—legislation Frankfurter often had a hand in preparing or defending—Thayer's doctrine of self-restraint easily coincided with and reinforced Frankfurter's liberalism.

More importantly, Thayer was, in Frankfurter's mind, endorsed and applied by Holmes and Brandeis. Frankfurter thought of himself as a member of a select legal fraternity whose members understood the true gospel. He often wrote of "the experience that I have had down here [on the Supreme Court], which so decisively confirms the philosophy in which Mr. Justice Holmes, Judge Learned Hand, Mr. Justice Brandeis and I were bred, to wit: James B. Thayer's outlook on the reviewing power of this Court." [4] Thayer's self-restraint, Frankfurter was convinced, provided the only assumption upon which a liberal and democratic jurisprudence could be based. The fact that he perceived agreement between himself and the giants of his world—Holmes, Brandeis, Hand—powerfully reinforced his convictions.

Frankfurter was committing a giant oversimplification, however, when he blithely combined Brandeis and Holmes under the banner of Thayer and attributed to both of them beliefs and premises coinciding with his own. Although both Holmes and Brandeis endorsed Thayer, they did so for different reasons and to a different extent. Moreover, when it came to the all-important question of how self-restraint should be reconciled with the protection of civil liberties, Brandeis significantly modified Thayer, while Holmes was both confused and contradictory.

Both Brandeis and Holmes believed that the executive and legislature should be given wide latitude in the formulation of social and economic policy, but the assumptions supporting this political premise were different for each of them. For Brandeis, this stance was in large part a function of his belief in the power of scientific expertise to solve social problems. Since the government —at least theoretically—had access to knowledge, it must be allowed to apply that knowledge in the most efficient manner without judicial interference. Brandeis's pre-Court career had been in large part devoted to making social "facts" available to the judiciary; he believed, writes his biographer Alpheus T. Mason, in the existence of "certain standards of social justice established prima facie by the facts." [5]

Holmes, on the other hand, was a skeptic.[6] He endorsed judicial self-restraint not because he believed in knowledge but because he believed in power;[7] legislative majorities, Holmes felt, had the right to shape public policy whether they were right or wrong, whether their preferences were based on facts or on prejudice. Unlike Brandeis, Holmes had no faith in the possibilities of popular education; the function of the judge, Holmes felt, was to enforce the will of the sovereign political body, whoever or whatever that might be.[8] It is only because in American constitutional theory "the people" are sovereign that Holmes's jurisprudence could be described as liberal and democratic.[9] Thus, although Brandeis and Holmes often voted together on the Court, their judicial creeds rested on fundamentally different assumptions—assumptions that remained largely unexpressed and unnoticed.

Frankfurter's pre-Court ideology was, in fact, much closer to Brandeis's than to Holmes's. Like Brandeis, Frankfurter strongly believed in the efficacy of scientific expertise and the need for experts in government; like Brandeis, Frankfurter believed that irrefutable social facts could and should guide policy choices. Frankfurter conceived of his entire career as a professor of law to be one in which he would create a "scientific" civil service, armed with "scientific" facts, ready to take over the reins of power in Washington. Yet, as Sanford Levinson has argued, a curious anomaly emerges, for despite the fact that Frankfurter's pre-Court career and ideology were similar to Brandeis's, "his tenure on the Court was marked by a self-conscious attempt to make Holmes the model for the proper Justice." [10]

Frankfurter, moreover, often misunderstood and misinterpreted Holmes in ways that are difficult to explain. Grant Gilmore has written of Frankfurter's tendency to paint a false picture of Holmes:

Holmes is a strange, enigmatic figure. Put out of your mind the picture of the tolerant aristocrat, the great liberal, the eloquent defender of our liberties, the Yankee from Olympus. All that was a myth, concocted principally by Harold Laski and Felix Frankfurter, about the time of World War I. The real Holmes was savage, harsh and cruel, a bitter and lifelong pessimist who saw in the course of human life nothing but a continuing struggle in which the rich and powerful impose their will on the poor and weak. . . .

In this bleak and terrifying universe, the function of law, as Holmes saw it, is simply to channel private aggressions in an orderly, perhaps in a dignified, fashion.[11]

Similarly, Gary Jacobsohn has argued that Frankfurter misunderstood Holmes, placing him in the category of "statesman" in the tradition of John Marshall.* But it was Brandeis, not Holmes, who believed in "statesmanship," in the possibility of intelligently directing social policy toward a specific goal.[13]

As Jacobsohn hints, Frankfurter's "misunderstanding" of Holmes was complicated by psychological factors. Frankfurter's affection for Holmes was strong and genuine; Holmes's approval and friendship were Frankfurter's most cherished possessions. It was Holmes—not Brandeis—who personified for Frankfurter the Brahmin establishment. Agreeing with Holmes meant agreeing with that world; being accepted by Holmes meant being accepted by that world. Frankfurter "needed" Holmes psychologically in a way that he did not need Brandeis; despite his fundamental agreement with Brandeis, it was Holmes he adopted as his ideal. His attachment to Holmes was so strong that he ignored or rationalized any ideological differences between them and could not see any contradictions within Holmes's thought.

This factor—Frankfurter's perception that Holmes supported his jurisprudence in full, while in fact it was possible to read Holmes in other ways—became crucial when the true meaning of the Holmesian legacy surfaced as a point of contention between Frankfurter and his judicial opponents. Whatever the true relationship between Holmes's premises and his own, however,

---

*Jacobsohn writes:

For the liberals, of course, Holmes' skepticism (and the constitutional philosophy that it entailed) was an important weapon in the fight against the Spencerian interpretation of the Constitution. It was this happy alignment of skepticism on the side of liberalism that greatly attracted Frankfurter to Holmes. Beyond this political attraction lay a deep and abiding personal affection, and these two factors must be remembered in considering the numerous accolades to Holmes that are found throughout Frankfurter's writings. Psychological analysis can be left to others; suffice it to say that the ambiguity in Frankfurter's reflections on statesmanship is at least in part attributable to the complex nature of his relationship with Holmes.[12]

Frankfurter's perception of agreement between himself and his idol reinforced his certainty that his theory of constitutional interpretation was correct.

.   .   .

Public events further convinced Frankfurter that Thayer's doctrine of self-restraint had won the day. The Court-packing fight and the Court's relinquishment of control over economic legislation persuaded Frankfurter that the course of action he had always supported was now in fact operative.

Throughout the twenties and thirties, Frankfurter had decried the Court's strangulation of liberal social legislation. In 1921 he had written Learned Hand about the Court:

Tomorrow they might very easily knock out the Minimum Wage Law. And so I say—as I said recently in answer to Cardozo's direct question—the price we pay for this judicial service is too great, the advantages too slim for the cost. A Court *dominantly* composed of Holmes and Brandeis and Learned Hand and Cardozo—that's one thing, but taking the judicial fish as they run, we have no business to build our institutions on such problematic and unlikely happenings.[14]

Two years later, when the Court did overturn the Minimum Wage Law by a vote of five to three—after Frankfurter had argued the case before them—he again wrote to Hand: "And my own mind has about found lodgment where yours has; namely, that the possible gain isn't worth the cost of having five men without any reasonable probability that they are qualified for the task, determine the course of social policy for the states and the nation." [15] Frankfurter's attitude toward the judicial invalidation of the New Deal was, of course, similar.[16]

When the Court after 1937 began allowing social and economic legislation which could be construed as "reasonable" to pass constitutional muster, Frankfurter was sure that constitutional liberalism, as he understood it, had finally triumphed. He felt fully prepared for and capable of handling the type of case he thought would come before the Court—cases involving the relationship between the federal government and the states, cases requiring the Court to interpret federal statutes, and, especially, cases involving administrative agencies of the federal government. Frankfurter considered himself an expert on all of these subjects; he had, after all, taught them for over two decades at the Harvard Law School.

Yet in the area of jurisprudence that was in fact to become the main preoccupation of the post-1937 Court—civil liberties and civil rights—Frankfurter was unprepared for what was to come. Frankfurter did hold opinions about the Court's role in handling civil liberties, but these opinions were sometimes contradictory, extremely fuzzy, inarticulate, and unrefined. He did not expect the protection of civil liberties to become the self-defined role of the Roosevelt Court, and thus did not give the topic nearly as much thought or energy as he devoted to other subjects.

His guides on these matters, as on all others, were Holmes and Brandeis. But here again, the two disagreed. Brandeis, much more than Holmes, had consistently held that judicial self-restraint must be abandoned when fundamental values were threatened.[17] In the *Whitney* case in 1927,[18] Brandeis had explicitly endorsed the concept of fundamental values and had written eloquently about the fundamental nature of free speech.[19] Holmes's position on free speech, on the other hand, was ambiguous in the extreme. Holmes's Court opinions on the subject can be read like tea leaves, taking out of them whatever position one seeks.

On the one hand, there is Holmes's doctrine of "clear-and-present-danger," first announced in *Schenck*,[20] elaborated in his *Abrams* dissent,[21] in which he says:

The best test of truth is the power of the thought to get itself accepted in the competition of the market. . . . I think that we should be eternally vigilant against attempts to check the expression of opinions that we loathe and believe to be fraught with death, unless they so imminently threaten immediately interference with the lawful and pressing purposes of the law that an immediate check is required to save the country.[22]

But on the other hand, there is Holmes's 1923 dissent in *Meyer* v.

Nebraska,[23] in which he calls upon the Court to exercise the same self-restraint in civil liberties cases as in other areas of adjudication.*

Frankfurter's analysis of Holmes's position on civil liberties was as ambiguous and contradictory as the master's words themselves. In 1923 he endorsed Holmes's position in *Meyer*. In an unsigned editorial for the *New Republic*, entitled "Can the Supreme Court Guarantee Toleration?" Frankfurter compared the *Meyer* case, and those like it, to those cases in which the Court had used the due process clause of the Fourteenth Amendment to strike down economic legislation, a practice he abhorred.[25] In a passage that would find its way almost verbatim into his Supreme Court opinions twenty years later, Frankfurter wrote:

And this brings us to consider the intrinsic promotion of the liberal spirit by the Supreme Court's invalidation of illiberal legislation. It must never be forgotten that our constant preoccupation with the constitutionality of legislation rather than its wisdom tends to preoccupation of the American mind with a false value. . . . The tendency of focusing attention on constitutionality is to make constitutionality synonymous with propriety; to regard a law all right so long as it is "constitutional." Such an attitude is a great enemy of liberalism.[26]

But despite such pronouncements—in which he endorses a strong version of judicial self-restraint and, by clear implication, denies the need for the Court to protect any fundamental values—Frankfurter was later able to describe and embrace what he considered Holmes's belief that the Court should afford more protection to civil liberties than to economic liberty. In a book on Holmes published in 1938—just one year before his own appointment to the Court—Frankfurter wrote:

The various interests of human personality are not of equal worth. There is a hierarchy of values. And so we shall find that some manifestations of the human spirit seemed to Mr. Justice Holmes so precious that in specific instances he found no justification for legislative restrictions, tolerant though he was of the legislative judgment. . . .

[Holmes believed that] the liberty of man to search for truth was of a different order than some economic dogma defined as a sacred

---

*The case involved a 1919 Nebraska statute prohibiting the teaching of any language but English in any elementary school, public or private. The Court struck down the statute; the unlikely duo of Holmes and Sutherland dissented.[24]

right because the temporal nature of its origin has been forgotten. And without freedom of expression liberty of thought is a mockery. . . .

Naturally, therefore, Mr. Justice Holmes attributed very different legal significance to those liberties of the individual which history has attested as the indispensable conditions of a free society from that which he attached to liberties which derived merely from shifting economic arrangements.[27]

Brandeis—who clearly believed in such a hierarchy of values—had disagreed with Holmes in the *Meyer* case. Brandeis and Frankfurter often discussed cases; Frankfurter often kept notes of these conversations.[28] In the following fragment, Frankfurter clearly endorses the general concept of "fundamental values" and—despite his 1923 editorial—seems to agree with Brandeis's position in *Meyer*.

Long talk on the application of due process as to freedom of speech and foreign language cases. Agreed.
  1. Due process should be restricted procedural regularity and
  2. In favor of repeal* but
  3. While it is, must be applied to substantive laws and so as to things that are fundamental.
  Right to education
  Right to choice of profession.
  Right to locomotion,
are such fundamental rights not to be impaired on [illegible] except as judged by "clear and present danger" test. Holmes says [he] doesn't want to extend XIV [Amendment]. L.D.B. says it means—you are going to cut down freedom through striking down regulation of property but not give protection. Property, it is absurd Holmes says, to deem fundamental in the sense that you can't curtail its use or its accumulation or power. There may be some aspects of property that are fundamental—but not regard as fundamental specific limitations upon it. *Whereas right to your education and to utter speech is fundamental except clear and present danger.*[29]

Whether there were in fact fundamental values and a hierarchy of values in the Constitution, and whether the Court should afford special protection to the most important of these values, was to be

---

*Frankfurter had been in favor of repealing the due process clause of the Fourteenth Amendment because of its use in invalidating progressive social legislation.

the key question of constitutional law for the post-1937 Supreme Court. It was this basic question on which Frankfurter and the men who became his judicial opponents were to divide, with Frankfurter taking a position diametrically opposite to the one he sometimes attributed to Holmes, to Brandeis, and to himself.

The division over this question was foreshadowed in the late thirties, before Frankfurter's appointment. In a case in 1938, Justice Harlan Fiske Stone—of whom Frankfurter held the lowest possible opinion—presented the germ of a new jurisprudence in the most famous footnote in Supreme Court history. In *United States* v. *Carolene Products*,[30] in footnote four, Stone wrote:

There may be narrower scope for operation of the presumption of constitutionality when legislation appears on its face to be within a specific prohibition of the Constitution, such as those of the first ten amendments, which are deemed equally specific when held to be embraced within the Fourteenth. . . .

It is unnecessary to consider now whether legislation which restricts those political processes which can ordinarily be expected to bring about repeal of undesirable legislation, is to be subjected to more exacting judicial scrutiny under the general prohibition of the Fourteenth Amendment than are most other types of legislation. . . .

Nor need we enquire whether similar considerations enter into the review of statutes directed at particular religious . . . or natural . . . or racial minorities: . . . whether prejudice against discrete and insular minorities may be a special condition, which tends seriously to curtail the operation of those political processes ordinarily to be relied upon to protect minorities, and which may call for a correspondingly more searching judicial inquiry.[31]

But for this doctrine of preference, or "preferred freedoms," to develop from a footnote to a full-blown theory of constitutional interpretation took several years, and was not accomplished until after Frankfurter's appointment. In the meantime, Frankfurter paid little attention to the question or to the refinement of his own position; he did not expect the issue to be raised in dramatic or difficult form. He never worked out the contradiction in his own thoughts between his endorsement of judicial self-restraint and his belief in the existence of a hierarchy of constitutional values; he never saw the contradictions within Holmes's jurisprudence or gave much thought to the difference between Holmes and Brandeis illustrated by *Meyer*. He agreed with both of them; he agreed with the Holmes of *Abrams* but also with the Holmes of *Meyer*.

Frankfurter thus believed simultaneously in both self-restraint and in fundamental values. He did not expect these stances to be cross-cutting; he was convinced that the members of the Court in the past who had been hostile to economic liberalism were also hostile to civil liberties. In 1937 he wrote C. C. Burlingham: "The fact of the matter is that the Justices who resist the social obligations of property, and apply Herbert Spencer's 'Social Statics' instead of the Constitution, are also the Justices who have had no respect for civil liberties, i.e., for the protection of views that they regard as dangerous." [32] Thus it did not occur to Frankfurter that a jurisprudence was possible in which maximum judicial self-restraint was applied and maximum latitude was given to the legislature in the field of economic policy, while close judicial scrutiny would be applied to the protection of civil liberties.

Soon, however, Frankfurter was to be faced with just such a jurisprudence. But on the eve of his appointment to the Court, Frankfurter could not foresee what was coming. He was supremely confident that the assumptions in which he so firmly believed would carry the day, and that they were adequate to deal with any doctrinal situation; he was unaware of any inconsistency in his own positions. He was convinced of his ability to easily handle the intellectual business of the Court within the framework that he already understood.*

---

*There were many who expected Frankfurter the judge to become an ardent protector of civil liberties. In 1939, Archibald MacLeish, a close friend, wrote of Frankfurter's great devotion and sensitivity to civil liberties:

It would be impossible to overestimate the importance of that sensitivity and that devotion in the present constitutional crisis. . . . The question . . . [is] whether the Court can and will permit the legislature the widest latitude in framing economic measures altering property relations while sharply rejecting all attempts to curtail or restrict civil liberties. On that issue the position of Mr. Frankfurter is clear.

MacLeish then went on to quote Frankfurter's description of Holmes's attitude, quoted above, pp. 134–35.[33]

•   •   •

Frankfurter was also convinced that he could easily handle his judicial colleagues. Throughout his life Frankfurter had excelled at "personalia"—that process of flattering, cajoling, helping, advising, and needling—of which he was so proud. In every previous environment—in the White House, at Harvard, in Washington—Frankfurter's interpersonal skills had won for him what he wanted. Here, on the Supreme Court, was an arena in which his ability to handle men could once again powerfully aid his political goals.

Adding to his certainty that he would be able to handle his colleagues was the fact that he had watched the judicial process at work for so long and was sure he understood the secret of inter-Court exchanges. Brandeis, in particular, had shared with Frankfurter a multitude of Court gossip and inside information. For years, Frankfurter had watched Brandeis influence his judicial colleagues to achieve his desired results. In the notes of his conversations with Brandeis, Frankfurter often quotes Brandeis as making numerous comments about his ability to influence his brethren. "I could have had much influence with White," Frankfurter quotes Brandeis as saying. "I did in the beginning, but I made up my mind I couldn't pay the price it would have cost in want of directness and frankness. He required to be managed. . . ." [34] On another occasion Brandeis told Frankfurter:

Taft is the worst sinner in wanting to "settle things" by deciding them when we ought not to, as a matter of jurisdiction. He says "we will have to decide it sooner or later and better now." I frequently remind him of Dred Scott—Sutherland also had to be held in check. McReynolds cares more about jurisdictional restraints than any of them—Holmes is beginning to see it.

Frankfurter paid particular attention to the influence of Brandeis upon Holmes; they often discussed him.[35] And Brandeis often discussed the "limitations" of various members of the Court.

Spoke of intellectual limitations of Court—no one to talk with except Holmes and CJ. Sutherland was promising but soon ran dry . . . Van D. has "taken charge" of Pierce B. Latter has given no sign of anything except a thoroughly mediocre mind. Sanford very nice, but entirely bourgeois—McReynolds has taken him in tow.

From Brandeis, Frankfurter took the confidence of an insider that he understood the process by which judicial influence could be exerted. He understood the role "de facto leader of the Court"; he had watched Brandeis play the role and was now prepared to play the role himself.

Moreover, Frankfurter had already established personal relationships with many of the colleagues he would now seek to influence; he had every reason to believe that they would be susceptible to his skillful handling. Of the eight men with whom he would now interact, Frankfurter knew several: Stone, with whom he had corresponded for years; Douglas and Reed, with whom he had interacted during the New Deal. Within two years of his own appointment, three more New Dealers were appointed to the Court: Jackson, Byrnes and Murphy, all of whom Frankfurter knew well. There were only two members of the Court in January 1939 with whom Frankfurter could not hope to have influence—McReynolds and Butler. And they were soon gone.

Frankfurter applauded the appointments of Black and Douglas. Frankfurter and Douglas had known each other for some time, and had corresponded casually during the thirties. When Douglas became chairman of the Securities and Exchange Commission Frankfurter sometimes sent him suggestions and recommendations.[36] To Charles Wyzanski, Frankfurter wrote: "You do well to be glad over the appointment of Douglas. We shall have a man who is historic-minded about the law, but also knows that history is not a tale of dead things but part of a dynamic process." [37]

Frankfurter was also pleased at the appointment of Black in 1937, although he was less sure of Black's abilities. He was, however, convinced that Black could learn as he went along. To C. C. Burlingham, who had serious doubts about Black, Frankfurter wrote:

As to Black, I haven't suggested that we should "roll him as a sweet morsel under tongues." I have merely suggested that we shouldn't spew him out in a panic nor swallow him as though he were a bitter pill. I say this because the evidence of very sober witnesses and knowing folk converges to an estimate of Black as a man of really fine native ability, studious habits, absorptive powers, and the humility which leads to growth and understanding.[38]

Frankfurter was sympathetic about Black's difficulties concerning his past affiliation with the Ku Klux Klan.* "Poor Black," he wrote. "I suspect he long ago outgrew Klanism and couldn't tell the truth by merely telling the facts." [40]

After his confirmation, Black's unconventional judicial behavior—particularly his willingness to express his strong views in dissents—rankled some of his brethren.[41] In 1938, Stone appealed to Frankfurter for help. "Do you know Black well?" Stone inquired. "You might be able to render him great assistance. He needs guidance from someone who is more familiar with the workings of the judicial process than he is. With guidance, and a disposition to follow it until he is a little surer of himself, he might do great things." [42] Frankfurter was only too happy to supply Black with advice. In the spring, Frankfurter wrote a long and revealing letter to Brandeis about Black.

1. We had tea at the Blacks and dined with them at the Reeds, and I had some time with them alone. I took occasions to speak *en passant* about the importance of choosing one's grounds for dissenting, illustrating by my conviction that you and Holmes had not always dissented when you disagreed. I also got a chance to speak of the value of secretaries—and he is at least abstractly aware of it. . . .

2. I did have a good private talk with Mrs. Black about him, and she can be counted on, I think, to soften and not to encourage asperities and to mitigate his feelings and habits of isolation.

3. I hope for a chance to talk with you about the whole Black business, for I am rather deeply troubled about your concern over his dissents. Frankly I don't share your concern. Of course he is not technically equipped—but many good men in the Court's history started out with poor equipment in the field of the Court's special technical business. . . . [He] has, I am sure, a good head, works hard, will learn, or rather is capable of learning if he is rightly encouraged and not treated as though he is outside the fold. . . . It weighs with me that people who literally hate Black (and F.D.) should tell me, in fields in which they speak with special learning, that Black's dissent was

*As a young politician in Alabama, Black had briefly joined the Klan, which controlled the local votes in virtually every rural Alabama location.[39]

to be preferred to the Court's views. . . . Besides, in constitutional questions it will do no harm, as far as I can see, to have some pressure and jolts from what is called "the left." . . . I don't think we ought to be impatient with Black even though he does not have the wisdom to husband his resources and lacks the technical equipment which time ought not to put beyond him.[43]

As always, Frankfurter was sure that, with proper "education," people could be brought to do what they ought to do. He had no idea that Black and Douglas would not live up to his expectations; both, however, were highly independent and proud men who were not likely to take kindly to Frankfurter's style of instruction.

It was inevitable that Frankfurter in 1939 would think of himself as the intellectual leader of the Roosevelt Court. Members of the White House circle expected him to dominate; that was why he had been appointed. He expected himself to dominate. He was convinced that he held the doctrinal key to the legal universe; he was supremely confident of his ability to get on with and influence his colleagues. On every level, his self-image was intact and strong.

. . .

Frankfurter's first months on the Court were calm and pleasant, although he was a bit surprised by the work load and the pressure of opinion writing. "You can imagine the load of work I am under from the meagreness of my correspondence," he wrote Julian Mack.

But really, it is a very steady grind if one is to take this job as one should. The cases pile up one after the other, and if one is not to make a merely casual judgment on so many complicated and cloudy issues, it requires a good deal of reading and digging, and, what appears to be rather rare here—talking with some of the brethren. I don't have to tell you that even about matters about which I knew but little when I came down here, it is one thing to have views, and another thing to act on them.[44]

He was thrilled to be where he was. "For Marion and me it all seems so unreal," he wrote Learned Hand. "I can hardly believe that less than a month ago I was still having classes at Cambridge." [45]

From the start, Frankfurter enjoyed a cordial relationship with Chief Justice Hughes. Although Frankfurter had been highly critical of Hughes in the past—particularly during the Court-packing controversy [46]—the Chief Justice's commanding presence and serene temperament helped soften Frankfurter's feelings for him.[47] More importantly, Hughes was amenable to Frankfurter's influence, and it was difficult for Frankfurter to bear a grudge against one who could be made to see the light. Hughes welcomed Frankfurter to the Court warmly, telling him he was about to undertake work "for which you are so exceptionally qualified." [48] Hughes praised Frankfurter's earliest judicial outputs; "very clear and thorough. I agree," he would write on Frankfurter's slip opinions.* In the interests of harmony, the Chief Justice was often willing to accept points in a Frankfurter opinion about which he had reservations.[49]

Frankfurter flattered the chief justice, telling him that he "awaited with trepidation your scrutiny. . . . I am correspondingly relieved and heartened that you should approve." [50] When Hughes on one occasion called attention to a precedent supporting Frankfurter's opinion that Frankfurter had neglected to mention, Frankfurter responded: "I am rather ashamed of myself not to have cited the . . . case which fits so well into the analysis that I attempted." [51] Frankfurter played the role of the novice, seeking out the Chief's advice. "As a junior junior," he wrote Hughes, "I naturally should not like to have anyone, however unwittingly, have a feeling of displacement." [52] Slowly and subtly, Frankfurter began making suggestions to Hughes, which Hughes was often willing to accept.[53]

The characteristics Frankfurter evidenced in his treatment of Hughes were familiar parts of the Frankfurter style—flattery mixed with persuasion; claims of modesty mixed with claims of expertise. Although he was careful to be deferential to the chief justice, he was a bit more forthright in his relations with the associate justices. Stanley Reed, in particular, received instruction

---

*"Slip opinions" are early drafts of opinions circulated among members of the Court. Each member normally indicates whether he agrees or disagrees with the opinion, why, and often makes criticisms or suggestions.

from Frankfurter, in long letters detailing the validity of a Frankfurter opinion or the inadequacy of Reed's objections.[54]

Instruction was always mixed with flattery. In a case in which Reed had written the majority opinion, Frankfurter prepared a concurrence.* He sent Reed a copy of it, together with a note.

> I want you to see this before I circulate it not in order to soften the blow, for I have no doubt you will agree there is no blow. I want you to see it because that's the way I feel about you. No job is all beer and skittles—not even this one. Nothing in connection with the job here gives me more enveloping and continuous satisfaction than the disinterestedness of your friendship and fellowship. I have known a few people—very very few—in whom the instinct for work was as untarnished by any personal sensitiveness as is yours, but I have never known anyone in whom instinct was more finely or more constantly alive than in you. Therefore you never arouse in me any personal concern that whatever conscientious response I may make to your opinion will be interpreted by you otherwise than as the labors of co-workers in the vineyard.[55]

Although Reed did not incorporate Frankfurter's points into his opinion, Frankfurter eventually withdrew the concurrence.[56] Frankfurter paid Reed several visits to get his points across. Since the case involved the commerce clause—which Frankfurter considered one of his "special subjects"—he asked Reed whether he had read his book on the clause, which evidently startled Reed. Frankfurter attempted to soothe his feelings in yet another letter.

> When I asked you whether you had read my little book on the Commerce Clause, I meant to imply not a commentary on your opinion in the *Ford* case, but on my views regarding the problems raised by relation of the states to the Commerce Clause. I merely meant to indicate that my conviction as to the necessity for empiricism relates to the disposition of special variants of a particular case within a framework of general ideas and not to a denial of the indispensability for a philosophy regarding state-nation relations under the Commerce Clause. What my own philosophy is I have tried to state meagerly enough in my little book as a result of such understanding as I have been able to

---

*A member of the Court who concurs with the majority agrees with the precise legal holding of the case, although not necessarily with the reasoning of the majority opinion.

muster through the years. Heaven forfend that you should think that I am implying I have come to the end of my own possible wisdom.[57]

Other members of the Court received similar treatment. Stone, as one of the more senior members of the Court and, after the retirement of Brandeis, its most prominent liberal, was anxious to help Frankfurter along, and often made suggestions [58] which Frankfurter must have found patronizing, coming, as they did, from someone whose legal talents he considered inferior to his own. Frankfurter, in turn, applied his own treatment to Stone. As he had done throughout their long correspondence over the years, Frankfurter continued to flatter Stone.

You comfort me enormously in having found the opinion satisfactory. The ultimate tribunal is, of course, one's self, but as Holmes used to say, one needs the agreement of some other people for if you are a minority of one in the world you are likely to be shut up. And so one writes for a particular audience. It is true in everything I write that you are my touchstone, but it was particularly true [here] because of your great generosity in assigning it to me. And so I was deeply relieved to have your approval.[59]

As usual, instruction was often mixed with flattery.

In view of your encouraging words yesterday forenoon, I am tempted to put to you what was in my mind regarding the restricted nature of the issues on which [this case] turn[s]. Of course, I don't mean to imply that what I am about to say isn't old stuff to you, but I should like to express more freely than I was enabled to on Saturday what was in my mind.[60]

Sometimes, though, it was flattery for flattery's sake. "Your special significance," Frankfurter wrote Stone, "is that you embody in yourself to a more significant degree than has been true of anybody else who has been on this Court the three great branches of our profession,—scholarship, practice, judging." [61]

Frankfurter was invited by Stone to join the rump conference held by the liberal members of the Court as soon as he was appointed to the bench. The first item Frankfurter pasted in his Supreme Court scrapbook was a handwritten note from Stone: "You are invited to join the party at Brandeis home at 6 p.m. today." At the bottom of this note, Frankfurter wrote: "This was passed to me on the Bench by Stone, on Friday, February 10, 1939. That evening, at L.D.B.'s, I met Stone and Roberts and the four of us went over the cases that had been argued the week of February 6. We agreed on all." At the end of the 1941 term, Frankfurter added: "This practice continued at Stone's house, after Brandeis' retirement. When Douglas came on he was invited to join. Roberts dropped out the following fall, that is, October 1940. Thereafter Douglas and I went to Stone's and that was discontinued after Stone became C.J." *

Douglas and Roberts, as well as Black, often warmly endorsed Frankfurter's opinions during the 1938 and 1939 terms. "I heartily agree—you have cleared the situation admirably—a much needed job, perfectly done!" Roberts wrote on the slip opinion of one of Frankfurter's earliest products.[62] "Superb!" Douglas would write, or "You have done a magnificent job. I say 'yes' even more enthusiastically than I did before." [63] Black was equally enthusiastic. "Your best up to date. . . . I am delighted to agree." [64]

Despite the prevailing harmony, some faint signs of discord between Frankfurter and Black and Douglas appeared during the 1939 term. Early in the term, Frankfurter wrote Black an intriguing letter about an issue that would later become a major point of contention between them: the application of the Bill of Rights to the states, through its "incorporation" into the Fourteenth Amendment.† And in a case involving the taxing of Indians,

*Stone was appointed chief justice in the summer of 1941.
† Frankfurter wrote:

Dear Hugo:

Perhaps you will let me say quite simply and without any ulterior thought what I mean to say, and *all* I mean to say, regarding your position on the "Fourteenth Amendment" as an entirety.

(1) I *can* understand that the Bill of Rights—to wit Amendments 1–9 inclusive—applies to State action and not merely to U.S. action, and that *Barron v. Baltimore* was wrong. I think it was rightly decided.

(2) What I am unable to appreciate is what are the criteria of selection as to the nine Amendments—which applies and which does not apply.

This is not written to draw any comment from you—not that I should not have pleasure in anything you may say. But I have written the above merely to state, as clearly as I am capable of, what is in my mind.

F.F.[65]

Barron v. Baltimore is the famous case in which John Marshall, in 1833, declared that the Bill of Rights was not applicable to state action.

in which Frankfurter wrote for the majority, Black filed a concurring opinion. Douglas had originally endorsed Frankfurter's majority opinion, writing on the slip opinion "I agree. This is very deftly done—so deftly as to justify the C. J. in saying hereafter, 'Felix, *my* boy'!" Later, however, Douglas decided to join Black; on the recirculation of Frankfurter's opinion, he wrote: "I have decided to go with Hugo on this, not because I have the difficulty he has but for reasons I can tell you sometime. They do not really go to the [illegible] of your discussion, which I still think is an excellent one." *

Frankfurter attempted to dissuade Black from filing his concurrence. In a long and somewhat condescending letter, he told Black:

Just because we agree in result . . . and because no immediately important public issue is involved by our different approaches in reaching the same legal result, it is at once interesting and profitable to discuss the underlying jurisprudential problem. And so I venture to make some observations on your opinion, I hope in the same spirit and for the same academic purpose as I would were I writing a piece as a professor in the Harvard Law Review.

Some time ago at the end of a, to me, very stimulating talk between us, I told you that you were a Benthamite. Since I regard Bentham as the most fruitful law reformer of the Nineteenth Century, that was of course fundamentally a term of praise. But as is so often the case with a reformer who seeks to get rid of the accumulated abuses of the past Bentham at times threw out the baby with the bath.[66]

Black was not persuaded and filed his opinion.[67]

Later in the term, Frankfurter filed a concurring opinion in a case in which Douglas wrote for the majority, with Roberts and McReynolds dissenting.[68] The case involved a complex series of facts concerning business deductions for securities transactions. In his concurring opinion Frankfurter attacked Douglas's "hypothetical, litigation-breeding assumption that this taxpayer's activities, for which expenses were sought to be deducted, did constitute a 'trade or business.' "[69]

---

*At the bottom of Douglas's note, Frankfurter wrote: "Douglas *never* thereafter referred to this case, nor to his shift, nor to his reasons for going 'with Hugo.' FF June 12, 1942."

Black endorsed Douglas's opinion. In his scrapbook, Frankfurter reported the following exchange:

Black to FF (after Douglas opinion was circulated) "I'm sure you [illegible] are wrong. I swear I think [illegible] But is entitled to the deduction.

FF "Well for heaven's sake if you feel that way why don't you join Roberts. It would be a fine thing for the Court—I won't say for you."

Black "Bill wouldn't like me to dissent."

FF "Nonsense!!"

Black "No he wouldn't"

I then spoke to Douglas and I said that he—Douglas—wouldn't mind if Black dissented. To which Douglas "Hugo can do what he likes"!!! [70]

Yet despite these small hints of the traumas which were soon to come, the 1938 and 1939 terms were on the whole calm and pleasant for Frankfurter. He was doing what he had always done— slowly influencing the men around him to achieve the results he sought, by a combination of techniques including, most obviously, the application of flattery. He had good relations with all the liberal members of the Court. He saw his influence at work on Chief Justice Hughes, on Stone, Reed, Roberts, Black, and Douglas. He fully expected the Court to continue coalescing under his leadership. In a letter to Stone concerning Reed's opinion in one case, he said:

I have a strong feeling that we will do best for the time to decide these commerce-tax cases by further defining as little as possible the underlying general ideas. Gradually there will be more of a fusion of outlook among the brethren, and by comradeship in agreement on specific decisions we will be the more ready when the time comes, to deal with these issues more at large. [71]

. . .

At the end of the 1939 term the *Gobitis* case [72] presented Frankfurter an opportunity to make his first major statement of judicial philosophy. The case raised in dramatic form the issues that would soon tear the Court apart.

Gobitis involved the question of whether the children of Jehovah's Witnesses could be required to salute the flag in school. The Witnesses claimed that the flag salute was forbidden by their religion—because it constituted worship of a graven image—and thus violated their right to the free exercise of religion under the First Amendment. Thus several key issues were concentrated in this case, including the Court's role in protecting First Amendment freedoms and minority groups, and the Court's role in overturning legislative judgments. In stark and dramatic fashion, the Gobitis children were asking for protection from the majority decision of their community, a decision that violated their conscience.

For Frankfurter, the decision produced responses on multiple levels. It involved his dearly held belief that the Court should defer to majority judgment, even when that judgment was intolerant or repressive. It called forth his ardent patriotism, just as World War II was getting underway. And it involved his deeply held belief in the power and importance of national symbols— "we live by symbols" was a Holmesian phrase he quoted constantly.[73] And *Gobitis* called forth a response in Frankfurter on yet another point—his belief in the irrelevance of religious affiliation. Frankfurter was, in a very real sense, asking the Jehovah's Witnesses to make the same choice he himself had made—to accept the secular over the religious.[74]

Gobitis, moreover, offered Frankfurter an opportunity to prove himself a "disinterested" jurist. All of his life, this was the intellectual characteristic Frankfurter most valued—the ability to separate personal preference from what he defined as necessary action in a given situation; all of his life, Frankfurter felt this characteristic separated him from his opponents and enemies. Here, in a civil liberties case in which his personal sympathies would clearly incline him against the actions of the state, Frankfurter had a chance to bend over backwards and prove his fairness and impartiality— his "disinterestedness."

Frankfurter's opinion was an eloquent and moving document.

A grave responsibility confronts this Court whenever in course of litigation it must reconcile the conflicting claims of liberty and authority.

But when the liberty invoked is liberty of conscience, and the authority is authority to safeguard the nation's fellowship, judicial conscience is put to its severest test. . . .

The manifold character of man's relations may bring his conception of religious duty into conflict with the secular interests of his fellow-men. When does the constitutional guarantee compel exemption from doing what society thinks necessary for the promotion of some great common end, or from a penalty for conduct which appears dangerous to the general good? . . . To affirm that the freedom to follow conscience has itself no limits in the life of society would deny that very plurality of principles which, as a matter of history, underlies protection of religious toleration.[75]

He stressed the right of a state to induce patriotism in its citizens.

The ultimate foundation of a free society is the binding tie of cohesive sentiment. Such a sentiment is fostered by all those agencies of the mind and spirit which may serve to gather up the traditions of a people, transmit them from generation to generation, and thereby create that continuity of a treasured common life which constitutes a civilization. "We live by symbols." The flag is the symbol of our national unity, transcending all internal differences, however large, within the framework of the Constitution. . . .

The precise issue, then, for us to decide is whether the legislatures of the various states and the authorities in a thousand counties and school districts are barred from determining the appropriateness of various means to evoke that unifying sentiment without which there can ultimately be no liberties, civil or religious.[76]

He emphasized the deference the Court must show to democratic judgment, and the possibilities of tolerance in a democracy.

Except where the transgression of constitutional liberty is too plain for argument, personal freedom is best maintained—so long as the remedial channels of the democratic process remain open and un-obstructed—when it is ingrained in a people's habits and not enforced against popular policy by the coercion of adjudicated law. . . .

Where all the effective means of inducing political changes are left free from interference, education in the abandonment of foolish legislation is itself a training in liberty.[77]

The reactions to the first circulation of Frankfurter's opinion were enthusiastic from all his brethren—except Stone. On the slip opinion Hughes wrote: "I agree. You have accomplished most admirably a very difficult and highly important task—The Court is indebted to you." [78] Douglas echoed Hughes: "This is a powerful moving document of incalculable contemporary and (I believe) historic value. I congratulate you on a truly statesmanlike job." On a recirculation, Douglas wrote: "You have done a magnificent job on a subject which defies, because of the host of intangibles, conventional legal treatment. I agree." Roberts called the opinion "among the best ever prepared by a judge of this Court." Frank Murphy, the newest member of the Court, wrote: "This has been a Gethsemane for me. But after all the institution presupposes a government that will nourish and protect itself and therefore I join your beautifully expressed opinion." [79]

Stone, however, did not agree. He considered the case within the context of his *Carolene Products* footnote, and thus concluded that the Court had an obligation to uphold the religious rights of a minority. In dissent, Stone wrote:

Here we have such a small minority entertaining in good faith a religious belief, which is such a departure from the usual course of human conduct, that most persons are disposed to regard it with little toleration or concern. In such circumstances careful scrutiny of legislative efforts to secure conformity of belief and opinion by a compulsory affirmation of the desired belief, is especially needful if civil rights are to receive any protection. Tested by this standard, I am not prepared to say that the right of this small and helpless minority . . . is to be overborne by the interest of the state. . . .[80]

Frankfurter was surprised by Stone's dissent. A flag salute case had been before the Court several times before *Gobitis*. "In each instance," Mason reports, "they had disposed of the matter by *per curiam* opinion, for want of a substantial federal question. As late as April 17, 1939, Justice Stone joined his colleagues in denying appeal from the Supreme Court of California, upholding the flag salute." [81]

In a long letter, Frankfurter attempted to reason with Stone. "Were [this] an ordinary case," Frankfurter wrote, "I should let the opinion speak for itself. But that you should entertain doubts has naturally stirred me to an anxious re-examination of my own views, even though I can assure you that nothing has weighed so much on my conscience since I have come to this Court, as has this case." Frankfurter stressed that he agreed with Stone's points in footnote four of *Carolene Products*.

I am aware of the important distinction which you skillfully adumbrated in your footnote 4 (particularly the second paragraph of it) in the *Carolene Products Co.* case. I agree with that distinction; I regard it as basic. I have taken over that distinction in its central aspect, however inadequately, in the present opinion by insisting on the importance of keeping open all those channels of free expression by which undesirable legislation may be removed, and keeping unobstructed all forms of protest against what are deemed invasions of conscience. . . .

But Frankfurter here is missing the point. Stone's position did not turn on paragraph two—the safeguarding of the democratic process—but rather on paragraphs one and three—the protection of civil liberties under "specific prohibitions" of the first ten amendments, and the protection of minorities. These were points Frankfurter was unwilling to concede; he emphasized, instead, the need for judicial deference to legislative judgment:

What weighs with me strongly in this case is my anxiety that, while we lean in the direction of the libertarian aspect, we do not exercise our judicial power unduly, and as though we ourselves were legislators by holding with too tight a rein the organs of popular government. In other words, I want to avoid the mistake comparable to that made by those whom we criticized when dealing with the control of property.[82]

Stone was not moved. "I am truly sorry not to go along with you," he wrote Frankfurter. "The case is peculiarly one of the relative weight of imponderables and I cannot overcome the feeling that the Constitution tips the scale in favor of religion."[83]

It is tempting to speculate whether Frankfurter would have been more sympathetic to the preference doctrine—as outlined in paragraphs one and three of footnote four—under different conditions. Had the author of the footnote not been Stone, and had the issue not first been raised in such dramatic form in the *Gobitis* case, where it touched Frankfurter on so many different psychological and ideological levels, it is at least conceivable that Frankfurter might have gone the other way. As just noted, he had, in 1938, described Holmes as weighing economic and civil liberties differently; he himself had expressed belief in a hierarchy of constitutional values. Frankfurter quite conceivably could have elaborated Holmes's doctrine of clear-and-present-danger into a truly First Amendment-protective doctrine, as his opponents later did. His failure to do so at this crucial juncture in Supreme Court history boxed him into a corner, and, in Joseph Lash's highly appropriate words, "uncoupled him from the locomotive of history." [84] But in the context of the *Gobitis* case, and with Stone representing the opposition, such an outcome was impossible for Frankfurter. Every fiber of his being—his patriotism, his devotion to the symbols of American life, his belief in judicial deference to majority will, his ambivalence toward religion, his dislike of Stone, and his desire to appear "disinterested"—coalesced in *Gobitis*. The case resonated on every level, personally and jurisprudentially. Frankfurter was supremely confident that he was right. And he had carried seven other members of the Court with him.

. . .

At the beginning of the 1940 term, Frankfurter recorded in his scrapbook an exchange that foreshadowed the division that would soon erupt to destroy his accomplishment in *Gobitis*.

In the fall of 1940, after returning from the summer vacation, on the first meeting with Douglas this colloquy took place:

Douglas: "Hugo tells me that now he wouldn't go with you in the Gobitis case."

FF: "Has Hugo been re-reading the Constitution during the summer."

Douglas: "No—he has been reading the papers."

The public reaction to Frankfurter's opinion in *Gobitis* had, indeed, been overwhelmingly negative. Mason writes:

One hundred and seventy-one leading newspapers promptly condemned the decision; only a handful approved it. . . . Liberals far and wide, including some with whom Frankfurter had worked shoulder to shoulder before coming to the Court, deplored his "judicial self-restraint," regretted his misguided attempt to fortify national unity at the cost of freedom.[85]

Several of Frankfurter's closest friends, including Harold Laski, criticized his opinion and praised Stone's.[86] The attribution of concern with "the newspapers" to Black sounded a theme which would soon obsess Frankfurter. As he came under increasing fire, Frankfurter became correspondingly preoccupied with the motives of his judicial opponents. As had been true throughout his life, Frankfurter once again attributed opposition to improper motivation.

But for a while at least during the 1940 term, harmony within the Court continued to prevail. Black, Douglas, and Murphy continued to enthusiastically endorse Frankfurter's opinions.[87] Douglas, in particular, continued to praise Frankfurter's outputs. On slip opinions he would write: "Respectfully, yes! And to prove to you that I have read this carefully and thoughtfully let me say that I am particularly fond of that salty statement at the bottom of page 2." [88] Joining Frankfurter in a dissent, Douglas wrote: "No matter what the majority may cook up, I am with you. But your speed puts a young squirt to shame." [89]

Slowly, however, the trio of Douglas, Black, and Murphy began breaking away from Frankfurter's tutelage, as they cautiously moved toward an endorsement and elaboration of Stone's preference philosophy. For each of the three, their movement from deference to preference was accelerated by irritation with Frankfurter's style—by his constant prodding, which quickly became patronizing and condescending; by his never-ending stream of suggestions and corrections.[90]

The first real sign of the split was the *Meadowmoor Dairies* case, handed down in February 1941,[91] which involved an extension of the *Thornhill* picketing doctrine.* Frankfurter, for the Court, held that picketing "in a context of violence" loses its "appeal to reason" and upheld state power to enjoin picketing after prolonged violence in a labor dispute.

*In *Thornhill* v. *Alabama* [92] the Court held for the first time that the constitutional guarantee of free communication included peaceful picketing. The decision was written by Murphy, in his first major undertaking, and was praised by Frankfurter.[93]

Black, joined by Douglas, dissented, emphasizing the importance of First Amendment freedoms. His opinion was a striking statement of the preference doctrine; the opinion signified, in the words of Gerald Dunne, "the beginnings of his own judicial credo." [94]

In determining whether the injunction does deprive petitioners of their constitutional liberties, we cannot and should not lose sight of the nature and importance of the particular liberties that are at stake. And in reaching my conclusion I view the guaranties of the First Amendment as the foundation upon which our governmental structure rests and without which it could not continue to endure as conceived and planned. Freedom to speak and write about public questions is as important to the life of our government as is the heart to the human body. In fact, this privilege is the heart of our government. If that heart be weakened, the result is debilitation; if it be stilled, the result is death.[95]

Murphy, at this time just beginning to shift from the leadership of Frankfurter to the tutelage of Black, voted with Frankfurter, although not without misgivings.[96] Frankfurter, anxious to hold on to Murphy, was especially flattering when Murphy suggested additions to his opinion.

You know how very eager I have been—and am—to have our Milk opinion reflect your specially qualified experience and views. You also know how anxious I am to add not one extra word, and especially not to say anything that is absolutely avoidable by way of creating a heated atmosphere. So here is my effort to translate your various suggestions into terms that would fit into, and truly strengthen our opinion.[97]

By the end of the 1940 term, however, Frankfurter had "lost" Murphy. In the *Phelps Dodge* case,[98] Murphy, joined by Black and Douglas, dissented in part from Frankfurter's majority opinion.[99] Murphy criticized Frankfurter's opinion for requiring the National Labor Relations Board to follow certain remedies upon a finding of unfair labor practices. Murphy accused Frankfurter of usurping the power of another government body—a charge usually made by Frankfurter against his opponents.

Frankfurter had tried especially hard to hold the Court together in *Phelps Dodge*; he circulated a memorandum in which he said he was "anxious to elicit suggestions in the hope that the Court may reach unanimity on problems as to which discord is, of course, very undesirable." [100] Murphy was not moved; his "initial honeymoon with Justice Frankfurter," J. Woodford Howard reports, "was beginning to cool as a result of disagreements, some of which, as one clerk recalled of the *Phelps Dodge* dispute in 1941, set Murphy's eyes 'sparkling with true Irish deviltry.' " [101]

Throughout the spring of 1941, as Black, Douglas, and Murphy continued to agree with Frankfurter only in minor cases, Frankfurter stepped up his efforts at instruction. By the end of the term, Frankfurter was clearly exasperated with his colleagues. He wrote Harold Laski:

It's absurd to tell *you* of my days, these days. . . . But this job of mine did after all exact full time labor from Holmes, Brandeis and Cardozo. . . . And they had *nothing* like my problems, & draining time and energy, with colleagues with whom a common effort is not what you might expect it to be. . . . I'm not talking, of course, of differences as to views—I'm talking of the candor and disinterestedness of collaborative enterprise.[102]

. . .

The term that began in the fall of 1941 was a turning point. The liberal trio solidified in its opposition to Frankfurter, and personnel changes brought a new unsettledness to inter-Court relations. Suddenly, Frankfurter found himself watching a calm Court, amenable to his influence and leadership, slip away from him.

Although he had been partly responsible for Stone's elevation to the Chief Justiceship,* Frankfurter found his style at conference much less appealing than Hughes's. In contrast to Hughes's austere and commanding style, with its emphasis on quick disposition of business, Stone allowed ideological differences to dominate.[104]

---

*At the end of the 1940 term Chief Justice Hughes retired. In addition, McReynold's seat had been vacant since February. Roosevelt promoted Stone to the center chair and appointed Robert H. Jackson and James F. Byrnes to the two empty seats. Frankfurter was instrumental in convincing Roosevelt to appoint Stone, rather than Jackson, as Chief Justice. Frankfurter felt strongly that, with war on the horizon, it was important for FDR to appoint a Republican, rather than a close associate, as chief, even though Roosevelt had often told Jackson that he wanted to make him chief justice.[103]

Moreover, Stone's tolerance of, and contribution to, heated debate began just as Frankfurter's liberal opposition was crystallizing.

The *Edwards* case [105] provided the first example during the 1941 term of the divisions within the Court. The California legislature had passed an act making the transportation of migrant workers a crime. Although all the members of the Court agreed that the law was unconstitutional, there was sharp disagreement over the grounds on which to base the decision.

The two new justices—Byrnes and Jackson—and the liberal trio felt that the decision ought to rest on the privileges and immunities clause of the Fourteenth Amendment; Stone and Frankfurter, on the other hand, wanted the decision to rest upon the commerce clause.[106] The opinion was assigned to Byrnes, who, as a freshman, was anxious to please Stone and Frankfurter, who both urged him not to rest the decision on the Fourteenth Amendment. Frankfurter wrote:

Dear Jimmie:

I hope I left no doubt at the Conference that I feel as strongly as you do the unconstitutionality of the particular act in the *Edwards* case, but I should very much like to have the chance to talk with you more freely about "privileges and immunities" than was possible at the Conference. Precisely because I agree with your conclusion and should very much like to agree with the grounds on which it may be rested I do wish to talk to you.[107]

Frankfurter considered himself an expert on the Fourteenth Amendment; for many years before his appointment to the Court, he had planned a book on the subject. He wanted to make his point to Jackson as well as to Byrnes. "Dear Bob," he wrote, "I have asked Jimmie to give me a chance to talk to him about 'privileges and immunities' because he is writing the opinion in the *Edwards* case, and now I ask you for a similar chance because you are not! How often opposite reasons lead to the same conclusion!" [108] Frankfurter also sent a sarcastic note to Murphy.[109]

Byrnes was persuaded, and based his opinion on the commerce clause; Murphy, however, was not, and joined Douglas's concurrence, as did Black.[110] For years to come, the proper construction of the Fourteenth Amendment was an item of sharp contention between Frankfurter and his liberal opponents.

In the *Bridges* case,[111] the division between Frankfurter and the liberal trio over the First Amendment was dramatically displayed. This was, as Robert McCloskey points out, "the first really important case involving secular freedom of expression" during this period.[112]

The case involved a classic constitutional dilemma, free press versus fair trial. Harry Bridges, a California labor leader, had been found in contempt by a California court for sending and releasing to the press a telegram in which he warned the secretary of labor that there would be a strike tying up the Pacific coast if the state court's recent "outrageous" decisions in a labor dispute were allowed to stand.

The case was originally argued during the 1940 term. Frankfurter, Stone, Roberts, Hughes, and Murphy voted to uphold the contempt citation; Black, Douglas, and Reed voted to overturn it. The majority opinion was assigned to Frankfurter; Black prepared a dissent, using Holmes's clear-and-present-danger test to uphold Bridges's First Amendment rights. The key vote was Murphy's, and he began to waiver.

Murphy . . . voted to approve Harry Bridges' contempt citation under the admitted influence of Frankfurter's "beautiful statement" in conference defending judicial power to protect fairness of trial. Toward spring, however, when the opinions were nearing completion, the Justice began to share his clerk's doubts whether the trial judge had even been aware of Bridges' threats, much less whether they presented a clear and present danger to the trial.[113]

Ultimately, Murphy changed his mind, leaving the Court with a four to four deadlock.[114] When the case was reargued in the 1941 term, Hughes had resigned; Byrnes and Jackson had taken the empty seats. Byrnes voted with Frankfurter, but Jackson voted with Black, making the decision five to four for reversal of Bridges's conviction. Frankfurter thus found his majority decision turned into a dissent.

It was particularly galling for Frankfurter to watch the words of Holmes and Brandeis turned against him. Frankfurter, after all, had been intimate with them both for all those years; surely he, if anyone, knew what they meant by "clear-and-present-danger." As Frankfurter was about to lose Murphy's vote, he noted in his scrapbook:

According to my custom in sending Brandeis all my draft opinions *after* he retired—circulating to him as to the sitting Justices—I sent this [opinion] to him when shortly thereafter, I saw him he said "That's a very fine opinion of yours. I assume that you have a unanimous Court." "Certainly not" I replied and told him that I may not have even a majority and that Black was writing. To which he said "Black and Co. are going mad." [115]

By erecting the clear-and-present-danger formula into a truly speech-protective standard, Black's opinion in this case went far toward elaborating the preference doctrine for which he and his colleagues had been groping. Black said, in effect, that Bridges's threats did not even come close to posing a clear and present danger to the fair administration of justice; that, more generally, speech that poses only minor inconvenience cannot be controlled by the state; that even if the evil posed by speech is great, a mere "reasonable" tendency of the speech to bring about evil cannot justify restriction.[116]

Frankfurter, in dissent, argued that Bridges's speech constituted a "real and substantial threat" to a fair trial. And he accused the majority of misconceiving the idea of freedom of thought and speech.

Our whole history repels the view that it is an exercise of one of the civil liberties secured by the Bill of Rights for a leader of a large following or for a powerful metropolitan newspaper to attempt to over-awe a judge in a matter immediately pending before him. The view of the majority deprives California of means for securing to its citizens justice according to law—means which, since the Union was founded, have been the possession, hitherto unchallenged, of all the states. This sudden break with the uninterrupted course of constitutional history has no constitutional warrant. To find justification for such deprivation of the historic powers of the states is to misconceive the idea of freedom of thought and speech as guaranteed by the Constitution.[117]

Bridges cut deeply into Frankfurter's sense of well-being. He had lost the majority; he had lost Frank Murphy, probably for good; he had lost the vote of Stanley Reed, who had been a dependable ally; he had lost the vote of Robert Jackson, whom he knew well and had expected to follow his leadership. And his opponents were using Holmes against him. He was angry and agitated. When Reed rather good-naturedly wrote that his dissent was "beautifully done . . . I agree with it all except the conclusion. . . ." [118] Frankfurter responded sarcastically:

Thank you very much, dear Stanley, for your characteristic generosity. Apparently that which is fundamental with me is of no moment to you, namely, that striking down state action by declaring it *UN*constitutional entails a wholly different quality of judgment from that in letting state action prevail.[119]

On decision day, Frankfurter read his dissent orally, a highly unusual move for him. After doing so, Byrnes passed him a note: "What you have just done, justifies continuance of the practice of announcing Decisions. If you suffered in its delivery, you can be assured its delivery caused suffering to those who differed with you." [120]

The battle lines—and Frankfurter's battle mentality—were clearly forming. Frankfurter's self-image—as the intellectual leader of the Court, as a true liberal and an "expert" on constitutional law, as the ultimate interpreter of Holmes and Brandeis—was at stake. Frankfurter's references to his self-image increase noticeably in his correspondence during the 1941 term. "Long years of observation of the work of this Court before I came down here," he wrote Douglas, "have sensitized me against needlessly vague and rhetorical phrases." [121] "For a good many years before I came down here," he wrote Reed, "I have been on the alert against *ad hoc* statutory construction, and more particularly the construction of statutes unrelated to a general philosophy of law and to a realization that adjudication and legislation are two phases of what should be a harmonious process." [122] "For all I know," he wrote Reed on another occasion,

you probably think me very pernickety or, at least, academic in fussing about your reference to "constitutional facts." . . . Well, the fact is that I am an academic and I have no excuse for being on this Court unless I remain so. By which I mean that Harvard paid me a high salary for the opportunity of understanding the problems covered by the phrase "judicial review" and generations of the ablest legal brains in the country deprived me of any excuse for not having availed myself of that opportunity. And not even as powerful and agile a mind as that of Charles Evans Hughes could, under the pressures which produced adjudication and opinion writing, gain that thorough and disinterested grasp of these problems which twenty-five years of academic preoccupation with the problems should have left in one.[123]

Frankfurter's use of combat imagery increases; he compliments a Stone dissent, which he is joining, for "striking at the jugular of the majority opinion." [124]

Frankfurter struggles hard to hold on to Jackson and Reed, who are voting both with him and with his opponents; he flatters them and instructs them. When they disagree, he is sarcastic; when Jackson dissents from an opinion of his, he writes:

I do not give a plugged nickel about the way in which you will come out of the mess of molasses. But I do care a lot that this Court should not put lawyers, litigants, and law further into the mess of presumption. And so please, Mr. Jackson, do find time to read, if you have not already read, the chapter on Presumption in J. B. Thayer's Preliminary Treatise.[125]

When Jackson agrees with him, however, Frankfurter flatters him: "For the moment I should like merely to say that the conception of your opinion—the wise *ad hoc* way in which you have dealt with problems in which balancing of competing interests has to be made—strikes me as just right." [126]

To Jackson and Reed he would make deprecating comments about his opponents. "When you get around to it," he wrote Jackson, "I would like to have a word with you about Bill's sudden conviction that judicial review should have a checkrein on the administrative process." [127] A disputed point, he wrote Reed, "I assume you will agree, [is] a question of Texas law and not of Bill Douglas law." [128] When this case goes against him and he dissents—Reed voting with the majority—Frankfurter passes along to Reed (as well as to Stone and Byrnes, who joined his dissent) the comments of Learned Hand critical of the majority.

Dear Stanley,

I know you will not think me moved by any I-told-you-so motive in passing on to you the quotation below from Learned Hand. . . . "I really think that the *Pearce* decision was unpardonable. . . . These bozos don't seem to me to comprehend the very basic characteristic of their job, which is to keep some kind of coherence and simplicity in the body of rules which must be applied by a vastly complicated society." [129]

When even Reed disagrees, Frankfurter instructs him: "I would like to ask you to read or reread in cold blood the following cases," Frankfurter writes him on one occasion, hoping to persuade him to change his mind. [130]

The end of the 1941 term brought two cases that dramatically symbolized the widening split within the Court. In *Jones* v. *Opelika* [131] the Court, speaking through Reed, upheld the power of a municipality to tax the sale of religious literature by Jehovah's Witnesses. The case brought two vigorous dissents—one from Stone, the other from Murphy [132]—and an astonishing statement by Black, Douglas, and Murphy indicating that they had changed their minds about their votes in *Gobitis*, the original flag salute case.* And in *Betts* v. *Brady*,[134] the Court, speaking through Roberts, said that the Sixth Amendment right to counsel was not incorporated into the due process clause of the Fourteenth Amendment, and thus was not applicable to state criminal proceedings. Black, Douglas, and Murphy dissented; in an opinion written by Black, the trio began their campaign to make the entire Bill of Rights applicable to the states by way of the Fourteenth Amendment.

---

*They wrote:

The opinion of the Court sanctions a device which in our opinion suppresses or tends to suppress the free exercise of a religion practiced by a minority group. This is but another step in the direction which *Minersville School District* v. *Gobitis* . . . took against the same religious minority, and is a logical extension of the principles upon which that decision rested. Since we joined in the opinion in the *Gobitis* case, we think this is an appropriate occasion to state that we now believe that it was also wrongly decided. Certainly our democratic form of government, functioning under the historic Bill of Rights, has a high responsibility to accommodate itself to the religious views of minorities, however unpopular and unorthodox those views may be. The First Amendment does not put the right freely to exercise religion in a subordinate position. We fear, however, that the opinions in this and in the *Gobitis* case do exactly that.[133]

By the end of the 1941 term, a watershed had clearly occurred. Examining the results of the term quantitatively, C. Herman Pritchett has written:

Some startling changes in judicial divisions occurred . . . and the Court began to give the appearance of flying apart in all directions. The rate of disagreement shot up to 36 percent. . . . Frankfurter issued more than twice as many dissents in this one term as he had during his three preceding terms. . . .

In spite of the general melee, a definite liaison was preserved on the left among Douglas, Black, and Murphy. Reed, Jackson and Byrnes spread themselves rather evenly over the entire spectrum of judicial opinion. Frankfurter slipped definitely into the right wing, developing a close affiliation with the Chief Justice. . . . Looking backward it is clear that the 1941–42 term was definitely a turning point for the Roosevelt Court.[135]

•   •   •

During the 1942 term—one of the most ideologically divisive terms in Supreme Court history—Frankfurter lost to his opponents in several highly dramatic cases. By the beginning of the term it was obvious to Frankfurter that an opposition bloc had formed. Composed of three votes—Black, Douglas, and Murphy—they needed to recruit only two other votes to form a majority; at one time or another virtually every other justice had joined them in an important case. It was obvious to Frankfurter that he needed help.

His opportunity came with the resignation of Justice Byrnes, at the beginning of the 1942 term, to become the director of the Office of Economic Stabilization. Frankfurter began an intensive campaign to have Learned Hand appointed to the vacant seat, someone he was sure he would be able to count on. Hand was, Frankfurter wrote FDR, "the only man worthy to rank with Holmes, Brandeis and Cardozo." [136] Throughout the fall and winter, Frankfurter urged various people to write or speak with Roosevelt on Hand's behalf.

In the meantime, Frankfurter's relationships with the members of the opposition bloc were deteriorating. Relations with Murphy continued to regress; Murphy was openly sarcastic to Frankfurter's still constant stream of suggestions. "Thank you for your engaging and wonderfully clear letter," he wrote in November, "so simple that even my untutored mind instantly perceived the point. I can but conclude that you must have spent a summer as an exchange professor at some midwestern school." [137] In December, the liberal trio dissented from Frankfurter's opinion in a right to counsel case,[138] one of a series of cases that foreshadowed a deep division on the Court on the question of what power federal judges should have in formulating standards of criminal justice.[139] And Frankfurter continued to cultivate carefully the other members of the Court, particularly Jackson.[140]

Increasingly, Frankfurter accused his opponents of acting on the basis of nonjudicial motives. During the 1942 term, Frankfurter kept a detailed diary in which he would often record his anger or frustration.* In February, he recorded an exchange with Roberts concerning the assignment of two politically charged cases to Douglas. The cases concerned the convictions of two political bosses, one Democrat and one Republican.[141] Roberts thought that "it wasn't fair to make Douglas write that opinion whereby it would appear that he let the Dem. boss out but kept a Rep. boss in prison," [142] and had urged Black to speak to Stone about the problem. Frankfurter recorded that, when Roberts discussed the situation with him,

I had to think fast in order to decide how to deal with this extraordinary recital. I had to decide quickly in my own mind whether to tell Roberts how shocked and outraged I was—the very notion of thinking about men after they were on this Court in terms of the New Deal or Old Deal; the shocking irrelevance of whether any Justice would or would not be criticized for doing his duty, reaching the conclusion in a case that conscience required and writing on behalf of the Court the views of the Court whenever that task was assigned to him by the Chief Justice; the fantastic and repulsive implication that in writing the opinion in the Pendergast case it mattered that Douglas was a "New Dealer" and Pendergast a Democratic boss, and that in writing in the

*The fact that Frankfurter kept a diary during 1943 is in itself significant. The years during which he keeps a diary are highly emotional years: 1911, when he first goes to Washington; 1927–28, the years of Sacco-Vanzetti; 1933, the year Roosevelt becomes president; 1937, the year of the Court-packing scheme. The diaries for 1927 and 1937 have been stolen from the Library of Congress and have not yet been recovered.

Johnson [case] that Douglas was a New Dealer and Johnson was a Republican boss, and that perhaps it was all right if we left all bosses of all parties off, that the only possible ground for any thought of unfairness in any criticism that might come to Douglas for being the organ of the Court could only derive because it might be unfair to political ambitions of Douglas. . . . To raise them would involve at least a tacit criticism of Roberts for not being shocked himself by the game that Douglas and Black were playing in this business, and it would also involve opening up the scheming of these two about which Roberts is as innocent as a newborn babe.[143]

There are several noteworthy things about this passage: Frankfurter's references to Douglas's political ambitions and to the "game" of Black and Douglas, themes he will return to again and again; his calculation that it would be best not to antagonize Roberts, who was one of his most reliable allies. One of the most fascinating and startling things about Frankfurter's diaries is the extent to which he accuses his opponents of activities of which he was himself a master. "In their cultivation of Roberts," he writes, "Black and Douglas go to perfectly fantastic lengths." [144] He also writes of "the Douglas technique" of flattery: "Except in cases where he knows it is useless or in cases where he knows or suspects that people are on to him, he is the most systematic exploiter of flattery I have ever encountered in my life." [145] Frankfurter continues:

He tried it on me when he first came on the Court—every opinion of mine that he returned, he returned with the most extravagant praise, all of which ceased after I left him in no doubt that I did not come on the Court to play politics on the Court but to vote in each case as my poor lights guided me.[146]

Frankfurter was convinced that Black, Douglas, and Murphy were playing hardball with their votes, that they would not vote with him even when they agreed with him. When Frankfurter prepared a dissent in the *Monia* case,[147] dealing with immunity from prosecution under the Sherman Act, he recorded the following:

On the bench today Black volunteered the following: "I think your dissent in the *Monia* case is very strong. I do not believe that anyone could write a stronger one. And I told Roberts that if you got a majority of the Court with you, I certainly would not dissent. But inasmuch as the privilege against self-crimination [*sic*] was written into the Constitution, I am in favor of giving a liberal construction to the statutes which deal with that privilege."

A little later Murphy said: "If I could only write one such opinion as your dissent in the *Monia* case I would feel my whole year was well spent. Your paragraph on statutory construction will remain immortal in legal literature."

To which I replied: "Them is big words but I infer you think the rest of the opinion dilutes the immortal paragraph."

F.M.: "Not at all. I think it is a very persuasive opinion."

F.F.: "It is so persuasive that it does not persuade anyone." [148]

By mid-term, Frankfurter was fighting hard. He wrote Reed, who joined a dissent by Black from a Frankfurter opinion: "Were I still at Cambridge I would be saddened to note that you underwrote an opinion like Black's dissent in the *Chenery* case.[149] I don't think I should be less saddened because I am your colleague. I hate to see you 'bogged down in the quagmire' of Populist rhetoric unrelated to fact." [150]

In his diary Frankfurter refers to a "harangue" by Black at conference, "worthy of the cheapest soapbox orator. . . . Douglas and Murphy contenting themselves with the usual 'I agree with Justice Black.'" [151] In the same diary entry Frankfurter mixes an assertion of his own self-image with his anger at his opponents.

Since the history of this Court was my business for a quarter of a century, I knew all there was to know, so far as print could convey it, on what had gone on behind the scenes and beginning with my friendship with Holmes in 1911, greatly reinforced during the course of the years, I learnt a good deal, of course, about the Court's doings since the time Holmes came on in 1902, and after Brandeis came here in 1916 and Cardozo in 1932, I learnt with cumulative intimacy from them about the inner workings of the institution and the behavior of the various personalities. As a result, I made one pact with myself when I came on the Court: that I would try to my utmost to continue to behave here as I did as an independent scholar at Cambridge, that is, act on the best judgment I am able to summon with reference to a particular case regardless of where it would land me in relation to votes of other people on the Court and to eschew all combinations or machinations, active or tacit playing of politics on the Court. This of course does not mean that I would always express a dissent—many considerations enter into the expression or withholding of a dissent. Nor does it meant [sic] that the views that I reached independently might not be altered in disinterested discussion with one or more members of the Court or after Conference. That is the very essence of the Court, namely, that the views of individuals should be shared to the end that a collective conclusion may be achieved. That is why the Conferences should be the most important aspect of our labors, the free and full canvassing of all relevant considerations in the disposition of a case. But that is a wholly different thing from hunting in packs, presenting a solid phalanx, as part of a general parting within the Court as was true of what Learned Hand used to call "the four mastiffs"—VanDevanter, McReynolds, Sutherland and Butler, and as is true now of what everyone calls "the Axis"—Black, Douglas and Murphy. It is in this aspect of the matter that Jimmie Byrnes' remark reveals such an ominous situation—his remark that in the Senate Black controlled one vote, his own, out of 96 votes; on the Court he controls three votes out of nine in all important matters.[152]

At the end of the 1942 term came a devastating series of blows. It began when Frankfurter's campaign to have Learned Hand appointed to the empty seat failed; it failed, moreover, in part because Frankfurter pushed Roosevelt too hard.[153] Instead of Hand, Roosevelt appointed Wiley Rutledge, who quickly joined the liberal opposition. Thus instead of an ally, Frankfurter got only another opponent.

Four days after Rutledge took his seat, the Court granted *certiorari* in the *Murdock* case [154] and ordered reargument in *Opelika*, both dealing with the First Amendment rights of Jehovah's Witnesses.[155] At the end of the 1941 term, *Opelika* had gone against the Witnesses; the Court had held that a town ordinance licensing and taxing street vendors did not violate the First Amendment when applied to Witnesses selling religious literature. Now, Rutledge joined Black, Douglas, Murphy, and Stone in reversing that outcome. Frankfurter, Reed, Roberts, and Jackson dissented; Reed, Jackson, and Frankfurter all filed dissenting opinions. On the same day, the Court handed down its opinion in *Martin v. Struthers*,[156] in which Black, for the majority, held that an ordinance requiring a license for door-to-door circulation of pamphlets violated the Witnesses' freedom of speech and press.

Black had originally voted with Frankfurter in *Struthers*, making it five to four against the Witnesses. He was assigned the opinion and drafted one. Frankfurter recorded what happened in a memorandum he titled "The Story of Struthers."

At the conference . . . at which this case was discussed, Black spoke at length and at his most vigorous in sustaining the right of the city to pass the challenged ordinance. He said that in modern times it was even more important than it was in ancient times to treat a man's home as his castle, and spoke especially of the dangers and difficulties presented by house-to-house canvassing to people living in tenement houses.

Brother Reed told me that Black would not stick to his opinion because he would not want to be placed in a position of deciding against "free speech and freedom of religion" with the Chief, Douglas, Murphy and Rutledge appearing to be greater champions of liberty than he is. At the same time I was informed that Black's law clerk was laboring with him and bearing down hard on him with arguments that he would be much criticized by "liberals" if he let his opinion stand. . . . In due course Black reversed himself on paper and circulated an opinion . . . invalidating the ordinance. I thereupon drafted and circulated a short opinion pointing out the conscious ambiguities of Black's opinion. . . .[157]

Once again, Frankfurter had attributed a loss to the unholy motives of his opponents. Roberts shared his perceptions, and sent Frankfurter a note about Murphy: "The Saint * said to me at luncheon that the reason for his vote and voice in *Struthers* was that he wanted always to err on the side of religion. I replied that as we are judges it is our business not to err on either side. This seemed a new thought to him. He made no reply but rushed out!" [158] Frankfurter recorded in his diary that Stone was ashamed of the opinions by Black, Douglas, and Murphy in these Jehovah's Witnesses cases.

Jackson reported the Chief as saying that he was very sorry about the majority opinions in the Jehovahs Witnesses cases last Monday, that as opinions they were inexcusable, they did not properly formulate or discuss the issues, that he was in an impossible situation in that having said all that he had to say in his dissent in the *Opelika* case last term, he could not now rehash what he had said, he could not make

*A term used by Frankfurter and Roberts to describe Frank Murphy, the Court's only Catholic member.

those who were writing the majority opinions in which he agreed with the results, write opinions to suit his views, and so he was in a practical box of having to agree to opinions that he was ashamed of.[159]

Whether this conversation took place is impossible to verify; it is significant, however, that Frankfurter perceived Stone as something of an ally against the liberals even though he voted with them. Elsewhere in his diary, Frankfurter wrote:

The Chief asked to see me and apparently all he wanted was to relieve his mind about the difficulties that the present situation on the Court presents, and especially the difficulties of making assignments of cases when he is so limited in choice by reason of the fact that three members—he laughingly said "the Axis" which is now a common sobriquet of Black, Douglas and Murphy—are practically a solid block on any question that divides the Court, and a solid block at that through their strange subservience to Black.[160]

·   ·   ·

The end of the 1942 term brought two highly emotional and divisive cases—*Schneiderman* and *Barnette*.[161] *Schneiderman* was both a complex and an ideologically important case. William Schneiderman, a Communist party leader in Minnesota, had been stripped of his naturalized citizenship in 1939 under a statute that authorized cancellation of citizenship on proof of fraud or illegal procurement. The government had dropped charges of fraud against Schneiderman and had admitted that he had violated no laws, but still advanced the convoluted argument that his citizenship had been illegally obtained because he did not satisfy a requirement of "attachment to the Constitution" in the five-year period prior to his naturalization in 1927.[162] Howard comments:

Imputing lack of attachment retroactively from his subsequent membership in the party and from his active dissemination of communist ideas, the proceedings presented an early forerunner of vexatious issues which plagued the Court for the next two decades. . . . And Schneiderman's case presented a[n] . . . explosive issue at the very peak of the nation's flirtation with its Soviet ally—did the Communist party advocate forcible overthrow of the United States government? [163]

The case evoked all of Frankfurter's patriotic fervor—as well as his own very personal sense of the importance of the naturalization process; at conference, he spoke of his own family experiences. In notes he prepared of the conference discussions of this case, Frankfurter recorded himself as saying:

I am saying what I am going to say because perhaps this case arouses in me feelings that could not be entertained by anyone else around this table. It is well known that a convert is more zealous than one born to the faith. None of you has had the experience that I have had with reference to American citizenship. I was at college when my father became naturalized and I can assure you that for months proceeding it was a matter of moment in our family life, and when the great day came it partook for me of great solemnity. Later on, as an Assistant United States Attorney in the Southern District of New York—with all that New York implies in the making of new citizens I represented the government in naturalization proceedings in the federal court. As one who has no ties with any formal religion, perhaps the feelings that underlie religious forms for me run into intensification of my feelings about American citizenship. I have known, as you hardly could have known, literally hundreds of men and women of the finest spirit who had to shed old loyalties and take on the loyalty of American citizenship.[164]

The case brought to the fore Frankfurter's deep love of the Constitution, his belief that "American citizenship implies entering upon a fellowship which binds people together by devotion to certain feelings and ideas and ideals summarized as a requirement that they be attached to the principles of the Constitution." [165]

The case produced a sharp and highly unusual public exchange on the bench between Frankfurter and Black, the result of tensions that had been building for months. While the case was being argued, Frankfurter recorded,

The Chief Justice asked Mr. Fahy, the Solicitor General, a series of questions and answers according to which Schneiderman appeared to have expressed his personal acceptance of what are deemed to be "principles" opposed to those principles of the Constitution. Brother Black then asked "Is there anything more than his agreement to general political talk?" To which Fahy said, "There is nothing more than Schneiderman's agreement with this general political talk." I followed that question up by asking Fahy, "Is it suggested that the Communist party has no principles?" At which Black turned to me with blazing eyes and ferocity in his voice and said, "The Hearst press will love that question." I replied, "I don't give a damn whether the Hearst press or any other press likes or dislikes any question that seems to me relevant to the argument. I am a judge and not a politician." "Of course," replied Black, "you, unlike the rest of us, live in the stratosphere." I made no further comment but resisted the impulse to say that in any event I do not change my views and votes on cases before this Court because of newspaper criticism.[166]

Frankfurter, Stone, and Roberts voted to uphold the revocation of Schneiderman's naturalization; Stone wrote a bitter dissent which Frankfurter and Roberts joined. Once again, Frankfurter attributed the majority's actions to nonjudicial "political" considerations. He wrote Stone in praise of his dissent:

As I have indicated to you on several occasions, I look forward with entire confidence to your dissent in the *Schneiderman* case—confidence, that is, that as becomes the Chief Justice of the United States, you will vindicate the historic fact that there are "principles of the Constitution of the United States." . . . And so, after reading Murphy's opinion, I make the following summary observations merely to tell briefly the thoughts that were stirred in me by that opinion, and to repeat the confidence that you will blow away the gossamer web of evasion and word-juggling and casuistry, ill befitting the Supreme Court of the United States, which is, in effect, the proposed opinion of the Court.

It is very painful for me to say so, but I do not think there is the slightest doubt that if the same kind of a record had come up with reference to a *Bundist*, the opposite result would have been reached. . . . What is plain as a pikestaff is that the present war considerations—political considerations—are the driving force behind the result of this case.[167]

Frankfurter sent a sarcastic letter to Reed, accusing him of voting with the majority because of concern for the Soviet Union; [168] and he sent Murphy the following note:

Thorough and comprehensive as your opinion in *Schneiderman* is you omitted one thing that, on reflection, you might want to add. I think that it is only fair to state, in view of your general argument, that Uncle Joe Stalin was at least a spiritual co-author with Jefferson of the Virginia Statutes for Religious Freedom.[169]

He followed this up with another:

In view of its importance I have prepared the following draft head-
note to the *Schneiderman* opinion. I should very much appreciate
your comments:

"The American Constitution ain't got no principles. The Communist
Party don't stand for nuthin'. The Soopreme Court don't mean nuthin'.
Nuthin' means nuthin', and this country don't mean to us what Russia
means to the Bolshies."

Respectfully yours,
F. F. Knaebel [170]

Murphy responded: "Many thanks for your original and revised
headnotes in the *Schneiderman* case. Not only do they reveal
long and arduous preparation, but best of all, they are done with
commendable English understatement and characteristic New
England reserve." [171]

.　　.　　.

In the *Barnette* case, the Court dramatically reversed its stand in
Gobitis; Frankfurter was once again cast into the role of dis-
senter after watching a majority slip away from him. Here, in
Barnette,* he took his stand; he confronted his opponents on several highly charged issues—preferred freedoms and deference to
the legislature; the content of Holmes's jurisprudence; the importance of symbols for national unity. Once again, as in *Gobitis*, the
opinion resonated for Frankfurter on many levels at once; this
time, however, there was the additional factor of having lost, of
being forced to write in dissent what had so recently been the opinion of the Court. The result was a long, personal, emotional opinion, one that hardened Frankfurter's stand on the question of
judicial review and thereby set the tenor of his entire philosophy
of law.

Jackson wrote the majority opinion in *Barnette*; he had previously voted with Frankfurter in several First Amendment cases

---

*The facts in the *Barnette* case were precisely the same as in *Gobitis*: the
children of Jehovah's Witnesses were required to salute the flag in school, an act
forbidden by their religion.

and had, on several occasions, indicated his personal distaste for members of the liberal bloc.[172] Frankfurter was clearly coming to think of Jackson as a staunch ally; when Jackson sharply criticized the majority holding in *Struthers*, Frankfurter warmly endorsed his opinion.[173] Here, however, Jackson joined the liberals and authored a striking endorsement of the preference doctrine; moreover, he linked the concept of preferred freedoms to Holmes's clear-and-present-danger test. Although Stone's dissent in *Gobitis* had rested upon the minority status of the Witnesses and their freedom of religion more than their freedom of speech, Jackson here emphasized the free speech aspects of the case. In ringing phrases, he defended a broad concept of freedom of belief.[174] Jackson quoted—and explicitly attacked—that portion of Frankfurter's opinion in *Gobitis* dealing with his most cherished tenet: that judicial deference is required by devotion to democratic principles. In some of the most eloquent words ever written by a member of the Supreme Court, Jackson wrote:

The very purpose of a Bill of Rights was to withdraw certain subjects from the vicissitudes of political controversy, to place them beyond the reach of majorities and officials and to establish them as legal principles to be applied by the courts. One's right to life, liberty and property, to free speech, a free press, freedom of worship and assembly, and other fundamental rights may not be submitted to vote; they depend on the outcome of no elections.[175]

Frankfurter's dissent took him a long time to prepare; at one point, he noted in his diary, "Worked until 2 A.M. on *Flag Salute* case." [176] He held up the delivery of the opinion and apologized to Jackson for doing so.

Dear Bob:

I am sorry, very sorry, that I must hold you up some more . . . on the *Flag Salute* case [and other cases.] I have no mitigating circumstances to offer—for despite all the sidetracking of the last few days I should have at least got out what I am going to say in the *Flag Salute* case. For that won't be in the realm of research—it will be the expression of my credo regarding the function of this Court in invalidating legislation. But perhaps it is because it is credo and not research that the expression of it is so recalcitrant.[177]

Frankfurter's opinion—as eloquent as Jackson's—opened with an extraordinary personal reference. He claimed, as he had throughout his life, that he was "disinterested," that he was capable of divorcing his personal opinions from a necessary action; he did so, moreover, by referring to the fact that he himself was the symbol of a minority. He defended his past record as a civil libertarian. Unmistakenly, his self-image was on the line.

One who belongs to the most vilified and persecuted minority in history is not likely to be insensible to the freedoms guaranteed by our Constitution. Were my purely personal attitude relevant I should wholeheartedly associate myself with the general libertarian views in the Court's opinion, representing as they do the thought and action of a lifetime.[178]

As he had in *Gobitis*, Frankfurter discussed at great length the duty of judges to decide cases without reference to their personal predilections; he once again stressed that the standard the Court must apply is only whether the legislature had chosen a reasonable means to achieve a legitimate end.

It can never be emphasized too much that one's own opinion about the wisdom or evil of a law should be excluded altogether when one is doing one's duty on the bench. The only opinion of our own even looking in that direction that is material is our opinion whether legislators could in reason have enacted such a law. . . . I cannot bring my mind to believe that the "liberty" secured by the Due Process Clause gives this Court authority to deny to the State of West Virginia the attainment of that which we all recognize as a legitimate legislative end, namely, the promotion of good citizenship, by employment of the means here chosen.[179]

Frankfurter discussed in great detail the importance of national symbols, as he had in *Gobitis*: "We are told that symbolism is a dramatic but primitive way of communicating ideas. Symbolism is inescapable. Even the most sophisticated live by symbols." [180]

He stressed that the same issue had been decided many times; he explicitly referred to the switched votes of Stone,[181] Black, Douglas, and Murphy.

I am fortified in my view of this case by the history of the flag salute controversy in this Court. . . . Every Justice—thirteen in all—who has hitherto participated in judging this matter has at one or more times found no constitutional infirmity in what is now condemned. Only the two Justices sitting for the first time on this matter have not heretofore found this legislation inoffensive to the "liberty" guaranteed by the Constitution.[182]

In all of this, Frankfurter was recounting familiar themes. But in some crucial ways, this dissent went significantly beyond what he had said previously. It was supremely painful for Frankfurter to have Holmes used against him; he was thus at great pains to dissociate Holmes from the majority's stance. To do this, he takes a fateful step—he describes Holmes, and himself, as being unwilling to rank constitutional values. In direct contradiction to his statement in his 1938 book on Holmes,* he describes Holmes as treating all constitutional values with equal weight. By doing this, he is explicitly denying his own belief in fundamental values and hardening his concept of judicial deference.

When Mr. Justice Holmes, speaking for this Court, wrote that "it must be remembered that legislatures are ultimate guardians of the liberties and welfare of the people in quite as great a degree as the courts," . . . he went to the very essence of our constitutional system and the democratic conception of our society. He did not mean that for only some phases of civil government this Court was not to supplant legislatures and sit in judgment upon the right or wrong of a challenged measure. He was stating the comprehensive judicial duty and role of this Court in our constitutional scheme whenever legislation is sought to be nullified on any ground. . . .[183]

He accused the majority of taking the concept of "clear-and-present-danger" out of its original context.

To measure the state's power to make such regulations as are here resisted by the imminence of national danger is wholly to misconceive the origin and purpose of the concept of "clear and present danger." To apply such a test is for the Court to assume, however unwittingly, a legislative responsibility that does not belong to it. To talk about "clear and present danger" as the touchstone of allowable educational policy by the states whenever school curricula may impinge upon the boundaries of individual conscience, is to take a felicitous phrase out of the context of the particular situation . . . for which it was adapted.[184]

* See pp. 134–35.

Frankfurter almost denies the Court any role in enforcing the Bill of Rights; it is the Court's major function, he says, to umpire federalism.

> The attitude of judicial humility which these considerations enjoin is not an abdication of the judicial function. It is a due observance of its limits. Moreover, it is to be borne in mind that in a question like this we are not passing on the proper distribution of political power as between the states and the central government. We are not discharging the basic function of this Court as the mediator of powers within the federal system.[185]

Frankfurter denies that the Court has any special function in protecting minorities; the framers of the Constitution, he states blandly, "knew that minorities may disrupt society." [186]

Frankfurter's dissent in *Barnette* was extraordinarily important to him. He sent copies of it to the retired Chief Justice Hughes and to the president; he suggested to FDR that both his and Jackson's opinion should "find proper lodgment in the Hyde Park Library. They ought to furnish to the future historian food for thought on the scope and meaning of some of the Four Freedoms—their use and misuse." [187]

He was concerned about what the press reaction to the decision and his dissent would be; he wrote his friends Bruce Bliven of the *New Republic* and Frank Buxton of the *Boston Herald*, asking them to be sure to read the full text of his opinion themselves.[188] To Erwin Griswold of the Harvard Law School, he expressed his concern about the *Harvard Law Review's* "recent tendency . . . to deal with divisions in the Court as though they were the score of a baseball game. . . ." [189] He was always quick to point out that Learned Hand and Brandeis had agreed with his opinion in *Gobitis*.

> I know what the Hands thought of it. I know what Learned Hand thinks because he wrote me. I also know that it was okayed by Brandeis before I delivered it. It was also okayed by those great libertarians until they heard from the people, Justices Black and Douglas, because they told me and wrote me what they thought about it in strong terms of approval.[190]

The *Barnette* case marks a clear transition for Frankfurter and for the Court. The lines of battle have been sharply drawn; positions have been elaborated; sides have been chosen and stances taken. In a sense, Frankfurter will devote his remaining years on the Court to refighting the battle—and the opponents—of *Barnette*.

Psychologically, the period marked off by *Barnette* and the end of the 1942 term produced in Frankfurter a sense of being under seige. Unexpectedly, he found himself in a position of opposition; his leadership had been rejected. He would react in a manner that had become a familiar part of this psychological makeup. The reaction would be particularly bitter, for this time his opponents were former allies; the challenge was in a domain where he had every reason to anticipate complete success; and he had no choice but to remain where he was and fight it out.

This set of conditions affected the two vital aspects of Frankfurter's tenure on the Supreme Court—his relationships with his colleagues and the content of his jurisprudence.

CHAPTER 6

Dénouement

THE REMAINDER of Frankfurter's tenure on the Supreme Court was, in a very real sense, the inevitable result of his behavior in the early forties. Both in his relationships with his brethren and in the development of his judicial doctrines Frankfurter was left to play out the scenario he had written for himself. New justices came and went, new issues preoccupied the Court, but Frankfurter could neither change his political style nor dig himself out from under the hardened ideological commitments he had made.

. . .

After the seige of his first five years on the Court, Frankfurter would mentally divide his colleagues into three categories—adversaries, allies, and potential allies. He would react to adversaries as he had throughout his life—with heated anger and frustration, with attacks on their integrity and motives, with a search for vindication.

His major adversaries, throughout his tenure, were Black and Douglas. His greatest anger was reserved for Douglas, whose putative political ambitions during the forties became an obsessive concern.* As Lash suggests, there were several complicated emotions

---

*Douglas was considered by many Democratic party insiders as a prominent candidate for vice-president in 1944 and for both vice-president and president in 1948. Frankfurter's diaries and correspondence are full of comments critical of Douglas's political "ambitions." [1]

involved in the Douglas-Frankfurter clash: Douglas had always been Frankfurter's rival for FDR's affections; Douglas, moreover, was capable of seeking office himself, an option foreclosed to Frankfurter because of his foreign origins.[2] And Frankfurter had always strongly disapproved of extrajudicial ambitions on the part of judges. All of these factors, added to the ideological separation of the two men, created the strongest possible animosity and strain. Frankfurter's anger at Douglas even brings him, for the first time, to the brink of anger at FDR. During the 1944 presidential campaign, when many politicians and writers were touting both Douglas and James F. Byrnes as prominent candidates for vice-president, Frankfurter wrote Marion:

Had old-fashions with the Byrnes's . . . and learned the detailed Chicago* story. As I already knew in essentials, Jim was needlessly mistreated. F.D. wanted Jim and did not take sufficient and sufficiently candid care in the matter. Ed Flynn† really dished it. The more I hear of these "practical" men, including the President, the less impressed I am that their practicality has any long-range wisdom. Jim thinks that F.D. finally wanted Bill—but the leaders and rank and file would have none of him.

As for Bill—Jackson tells me that the Henry Wallaces have fierce feelings against Bill for they know it wasn't the pols, but the "liberals" that undermined Henry‡ with F.D. in Bill's interest. And instead of getting Bill, they, the Harold Ickeses, are sore to have got Truman! What a child that sophisticate Harold is.

And further as to Bill—I shall reserve for talk the proof Jim Byrnes gave me of Bill's astute but not astute enough, crookery.[3]

The tone of the Frankfurter-Douglas relationship after the early forties was polite but often strained; there was none of the mutual, good-natured friendliness of their first exchanges. Frankfurter continued to comment upon Douglas opinions and to offer suggestions; he often did so, however, with indignation. "What I have tried to say in this letter about the use of certiorari," he wrote on one occasion, "represents the practice of this Court sofar [sic] as I have been able to gather it through preoccupation with the subject for

---

*The site of the Democratic convention.
†Flynn, former secretary of New York State, was a Roosevelt strategist.
‡Henry Wallace, vice-president from 1941 to 1945.

almost a lifetime." [4] Frankfurter often concurred rather than join a Douglas opinion, or threatened to do so in the hopes of winning changes. On one occasion Frankfurter wrote dryly: "I hope you will be agreeable to such a change in your opinion, because I have no desire to write anything in explanation of my agreement with your result." [5]

For his part, Douglas bristled at these never-ending efforts to teach him the law, and dished it back to Frankfurter whenever he could. "Dear Felix," he wrote on one occasion. "Why do you need the paragraph beginning on p. 8 of your opinion? . . . Isn't that adequately covered by the paragraph beginning at the bottom of page 2?" [6] When he concurred with Frankfurter, Douglas would most often write a simple "I agree" on slip opinions, without the praise that would come from other members of the Court. Frankfurter grew more and more exasperated; "Apparently I am unable to convey what is crystal-clear to me," he wrote once. "Let me try once more. . . ." [7]

Frankfurter's relationship with Black was warmer than with Douglas, although also strained and difficult. Their battle over the relationship of the Bill of Rights and the Fourteenth Amendment preoccupied both during the mid-forties. Frankfurter won and Black lost their battle in *Adamson* v. *California*.[8] In one of the most significant cases of the decade, the Court ruled in 1947 that the due process clause of the Fourteenth Amendment did not "incorporate" the first eight amendments of the Constitution and make them fully applicable to state action. Black (joined by Douglas, Murphy, and Rutledge) dissented, stating that his study of the history of the Fourteenth Amendment led him to the opposite conclusion. It was a triumph for Frankfurter; he sent copies of his concurring opinion in the case to his friends, one of whom congratulated him for his "devastating attack on Blackism." [9] His victory over Black left Frankfurter with a sticky dilemma, however; he now had to come up with a way of deciding exactly which safeguards of the Bill of Rights *were* so fundamental as to constitute a necessary part of "due process of law." *

The disagreements between Frankfurter and Black continued throughout the fifties. To Learned Hand Frankfurter often com-

* See pp. 196–97.

plained of "that essentially lawless Black." [10] "It really is hard to believe," Frankfurter wrote Hand on one occasion, "what I hear with my own ears and know, as I know anything, as to the lengths Hugo will go to make a negligence plaintiff succeed." [11] It was only very late in both of their careers—when Black began to dissent from some of the more liberal decisions of the Warren Court—that their relationship improved dramatically.[12]

The liberal justices who allied themselves with Black and Douglas were subjected by Frankfurter to the same harsh judgment and treatment. Quickly, Frankfurter came to a set attitude about his opponents—the men he sneeringly referred to as "the liberals" or "the children of light," or, on one occasion, "my Sans Culotte and Brave Heart brothers." [13] In this category he included Frank Murphy [14] and, eventually, Earl Warren and William Brennan.

Frankfurter was convinced that his opponents did not really believe in their judicial philosophy; that they only wanted to appear "liberal" in law reviews and in history. Frankfurter would often pour out his anger at them to Learned Hand.

Regarding your "Four Horsemen" or "Battalion of Death," McReynolds & Co.,* one must in all fairness attribute to them the enforcement of their convictions. Indeed that was the trouble with them: they found their economic and social convictions in the Constitution. To a very considerable degree that cannot be said of too many of their successors. If I gave you a bill of particulars of what I have lived through in these now nearly twenty years, even you with all your knowledge and discernment would realize that you don't know nuthin'. "I could unto you a tale unfold" that would shock you, hardened character that you are. By way of a sample, let me refer you to Hartzell v United States, 322 U.S. 680, one of those noble civil liberties opinions of St. Frank. The fellow actually came to me to say that it was all wrong to reverse the conviction in that case. "The court mustn't do that," he insisted and begged me to try to get one other person to make a majority for affirmance. When in as soft a voice as I could muster I said, "Well, haven't you a vote—wouldn't that make five of us?" he replied, "Oh, but you know me. I want to be for free speech and I want to write a dissenting opinion in that case. But I think it is wrong to reverse the conviction." You probably will be prompted to say to yourself as I did when I was given that answer,

---

*Frankfurter is referring to the conservative members of the Court who had nullified progressive social and economic legislation in the twenties and thirties.

"And who's looney now?" I can assure you that while in the *Hartzell* case inadmissible considerations were spelled out in this fantastic way, "the judicial process" which it illustrates would have warranted Cardozo to say about these civil liberties cases as he said about cases involving economic issues in his time, "This is not a court of law." [15]

It is impossible to verify Frankfurter's story about Murphy; what is significant, however, is the attitude it represents. Frankfurter often compared his situation to the situation of Cardozo, Brandeis, and Holmes, who had opposed the judicial nullification of the New Deal on the part of their conservative brethren.

In counting your blessings you [should] rank high that you were not one of the Nine! I happened to see Ben Cardozo after the *Tipaldo* decision in 36 and with tears in his eyes, I'm being literal and accurate, he deprecated that he "was brought down from Albany." "This is not a Court now—this is a political body" he moaned. In his day there were four who were the "hard core" of the Court. They were narrow-minded economic sectarians. No such doctrinal cohesion binds together the present "hard core" "liberal" wing of the Court. Their common denominator is a self-willed self-righteous power-lust, conditioned by different causes, internal and external, undisciplined by adequate professional learning and cultivated understanding.

In this letter to Hand, Frankfurter discusses his newly appointed brother, John Marshall Harlan.

He makes me wince when he talks about questions being "in the First Amendment area" and having "an instinct" that this or that "power of Congress is extremely limited"—limited that is, by the goulash of narrow minded prejudices of Earl & Black & Douglas & Douglas [*sic*], their prejudices and their respective pasts and self-conscious desires to join Thomas Paine and T. Jefferson in the Valhalla of "Liberty" and in the meantime to have the avant garde of the Yale Law School and the Edmond Cahn's praise them!

About Harlan, Frankfurter writes:

With all his judicial aims and character, he really has not had the appropriate intellectual background of reading and reflection for the ultimate task, that of passing on constitutionality. . . . Moreover, he is not meant for battle, represents at its best what I'm told (by an esteemed Princetonian) is the dominant Princeton ideal, to be nice, and is just the kind of person who is too ready to have a bully like Black and a martignet like Warren have their way.

Frankfurter then discusses a specific opinion of Warren's: "It was a sufficient weakness on my part even to have joined quali-fiedly—by way of an interpretation of its holding—Warren's mush and excessive and poor rhetoric (by way of a wooly-headed law clerk)." Frankfurter added a concurrence to Warren's opinion, over Harlan's objections. Frankfurter responded:

John, you can always have what is called peace if you yield to the bullies and the irrationalists. I don't mean to be extravagant, but because of such yielding to Hitler the world is now what it is. . . . When [Harlan] went off the other day I put a copy of J. B. Thayer's essay . . . into his hands, with the remark, "Please read it, then reread it, and then read it again and then think about it long." [16]

Frankfurter's letters to Hand were often quite biting. After calling Robert Jackson "the oasis in my desert," Frankfurter says:

Look at them. Hugo is a self-righteous, self-deluded part fanatic, part demagogue, who really disbelieves in law, thinks it is essentially manip-ulation of language. Intrinsically, the best brain in the lot, but un-disciplined and "functional" in its employment, an instrument for supporting a predetermined result, not a means for responsible inquiry. Withal, he is quite devoid of play and humor. Reed is largely vegeta-ble—he has managed to give himself a nimbus of reasonableness but is as unjudicial-minded, as flagrantly moved, at times, by irrelevant con-siderations for adjudication, as any of them. He has a reasonable voice in the service of a dogmatic, worldly, timid mind. Bill is the most cynical, shamelessly immoral character I've ever known. With him I have no more relation than the necessities of court work require. He is too unscrupulous for any avoidable entanglement.[17]

As he does in his diaries, Frankfurter in his correspondence ac-cuses his opponents of maneuvering for votes. "The non-judicial twain of Justices," he writes of Black and Douglas, "are crafty on the job—I'm watching their effort on John [Harlan]. It's hard for a decent man to realize how indecent people operate." [18]

When friends agreed with his opponents, Frankfurter bristles; [19] this was especially true when anyone criticized the extent to which

Frankfurter had carried his concept of judicial deference.[20] And to his faithful disciples, Frankfurter expresses pleasure whenever they criticize "the liberals." Complimenting an article by one of his most prolific disciples—Alexander Bickel—Frankfurter writes:

I can assure you that explicit analysis and criticism of the way the Court is doing its business really gets under their skin, just as the praise of their constituencies, the so-called liberal journals and well-known liberal approvers only fortifies them in their present result-oriented jurisprudence. . . . You law professors really should sharpen your pens so that there is no mistaking as to what the trouble is and where the blame lies. I can give you proof that if you would speak out, you would get under their skins. . . .[21]

. . .

Frankfurter allied himself with whoever would agree with him in opposition to the liberals; during the forties, this meant Roberts, Reed, and Jackson.

In spite of his harsh words about Roberts's behavior during the Court-packing fight, Frankfurter found him a congenial and friendly colleague. During the Court term they often exchanged friendly notes on the bench; during the summers they would visit each other and occasionally write. Roberts, a former Philadelphia attorney, represented the Yankee elite of the American bar, a group for whom Frankfurter had always felt an ambivalent yet strong attraction.[22] Roberts often praised Frankfurter's opinions lavishly. By the 1942 term they were voting together frequently; [23] by the 1944 term, even more often.[24] And they were united in their disapproval of Black and Douglas. In 1943, Frankfurter recorded in his diary that, at the end of a conference,

Brother Roberts came into my room and said that on Saturday he went home after the long Conference tired and dispirited, and yesterday he went home after another long Conference tired and dispirited again. "Just because," he said, "of what we did on Saturday and yesterday, and the way we tear up the law with complete indifference to the precedents or the consequences. Black with his vehemence and vitality and lack of savoir faire and ruthlessness and unflagging industry will before long absolutely control the Court. . . ." [25]

During the 1943 term, as the split between Frankfurter and the liberals was widening, Roberts, in an obscure and unrelated case dealing with admiralty law, lashed out at the liberals for their switch in the Jehovah's Witness flag salute cases. In a dissent—which Frankfurter joined—Roberts sarcastically suggested that the public recantation of their *Gobitis* position by Black, Douglas, and Murphy might be a practice the Court should adopt, since they were wreaking such havoc upon the law:

The tendency to disregard precedents . . . has become so strong in this court of late as, in my view, to shake confidence in the consistency of decision and leave the courts below on an uncharted sea of doubt and difficulty without any confidence that what was said yesterday will hold good tomorrow, unless indeed a modern instance grows into a custom of members of this Court to make public announcement of a change of views and to indicate that they will change their votes on the same question when another case comes before the court. This might, to some extent, obviate the predicament in which the lower courts, the bar, and the public find themselves.[26]

Roberts often warmly praised Frankfurter's opinions; "better and better" he wrote, quite characteristically, on the recirculation of one of Frankfurter's efforts.[27] "My God!" Roberts wrote after Frankfurter delivered his dissent in an important case. "*No* justice ever did a greater job! I was deeply moved by it. Bravo!" [28] In his scrapbooks, Frankfurter marked numerous passages in opinions by Roberts as "written by FF." [29]

When Roberts retired from the Court at the end of the 1944 term, the phrasing of the letter from the other members of the Court to him became an occasion for another eruption of hostilities. The letter was drafted by Stone; Black insisted that the line "you have made fidelity to principle your guide to decision" be removed. At Stone's suggestion, Black redrafted the letter. Frankfurter refused to sign Black's letter, and the situation rapidly reached absurd proportions.[30]

Stanley Reed, despite Frankfurter's later judgment that he was "largely vegetable," was also an ally, although Reed kept his lines of communication with the liberal wing of the Court more open than either Roberts or Frankfurter. Reed and Frankfurter had worked together during the New Deal and their relations were friendly. Frankfurter clearly judged Reed his intellectual inferior and instructed him accordingly. Frankfurter sometimes got exasperated with what he judged to be Reed's stubbornness; he once described him to Learned Hand as "the most reasonable-sounding and least judicial as well as the stupidest." [31] Frankfurter was sometimes impatient with the amount of time he had to spend instructing Reed; he wrote Chief Justice Vinson in 1949:

I don't know how many times I have told Stanley to his face that while there is about him an aura of sweet reasonableness, he is one of the most obstinate of men. . . . *York* v. *Guaranty Trust Company* is a good illustration. I talked with him about that case almost hours on end before he finally concurred in the opinion. But it was like the proverbial pulling of teeth. . . . [32]

Despite his sometime recalcitrance, Reed often yielded to Frankfurter's lessons. And Frankfurter clearly perceived Reed as someone whose vote he could win, unlike others; on one occasion, he wrote Reed:

Add this to your collection of *Incredibilia*:

A few minutes after I finished my concurring opinion in the *Flagler Estate Tax* case, Frank* turned to me and said: "I think you ought to know that Wiley† and I have talked it over and are now convinced that we should have gone with your opinion."

'S wonderful! 'S marvelous. . . . [33]

By far, the ally with whom Frankfurter felt the closest affinity was Robert Jackson. The relationship between Frankfurter and Jackson seems to have deepened in proportion to the deterioration of relations between Jackson and Black, culminating in their celebrated feud in 1946.‡ Jackson's voting pattern during his first term

---

*Frank Murphy.
†Wiley Rutledge.
‡The personal animosity between Black and Jackson culminated in a complicated series of events centering around the vexing issue of whether justices could take part in cases in which they had had some personal connection. In the *Jewell Ridge* case,[34] decided in May 1945, Black joined the majority of the Court in holding that time spent by coal miners traveling underground to and from the mines constituted "work" under the Fair Labor Standards Act. Jackson dissented; in his opinion, Jackson quoted assurances by *Senator* Black in 1937 that wage contracts such as the one under examination would not be open to

on the Court was not terribly coherent, but he gradually moved closer to Frankfurter's position.[36] After Jackson's return from Nuremburg, and the climactic Jackson-Black outbursts, the relationship continued to improve.

Frankfurter supported Jackson in the feud with Black. On June 9, 1945, the Court met in conference to consider the *Jewell Ridge* petition for rehearing, and "argument grew so heated that the Chief Justice accepted Murphy's suggestion that final decision be postponed one week." [37] On the same date, Frankfurter sent Jackson the following note:

What do you say to adding this sentence: "The members of this Court have no right to sit in judgment on one another's participation in any case." Of course, that is the burden of what you are saying, but I thought this compendious sentence distributes favors all around in such a way as to indicate that the rule is invoked on your behalf as well as impliedly against another.[38]

After Jackson's outburst from Nuremburg, Frankfurter wrote Learned Hand:

I have a sense of guilt when I hear and read so much ignorant, shallow and malicious condemnation of Bob Jackson. The key to my state of mind you will discover in what was almost my first comment to Marion on hearing of the Nuremburg statement: "In some ways my

interpretation. Black vigorously protested that his earlier statements were being quoted out of context, but to no avail. After losing its case, the Jewell Ridge Corporation petitioned the Court for a rehearing on the grounds that Black should not have participated in the case because the winning attorney was his former law partner, and because he had been so instrumental to the passage of the legislation. The Court denied the petition, but Jackson, in an unusual move, added a brief concurrence to the denial, explaining that disqualification was a matter for each individual justice to decide for himself, not for the Court as a whole. Frankfurter joined Jackson's concurrence. The issues and animosities raised by the case simmered for nearly a year and then exploded. In June 1946, while Congress considered the nomination of Fred Vinson to be chief justice, and while the press speculated that both Black and Murphy had threatened President Truman with resignation if he appointed Jackson as Chief Justice—an honor promised him by FDR—Jackson, who was absent from the Court to serve as the American prosecutor at Nuremburg, burst out. He cabled the congressional committees, stating that the practice of ex-law partners of justices trying important cases was bringing "the Court into disrepute," and threatened that if such a series of events were "ever repeated while I am on the bench I will make my Jewell Ridge opinion look like a letter of recommendation." Jackson's outburst, in Howard's words, "shocked the country"; the entire episode represented "the most rancorous display of judicial temper in nearly a century." [35]

deepest feeling is that Bob had more guts than I had." For the fact is that I have for a considerable time been carrying myself with the thought that, perhaps, the best service I could render an institution that has semi-sacred implications for me was to resign and state fully my reasons—including Stone's major responsibility for the state of things.

The trouble with poor Bob was his difficulty in telling the real story— the deep elements of the situation of which he felt propelled to expose one surface outcropping. I wouldn't have done it, and I would, had he consulted me, have doubtless advised him against it, but—I so completely understand what made him do it, especially as his year's experience made him a deeper nature and more sensitive to the evil that acquiescence in skulduggery and lies and brutality brings upon the world.[39]

The correspondence between Jackson and Frankfurter in the years after Nuremburg reveals a deepening friendship, a common ideological outlook, and a common antipathy toward Douglas. They would exchange newspaper clippings about Douglas together with sarcastic comments; "the clippings were priceless," Jackson wrote on one occasion.[40] When a Drew Pearson article appears speculating on Douglas's distaste for Truman and Truman's aides, Jackson writes Frankfurter:

Bets are here divided as to what will be the nature of the correction Pearson will make to his story of today about Douglas. Some bet that tomorrow he will announce that our candidate left a meeting because a fellow told a dirty story.

Others bet that his indignation at finding that Presidential aides began drinking at noon was because he thought it should start at breakfast.

Take your choice.[41]

Frankfurter sent a steady stream of memoranda to Jackson with suggestions and corrections for his Court opinions. Their exchanges were often good natured.

Dear Bob:

Since I was a professor I might as well be hung for an old professor as for a young Justice. At all events attribute it to the pedantry of a professor that I want to waste some more time, not only mine but yours, regarding your concurring opinion in the *West Virginia Compact Case*. It isn't that I want to woo your vote—I might if I needed it. I write what follows purely as a matter of disinterested benevolence to seduce you into taking a little more thought not to emit an opinion, the analysis of which is so vulnerable.[42]

When Frankfurter did need Jackson's vote, however, he lobbied hard, using whatever tactic was necessary. Sometimes Frankfurter would alter his opinion to please Jackson; "Bob, will this do?" he wrote concerning a paragraph he had added for Jackson's benefit in one case. "If so—I'll recirculate with this in it. If not—I remain your obedient servant." [43] Sometimes he let Jackson know in advance that he would dissent from the Court's holding, hoping that Jackson would join him. "You may care to know," he wrote, "that I shall before very long circulate a dissent in No. 850, *Williams* v. *Austrian*, and you may therefore want to withhold your return to the Chief's opinion until you see what I have to say." [44] Quite often, Jackson was more than willing to go along with Frankfurter; "May I join the devastating work of your pen?" he wrote about one case, in a typical example of his praise for Frankfurter's efforts.[45] Sometimes, Jackson would withdraw an opinion he had written after seeing Frankfurter's work.[46]

Frankfurter felt Jackson was his intellectual equal, a judgment he did not offer easily. After Jackson's death, Frankfurter contrasted Jackson with Harold Burton.

Burton has purity of character. . . . He is the most open-minded colleague. . . . One has an easy, and inviting access to his mind. The difficulty is with what one finds when one is welcomed to enter it. And he has no humor, no esprit. . . . I shall now be sitting next to him—and while Bob and I had no end of fun in sitting next to one another, I shall now be looking down, as it were, my navel.[47]

Frankfurter was in constant search for new recruits; he treated every newly appointed justice as a potential convert and ally. Burton, Vinson, Minton, Clark, Warren, Harlan, Brennan, Whittaker, and Stewart—all received the familiar Frankfurter treatment—flattery and instruction. He often appealed to them by portraying his opponents in the worst possible light; "I beg of you," he wrote Harlan melodramatically, not to allow yourself to go in for heartbreaks by operating under the illusion that everybody has the same belief in the processes of law that guide you. There is all the difference in the world between starting with a result and clothing it in some appropriate verbal garb, and starting with a problem and letting it lead you where it will.[48]

That Black and Douglas "started with a result" was a common Frankfurter complaint. To Minton, who responded warmly to Frankfurter, he wrote, "Since you and I are on the same, even though *un*crusading team, you will not mind a comment of mine based on respect for the work of the team." [49] Minton, Frankfurter believed, disliked Black; at one conference he passed Frankfurter a note calling Black a demagogue.[50]

Frankfurter constantly instructed new brethren, telling them to read this case or that article, calling attention to the inadequacies of their opinions, wooing their votes. "Dear Harold," he wrote Burton soon after his appointment,

I have now read and read twice your recirculation in No. 45. I hope I appreciate the labor you have put into it and therefore I hate to bother you further. Certainly I try hard not to make points that involve merely choice in phrasing. But, after all, opinions consist of phrasing and differences in phrasing often carry substantial differences in implications. And so, without further ado, let me put to you the following. . . .[51]

Frankfurter's tone with those he considered his intellectual inferiors could be breathtakingly brusk and condescending. "Dear Shay," he wrote Minton—quite typically—about one of his first opinions, "I am sorry to have to suggest a slight modification in your revision of *Hazeltine*. . . ." [52]

With Chief Justice Vinson, appointed after Stone's death in 1946, Frankfurter feigned deference and sought influence. "Dear Felix," Vinson wrote soon after his appointment,

Now that I am one of you, I want to tell you how happy your letter made me, and how much I welcomed your generous prophecy in regard to my conduct of the office of Chief Justice. I am looking forward to our association and know that it will be a happy and stimulating one. . . .[53]

Quickly, Frankfurter began applying his treatment to Vinson.

I have reconsidered, as carefully as I can, your opinion in the Lewis case. I say reconsidered, because I have had the advantage of hearing your views not only at Conference but in the two talks we have had. The great public interest involved in these cases, my deep concern for the vindication of the law . . . and my strong feeling that the opinion of the Court should be voiced by the Chief Justice, have all combined to make me give your views and your opinion the most conscientious consideration. . . . The results of this consideration follow. . . .[54]

As with the other members of the Court, Frankfurter was not above threatening a concurrence against the chief justice. "Dear Chief," he wrote on one occasion,

Having assumed that your memorandum in *Culbertson* would become the Court's opinion, in the interest of time I prepared a concurring opinion. The printer tells me it will be ready after lunch, and I shall then promptly send you a copy. From it you will see what is in my mind. Of course I should be happy if the substance of what I have said in that proposed concurrence appeared instead in the Court's opinion. . . .[55]

Frankfurter was often hurt when a justice rejected his leadership; this was especially true of Brennan, a former student who, almost immediately upon coming to the Court, aligned himself with Black, Douglas, and Warren. By the late fifties and early sixties Frankfurter was referring to Brennan as "shoddy";[56] he refers to a liberal English judge as "the Black-Douglas-Brennan of the English judiciary."[57] Although initially Frankfurter had high hopes for Earl Warren, the Chief Justice's liberalism proved a major disappointment; by 1957, Frankfurter was referring to Warren's work as "dishonest nonsense."[58]

Frankfurter measured every colleague by his alignment with what he regarded as the ultimate split within the Court—between his "disinterested" and scholarly belief in judicial self-restraint, and the "shoddy," "result-oriented," "demogogic" jurisprudence of his opponents. This division in his mind is the unmistakable thread tying together Frankfurter's later years on the Supreme Court.

Dénouement

. . .

This division within the Court—and the challenge to his self-image that it entailed—helped propel Frankfurter even further into jurisprudential corners from which he never extricated himself. By making a total commitment to Thayer's philosophy of deference and by using that commitment as his principal philosophic shield against his opponents, Frankfurter lost whatever chance he might have had to work out the contradictions in his own beliefs. Within those beliefs, before his Court appointment, had been an almost implicit commitment to greater judicial scrutiny of civil liberties than of economics, and a belief in the existence of fundamental values and a hierarchy of values in the Constitution. But now, Frankfurter had buried those strands of thought under the certainty and rigidly austere doctrine of Thayer. When his opponents challenged him by erecting the First Amendment into an absolute value, Frankfurter ignored the distinction between "absolute" and "fundamental" to defeat them. He thus choked off the opportunity for a truly creative jurisprudence; his total commitment to deference led him into contradictions and, ultimately, into absurdities.

The contradictions appeared most clearly when Frankfurter was forced to admit that certain values were "fundamental" despite his professed credo that all constitutional values were equally deserving of protection. Two values in particular he found so basic to his conception of constitutional government that he could not help but exercise judicial power over them—the separation of church and state, and academic freedom. Both values were central to his own life and personality.[59]

In a series of church-state cases in the late forties and early fifties, Frankfurter ignored some of his own basic values—legislative freedom from judicial control, wide discretion for local school boards—in favor of close judicial scrutiny over schemes purporting to "establish" religion. In *Everson*,[60] he dissented from the Court's holding—in an opinion by Black—that a New Jersey statute providing reimbursement to parents for transportation expenses incurred in sending their children to private school did not violate the establishment-of-religion clause of the First Amendment.[61]

The next establishment-of-religion case came up in the 1947 term. In *McCollum*,[62] the Court was faced with the constitutionality of an Illinois statute providing a "released-time" program for religious instruction. On this issue Black felt that the establishment clause had been violated, thereby making the vote five to four for striking down the statute. Black circulated a majority opinion in which he referred to his *Everson* opinion, which Frankfurter and the other *Everson* dissenters objected to. Frankfurter recorded what happened in his diary.

Very quickly Black circulated an opinion in which he referred approvingly to the *Everson* decision. The *Everson* dissenters, Jackson, Rutledge, Burton and myself, consulted as to the position we should take and as Jackson put it, "it would be stultification for us to join Black's opinion." It was accordingly agreed that we should state our grounds for finding the [Illinois] scheme an infraction of the constitutional requirement of separation of Church and State and the desire was expressed that I try to write such an opinion for the group. Accordingly I did so, and after very few minor suggestions from Rutledge and Burton, to all of which I assented, I secured agreement to my opinion from the other three. Then began efforts on Burton's part to try to get a Court opinion in addition to my opinion on behalf of the four by getting Black to omit every reference to the *Everson* case from his opinion and from mine. Burton is one of these men who thinks you can put evil out of the world by trying to shut your eyes to it. It literally hurts him to have me make a remark that brings to the surface behavior or motives that are not nice or sweet. He hasn't the remotest idea how malignant men like Black and Douglas not only can be, but are. And so he is always trying to cover up differences that lie just beneath the surface on the assumption that thereby you smother them. . . .

Of course, I would have found it ignominous to find the . . . released-time program unconstitutional, considering the *Everson* case, without being explicit about the relation between the two cases. But the upshot of these long discussions between Burton and Black and me was that Black took out of his opinion everything except the noble sentiments that Black uttered in the *Everson* opinion, so that Rutledge and Burton could join his opinion and thereby make it a court opinion. (Poor Burton does not seem to realize that it is a characteristic of Black to utter noble sentiments and depart from them in practice—a tactic of which the *Everson* opinion is a beautiful illustration.) [63]

Frankfurter filed his opinion as a concurrence; it violated nearly every assumption upon which his system of judicial belief supposedly rested. Although he did not refer to the separation of church and state as a "fundamental value" or a "preferred freedom," his point was the same; he called the establishment clause a "great American principle" [64] which required "close judicial scrutiny." [65] Gone were the concerns for federalism and the freedom of local school officials that underpinned *Gobitis* and *Barnette*. In *Barnette*, moreover, he had said explicitly that the age of the children involved was an irrelevant consideration; in *McCollum* he made special reference to the fact that the case involved young children.[66]

Frankfurter supported his conclusions concerning the importance of the establishment clause through an analysis of history and the "philosophy of freedom reflected in the First Amendment" [67]—exactly the type of analysis used by Black and Douglas in their assertion of other clauses of the First Amendment as fundamental. Frankfurter's reading of history convinced him that the separation of church and state was a "basic constitutional principle," [68] one of the "vital reliances of our Constitutional system," [69] just as Black's and Douglas's reading of history convinced them that the free-speech and free-exercise-of-religion clauses were "basic" and "vital." Frankfurter emphasized his belief in letters to his friends; to C. C. Burlingham he wrote: "I am impenitent in believing in the principle of Church and State as basic to our democratic society, not only as formulated by Jefferson and Madison, but also by Elihu Root...." [70]

Another value Frankfurter was especially willing to uphold as basic was academic freedom. In *Sweezy* v. *New Hampshire* [71] the Court struck down as violative of due process an investigation by the attorney general of New Hampshire into the teaching and political affiliations of an instructor at the state university. The Court divided over the grounds of its decision, however. Warren, Black, Douglas, and Brennan rested their holding upon the failure of the state legislature to authorize properly the investigation conducted by the attorney general. Frankfurter, in an opinion joined by Harlan, disputed this finding (on the grounds that "distribution of powers" on the state level was not a federal matter) but struck down the investigation on the basis of its violation of academic and political freedom.

In a long and eloquent opinion, Frankfurter once again upheld a constitutional value as "preferred" without calling it so. He stressed "the dependence of a free society on free universities"; [72] he called "political autonomy" a "basic" liberty.[73] He demanded that the state present a "compelling" interest, rather than invoking his usual test of "reasonableness."

For a citizen to be made to forego even a part of so basic a liberty as his political autonomy, the subordinating interest of the State must be compelling. . . . The inviolability of privacy belonging to a citizen's political loyalties has so overwhelming an importance to the well-being of our kind of society that it cannot be constitutionally encroached upon on the basis of so meagre a counterveilling interest of the State as may be argumentatively found in the remote, shadowy threat to the security of New Hampshire allegedly presented. . . .[74]

Once again, Frankfurter supported his claims with an analysis of history; he did not shirk from the exercise of judicial judgment, even though his conclusions rested on "balancing." He was convinced he had made a disinterested analysis of the values in conflict and reached the proper conclusion. Gone were assertions of judicial modesty, of the centrality of federalism and respect for state courts.

To be sure, this is a conclusion based on a judicial judgment in balancing two contending principles—the right of a citizen to political privacy, as protected by the Fourteenth Amendment, and the right of the State to self-protection. And striking the balance implies the exercise of judgment. This is the inescapable judicial task in giving substantive content, legally enforced, to the Due Process Clause, and it is a task ultimately committed to this Court. It must not be an exercise of whim or will. It must be an overriding judgment founded on something much deeper than personal preference. As far as it lies within human limitations, it must be an impersonal judgment. It must rest on fundamental presuppositions rooted in history to which widespread acceptance may fairly be attributed. Such a judgment must be arrived at in a spirit of humility when it counters the judgment of the State's highest court. But, in the end, judgment cannot be escaped—the judgment of this Court.[75]

Without doubt, the values Frankfurter upheld judicially in these and similar cases were values he cherished personally. His life had rested on two basic principles—the irrelevance of religion and the importance of free academic inquiry. In *McCollum* Frankfurter wrote movingly of the public schools as instruments and symbols of national unity in terms that came straight from the heart.

The non-sectarian or secular public school was the means of reconciling freedom in general with religious freedom. The sharp confinement of the public schools to secular education was a recognition of the need of a democratic society to educate its children, insofar as the State undertook to do so, in an atmosphere free from pressures in a realm in which pressures are most resisted and where conflicts are most easily and most bitterly engendered. Designed to serve as perhaps the most powerful agency for promoting cohesion among a heterogeneous democratic people, the public school must keep scrupulously free from entanglement in the strife of sects. . . . This development of the public school as a symbol of our secular unity was not a sudden achievement nor attained without violent conflict.[76]

This is Frankfurter the man talking, the man who found in the public schools of New York City and in his rejection of his religion the means of personal integration into American society.*

Similarly, in *Sweezy*, Frankfurter writes beautifully about the

---

*A fragment among his files suggests that the personal value Frankfurter attached to the importance of public schools as a means of integration into American society contributed significantly to his willingness to agree with the Court's revolutionary decision in *Brown* v. *Board of Education*.[77] On a scrap of paper in his files for an earlier desegregation case [78] is the following item, written by hand:

Segregation
Atlanta Journal, quoted as follows, in N.Y. Times, Sunday, Aug. 14 (Sec. 4, p. 67)

"If the Negro is to make his due contribution to the commonwealth, he must have the knowledge, the training and the skill which only good schools can vouchsafe." [79]

"Good schools" for a minority group—those words helped trigger in Frankfurter a willingness to ignore judicial self-restraint and cast the Court into the thorniest issue of the century.[80]

academic and political freedom necessary for the good society—
values he cherished and lived by for decades.

Progress in the natural sciences is not remotely confined to findings
made in the laboratory. Insights into the mysteries of nature are born
of hypothesis and speculation. The more so is this true in the pursuit of
understanding in the groping endeavors of what are called the social
sciences, the concern of which is man and society. . . . For society's
good—if understanding be an essential need of society—inquiries into
these problems, speculation about them, stimulation in others of
reflection upon them, must be left as unfettered as possible.[81]

This is Frankfurter the scholar, the teacher, the "expert," not
Frankfurter the judge. Frankfurter in these cases is doing precisely
what he never stopped accusing his opponents of doing—reading
his own values into the Constitution.

Similarly, when it came to the troublesome issue of which
provisions of the Bill of Rights should be made applicable to state
action, Frankfurter once again found himself forced to admit that
certain values were "fundamental." [82] He again avoided the ter-
minology of his opponents—as well as their claim that the entire
Bill of Rights should be incorporated into the due process clause
of the Fourteenth Amendment—and instead used justifications
such as "that consensus of society's opinion" [83] which "judges
must divine . . . as best they can." [84] On one occasion, certain po-
lice conduct he found "shocking" to his "conscience"; there were,
he held, "canons of decency and fairness which express the notion
of justice of English-speaking people. . . ." [85] Most commentators
and Frankfurter admirers have been forced to conclude that
Frankfurter's judgment in these cases was just as subjective as
those of his opponents; the formulas and standards he applied,
Arthur Sutherland writes, "left us as much at large as we were
with mere 'due process of law.' " [86] "It must be admitted," says
Louis Jaffe, "that the Frankfurterian formulation is somewhat
deceptive. . . ." [87] Although, Raoul Berger notes, Frankfurter was
an exponent of self-restraint, "now that he had donned the robe
he apparently was satisfied that such power was safe in his
hands. . . ." [88] In these cases Frankfurter found himself forced
once again to return to his belief in the existence of fundamental

values; his all-out endorsement of self-restraint during his first years on the Court, however, left him vulnerable to those who accused him of violating his own tenets in a hypocritical manner.

. . .

When his own most cherished values were not involved, however, Frankfurter allowed his total commitment to judicial deference to lead him to nearly absurd lengths. Two famous cases, separated by ten years, vividly demonstrate this point. In *Dennis*,[89] the infamous cold-war Smith Act case, Frankfurter stretches the concept of "reasonableness" to the point of breaking. And in *Baker v. Carr*,[90] the 1962 reapportionment case and his last major case before retirement, Frankfurter's rigid adherence to deference philosophy produces a strained dissent violating both logic and his own principles.

In *Dennis*, the Court destroyed the clear-and-present-danger test and upheld the punishment of alleged conspiracies to overthrow the government at some uncertain time in the future. Frankfurter concurred; in his opinion, as Levinson argues, "there is absolutely no relation between a finding of constitutionality and an opinion as to the wisdom of the measure. . . . The very meaning of judicial restraint is that Congress' own assessment be accepted as final, unless there can literally be presented no 'reasons' for it."[91] Frankfurter wrote:

Congress has determined that the danger created by advocacy of overthrow justifies the ensuing restriction on freedom of speech. The determination was made after due deliberation, and the seriousness of the congressional purpose is attested by the volume of legislation passed to effectuate the same ends.

Can we say that the judgment Congress exercised was denied it by the Constitution? Can we establish a constitutional doctrine which forbids the elected representatives of the people to make this choice? Can we hold that the First Amendment deprives Congress of what it deemed necessary for the Government's protection?

To make validity of legislation depend on judicial reading of events still in the womb of time—a forecast, that is, of the outcome of forces at best appreciated only with knowledge of the topmost secrets of nations—is to charge the judiciary with duties beyond its equipment.[92]

Frankfurter here is all but abdicating any judgment over legislative decisions—a judgment he has been willing and eager to make on other occasions.

In *Baker* v. *Carr*, the Warren Court said that apportionment of legislative districts raised justiciable questions under the equal protection clause of the Fourteenth Amendment. Frankfurter dissented; he reiterated, for nearly the last time, that social change must come not through the courts but through "an aroused popular conscience that sears the conscience of the people's elected representatives." [93] The point of the majority's decision in the case, of course, was that the political process by which the "people's representatives" were chosen was itself flawed. *Baker* was thus squarely within the confines of paragraph two of Stone's *Carolene Products* footnote—that special judicial protection must be given to individual rights when the democratic process was itself impaired—a concept Frankfurter had endorsed strongly. To Stone he had written: "I am aware of the important distinction which you so skillfully adumbrated in your footnote four (particularly the second paragraph of it). . . . I agree with that distinction; I regard it as basic." [94]

.   .   .

But by 1962 Frankfurter was completely beyond the ability to agree with his opponents. He was old and ill, and by now his mind was occupied by what history would record about him and his enemies. In his papers there are scores of letters, mostly to his protégés and disciples, in which Frankfurter attempts to leave his legacy by shaping history to agree with his interpretation of events.

Frankfurter had long been preoccupied by the selection of biographers for the important men in his past—Holmes, Brandeis, Jackson. He "ordered" Mark Howe to undertake the definitive life of Holmes; he selected Paul Freund for Brandeis, Andrew Kaufman for Cardozo, Philip Kurland for Jackson, Alexander Bickel for himself. He deluged all of them with a constant stream of suggestions, recollections, interpretations. In the months before his death he would often lie awake at night recalling events, and then, in the morning, dictate a letter. Sometimes, he attempted to write in his own feeble hand.

Very recently I spent a restless, indeed sleepless, night and finally awoke and realized that I was restless and sleepless because I was out-lining in my mind in great detail the kind of book that I would be writing if I had Phil Kurland's job to write a book on . . . Jackson. Eventually I woke up and had my nurse bring me my familiar yellow pad and a fountain pen and I wrote out five or six pages in my own best handwriting for use by Phil. . . . Last night I had a similar experience, a restless night, indeed a sleepless night, and I had running in my mind the kind of book I would be writing if I had your responsibility of dealing with the Hughes period on the Court.[95]

He was anxious when his disciples were tardy at their tasks.

Isn't it time you talked to with me about Jacksoniana? You see my doctor has given my nurses strict orders to limit the length of my talk with visitors and since of course you and I ought to talk on the problems that confront us for days, we better begin soon.[96]

Frankfurter wanted history to record that Stone was a failure as chief justice and that Hughes was a success; that Jackson was a great judge; that Roberts had, after all, not really switched his votes during the Court-packing fight.[97]

As for Holmes, Frankfurter was confused and disturbed by what he wanted history to record; he realized that what Holmes thought about free speech was a difficult question—it was trouble-some in fact, and had been especially difficult for him. Since "clear-and-present-danger" had been used by the liberals,[98] Frankfurter was forced to discredit it; he wanted to be sure that history discredited it as well. To Mark Howe he wrote:

I must burden you with a few more remarks about Holmes's unwitting disservice . . . in regard to his clear-and present-danger formula. He should have safeguarded himself against being a powerful promotor of his own well-known admonition that by resting on a formula the mind goes to sleep and arrests further thought that is critical analysis of the formula itself. How true this has been in the fate of his clear-and-present-danger formula. I could give him weightier proof out of my own experience of the way in which not only counsel but the members of the Supreme Court used his phrase as though it were abracadabra.[99]

"The more I write on this subject," he wrote to Howe a few weeks later, "the more I realize I am depicting a real wart on my hero." [100] Frankfurter's desire to have history support him and discredit his opponents had brought him, finally, to a willingness to criticize his idol.

There is something eerie and vaguely disturbing about these letters written in the last years of Frankfurter's life. During the New Deal, Frankfurter had created in Washington a network of individuals, connected by ideology, which spread his influence throughout the government. Now, ill and near death, he had assembled a network of scholars, connected by personal loyalty to him, to create his version of the past.

CHAPTER 7

Conclusion

FRANKFURTER'S REACTION to the challenge he faced on the Supreme Court was similar to the behavior he had exhibited at several points in his life. I have argued that the key to Frankfurter's political behavior was his attitude toward opposition, and that the vehemence with which he reacted to opposition was a function of the psychological process involved in the formation of his self-image. The hypothesis presented in chapter 2 is that because of the delays and ambiguities involved in Frankfurter's psychological maturation, he developed a compensating, idealized self-image and the type of neurotic personality described by Karen Horney.

The cause of neurosis in the Horneyan model is a desperate need for self-confidence, or what she terms "basic anxiety." Living in a competitive culture, the insecure individual feels a need to lift himself above others; to cope with anxiety, he will use his imagination to create an idealized self-image. "Gradually and unconsciously, the imagination sets to work and creates in his mind an idealized image of himself. In this process he endows himself with unlimited powers and with exalted faculties; he becomes a hero, a genius, a supreme lover, a saint, a god." [1] Eventually, through this process of imagination, the individual comes to identify himself with his idealized image; "imperceptibly he becomes this image: the idealized image becomes an *idealized self*. And this idealized self becomes more real to him than his real self, not primarily because it is more appealing but because it answers all his stringent needs." [2] Self-idealization is a tonic for feelings of anxiousness and inferiority; it provides a comprehensive solution to the individual's problems. "No wonder, then, that when he believes he has found such a solution he clings to it for dear life." [3]

This "clinging for dear life" is the quality of compulsiveness, and it is the dynamic of compulsiveness that is the essence of neurosis. "Compulsiveness" is a term common to differing schools of psychology, and, as Alexander George points out, there is a common core of agreement about what constitutes "compulsive" behavior:

Orderliness and stubborness in persons of this type are said to derive in part from a desire for power or domination, which in turn is said to be related to a more basic need for self-esteem, or security. Thus, according to the technical literature compulsives often show a marked interest in imposing orderly systems upon others, an activity from which they derive a sense of power. They also hold fast obstinately to their own way of doing things. They dislike to accommodate themselves to arrangements imposed from without, but expect immediate compliance from other people as soon as they have worked out a definite arrangement, plan or proposal of their own.

In the sphere of activity in which they seek power gratifications, compulsives are sensitive to interference. . . . Negativeness, secretiveness and vindictiveness are traits often displayed by compulsives.[4]

In Horney's formulation, the compulsive, neurotic personality is engaged in a "search for glory"; the individual is driven to *prove* the validity of his idealized self-image in action. However, because the dimensions of the idealized self are out of proportion to reality, failure is inevitable. The result of any failure to prove the idealized self in action is self-hatred; but this self-hatred is often "externalized"—that is, directed outward, toward those who have challenged the neurotic's image of himself. Thus it is inevitable that the neurotic will experience impaired relationships with those in his environment who challenge him. The result of such a challenge will be vindictive hostility and a search for triumph.

Conclusion

Horney describes three general subdivisions of the neurotic type based upon three possible solutions to the problem of basic anxiety: the expansive solution, the self-effacing solution, and resignation. Frankfurter's behavior places him within the expansive category, in which the individual "prevailingly identifies himself with his glorified self." [5] Horney further identifies three characteristic subdivisions of this expansive type: the narcissistic, the perfectionistic, and the arrogant-vindictive. These classifications, like all typologies in psychological literature, are abstractions from reality. Thus, for example, all neurotics are to some extent vindictive, but a vindictive *type* is someone in whom this trait reaches a high degree of intensity. Although he displays some characteristics of all three types, Frankfurter's behavior places him within the narcissistic category. The narcissistic type, Horney finds, is full of energy and charm:

The person is his idealized self and seems to adore it. This basic attitude gives him the buoyancy or the resiliency entirely lacking in the other groups. It gives him a seeming abundance of self-confidence. . . . He has (consciously) no doubts; he *is* the anointed, the man of destiny, the prophet, the great giver, the benefactor of all mankind. All of this contains a grain of truth. He often is gifted beyond average, early and easily won distinctions, and sometimes was the favored and admired child.

This unquestioned belief in his greatness and uniqueness is the key to understanding him. His buoyancy and perennial youthfulness stem from this source. So does his often-fascinating charm. . . . He is often charming indeed, particularly when new people come into his orbit. . . . He gives the impression to himself and others that he "loves" people. And he can be generous, with a scintillating display of feeling, with flattery, with favors and help—in anticipation of admiration or in return for devotion received. . . . He can be quite tolerant, does not expect others to be perfect; he can even stand jokes about himself, so long as these merely highlight an amiable peculiarity of his; but he must never be questioned seriously. . . .

His difficulties appear both in his relations to people and in his work. His being at bottom unrelated to others is bound to show in close relations.[6]

To discover the sources of these characteristics in Frankfurter's behavior, I have applied Erikson's theories concerning identity formation, which parallel and supplement Horney's model of neurosis. Horney does not completely elaborate her concept of the "basic anxiety" that propels the individual into the search for an idealized self. Although she initially defines the term to mean the anxiety of a child who lacks the committed love of his parents,[7] she elsewhere speaks of basic anxiety in adulthood and the possibility of "accretions" of basic anxiety as the individual matures.[8] Erikson, on the other hand, outlines a sequence of psychological steps he considers necessary for the creation of a healthy identity; at each step, he indicates the possibilities of dysfunction which can create just such a condition of anxiety. Erikson's concepts of identity crisis and identity diffusion are thus similar to Horney's description of the "accretions" of "basic anxiety."

In chapter 2 I presented a hypothesis concerning the origins of Frankfurter's identity diffusion in his early adulthood, and a description of the new self-image he constructed to bring himself out of his turmoil.* During his years in Washington and at Harvard, from 1911 to 1916, Frankfurter came close to achieving a coherent sense of self, in what Erikson would call a tentative crystallization of identity. Beginning in 1916, however, a series of events shattered his sense of well-being and plunged him into a period of psychological turmoil—the death of his father, complications in his relationship with Marion, pressure from his mother concerning that relationship, uncertainty about his career. Underlying these specific problems was a fundamental ambiguity about his place in the world—whether he was an insider in the Brahmin establishment, or an outsider because he was a Jew. During the years 1916 and 1917 Frankfurter was faced with uncertainty in every part of his life—in his career, in his intimate life, in his relationship to his family and the culture his family represented. He was under severe and constant strain. This period in Frankfurter's life corresponds precisely to Erikson's description of the time of breakdown for an individual who "finds himself exposed to a com-

---

*Whether there was in Frankfurter's childhood an even more "basic" anxiety than those I have described, which propelled him toward the events of his early adulthood, is a question I cannot answer on the basis of available data. Presumably, sufficient information about his childhood would reveal a psychological situation that helped create—or did not prevent—his later identity diffusion.

bination of experiences which demand his simultaneous commitment to physical intimacy. . . , decisive occupational choice, to energetic competition, and to psychosocial self-definition." [9]

Frankfurter rebuilt a new self-image during the period of 1917 to 1919, while performing various tasks in wartime Washington. In these roles, Frankfurter displayed traits of mastery and the ability to achieve the successful imposition of his goals upon others. He discovered a talent for directing people—"personalia," in his own words; he discovered an ability to trounce opponents. He was so successful (on ever-expanding stages, culminating, literally, on the world stage at the Paris Peace Conference) and the enjoyment and sense of well-being he derived from his success contrasted so sharply with the pain of his recent past, that he came to identify himself with his success and his talents. He suddenly found himself a competent, powerful individual after feeling helpless and alone.

This self-image he had constructed, however, was idealized and inflated. A middle-level bureaucrat in Washington, he believed the future of American industrial relations rested with him; a minor functionary in Paris, he believed the fate of the Jews and therefore the peace of the world was in his hands. He began to think of himself as a symbol—of disinterested truth-seeking, of righteous tolerance. He was arrogant and self-important, and he was always right. From that point forward, opponents became enemies; every cause became a holy crusade. Frankfurter went through the rest of his life proving that he was, indeed, "great," that he was who and what he said he was—an expert, a disinterested scholar—and jurist—a handler of men. He had staked his psychological well-being on success and achievement—on "winning." *

---

*There were, of course, elements of truth in Frankfurter's self-image: he *was* successful, he *was* good at handling men, etc. As Horney argues, the neurotic individual will idealize traits he does in fact possess. What is crucial, however, is the individual's exaggeration of and identification with those traits. It is interesting to note that Barber discovered that "the President with compulsive tendencies is far more likely to have developed a political style in some relatively short, dramatic period of compensation than is the President with tendencies toward a pattern of compliance." [10] In my interpretation, the period of 1917 to 1919 is such a "short, dramatic period of compensation" in Frankfurter's life. It should also be noted that it is possible to accept the explanation of Frankfurter's personality and political style offered in chapters 3 through 6 without also accepting the validity of the hypothesis concerning the *origins* of his personality presented

To win, someone must lose. Throughout his life Frankfurter finds or creates enemies to fight against—Lowell at Harvard (and in Sacco-Vanzetti); the First New Dealers in Washington; the "liberals" on the Supreme Court. Such enemies are necessary to prove his ability to triumph; they are hated because they challenge his self-image. Every time Frankfurter faces a strong opponent and risks "losing," he also risks a loss of his identity and a resurrection of the pain and doubt of his past. Unconsciously, he is experiencing self-doubt and self-hatred; he externalizes these feelings and reacts with vindictiveness against his opponents.

To those he did not perceive as enemies, Frankfurter was a warm and charming companion, a helpful and devoted friend. At the core of the self-image he constructed in the period of 1917 to 1919 was his perception of his ability to handle men; he developed a political style using his interpersonal skills that he then applied in different situations and environments throughout his life—in his private relationships, at Harvard, in Washington during the New Deal, and, eventually, on the Supreme Court. The most obvious manifestation of this style was his constant resort to flattery. He flattered Henry Morgenthau on their trip to Turkey; he flattered Stimson, Holmes, and Brandeis; he flattered Marion when she was ill; he flattered his colleagues at Harvard; he flattered FDR and the men around him; he flattered his brethren on the Court.

Together with flattery, a key element of Frankfurter's style was his penchant for behind-the-scenes maneuvering. Whenever he was

---

in chapter 2. That is, Frankfurter's adult behavior patterns can be described as "neurotic" whether or not the precise origins of that neurosis were, as I hypothesize, in the identity crisis of the years 1916 to 1917 and the self-idealization of the years 1917 to 1919. As George and Greenstein argue, there are two different levels of psychological analysis—dynamic and genetic. A dynamic explanation begins with a description of the subject's most readily observable traits and regular pattern of actions; the analyst asks why the subject exhibits that particular syndrome of behavior, which leads to a theory of the psychic process responsible for the observed behavior. A genetic explanation goes a step further, offering a theory of the origins and causes of the subject's personality traits.[11] Thus my "dynamic" explanation is that Frankfurter was a neurotic personality of a particular type; my "genetic" explanation finds the origins of his neurosis in the period of 1916 to 1919. Although I believe the hypothesis of chapter 2 is correct, the analysis of this later behavior could stand alone. As George argues, "an answer to the casual question is not essential. Whatever creates a given personality dynamism, the dynamism itself—which is what interests the biographer the most—can be fairly readily identified. . . ."[12]

out of the public eye and able to apply his charm to a single individual, he was successful. Because he depended on this characteristic, Frankfurter realized that his success required freedom to pick and choose his own battles and the potential targets of his charm; consequently, he was unwilling to commit himself to formal offices or roles—except that of "academic"—until his appointment to the Court. He constantly referred to this as his "need for a sense of freedom."

Frankfurter thus repeatedly resisted submerging himself in any institution, except Harvard—he avoided formal office in Brandeis's Zionist organization; he did not want to become an administrator at Herbert Croly's New School; he did not formally join the Sacco-Vanzetti Defense Committee, but rather "advised" it; he did not want a seat on the Supreme Judicial Court of Massachusetts; he declined FDR's offer of formal office during the New Deal. He preferred in each case to function as a free-lance; he thus maintained the power to pick out his opportunities for successful influence through "personalia." The only institution in which he held a formal position was the Harvard Law School, which made relatively few formal demands on his time and where he was generally free from interference.

On the Supreme Court, however, Frankfurter could not function as a free-lance advisor. The successful Supreme Court justice cannot treat his brethren as if they were students in a first-year law class at Harvard, nor as if they were young protégés seeking jobs in the federal government.

This characteristic that Frankfurter displayed until his appointment to the Court—an unwillingness to be tied down or to make formal commitments—is a trait often manifested by neurotic individuals. As George argues, an individual motivated by ego-defensive needs must function without interference if he is to prove himself "uniquely endowed"; that individual will therefore avoid a commitment that will prevent independent action.[13]

This need to be unique—to be the exception to the rule—is a classic characteristic of the narcissistic personality type Horney describes. A belief in his unique "specialness" manifests itself in the often startling gap between what the neurotic actually does and what he says he does, another recurring characteristic of

Frankfurter's behavior. He claimed not to have sought disciples at Harvard; he did.* He claimed not to have placed people in Washington during the New Deal; he did. He claimed not to have lobbied for votes on the Supreme Court; he did. As Horney argues, this trait, which is often present in neurotic personalities, can indicate that an individual regards himself as exceptional. It is not that he is lying; he really believes that he does the things he says he does, that he is the person he claims to be.†

.   .   .

I have analyzed three large patterns running through Frankfurter's life which support my hypothesis. There is, first of all, his history of difficult interpersonal relationships. Frankfurter's tendency to domineer the individuals closest to him is evident throughout his life; the characteristic was so evident that it contributed to mental breakdown in his wife. Although we cannot know the extent to which Marion's psychological condition arose independently, the evidence—their letters, the testimony of their friends (including a medical authority who knew them well), the diagnosis of Marion's psychiatrist strongly hinted at in her letters—suggests that Frankfurter's personality unquestionably intensified her condition. It is absolutely clear that Frankfurter dominated his wife and that this affected her profoundly.

Frankfurter's other personal relationships show evidence of disturbance as well. Frankfurter dominated anyone in a subordinate position to him—his students, his law clerks, his disciples. For many of these young men, the relationship was, without question, highly rewarding; for others, the rewards were mixed with high psychological cost. When a disciple showed signs of questioning Frankfurter's judgment on an important matter, he was cut off and vilified. With his peers, Frankfurter often quickly became self-righteous during a disagreement; many of his closest friends at one time or another experienced the sting of Frankfurter's displeasure and his dogged pursuit of disagreements.

*In his reminiscences, Frankfurter said "that is the great thing about the Harvard Law School. It doesn't make disciples." [14]

†Presumably with a straight face, Frankfurter once wrote: "While I have long been dubious about capital punishment, I would without doubt reserve it for the fawners and flatterers of those in power." [15]

There is, secondly, Frankfurter's lifelong pattern of intense conflict with an individual or group of individuals he identified as enemies, and the degree to which he thrilled at the chance to defeat them. Frankfurter displayed a comparable syndrome of behavior in different environments: in his government jobs, at Harvard, during the New Deal, on the Supreme Court. In each case, Frankfurter resented those who did not agree with him and did not succumb to his charm; he attributed opposition to ignorance or malevolence; he attempted to discredit the motives of his opponents and to defeat them; he self-righteously defended his own motives—especially his "disinterestedness"—and his own abilities; he felt exhilaration and pleasure when vindicated.

This sense of delight at "winning," this all-out enthusiasm for the heat of battle, is an important piece of evidence. As George has argued, evidence of pleasurable feelings supports a hypothesis that unconscious motives are guiding behavior in such circumstances.[16] Frankfurter's thrill is especially evident during the period of 1919 to 1920, when he first realizes that a battle is brewing at Harvard and that he will have someone to fight against—and thus an opportunity to prove his new self-image in action. "Gee but I feel happy!" he once wrote Marion from Paris when warned of trouble ahead. "Think not only of having something to fight for, but something to fight against. It's just sheer joy. . . ."[17]

Finally, there is the startling extent to which Frankfurter displayed a pattern of projecting his own characteristics onto others, while rationalizing his own behavior. The most glaring examples of this trait occur in his descriptions of his judicial colleagues. Although he, perhaps more than anyone, lobbied other members of the Court for votes, he never admitted doing so, but rather perceived his own actions as helpfully "advising" his brethren; his judicial opponents, however, were, in his view, cynical and evil spreaders of their own influence. Although he was directly and actively involved in politics while on the bench, he never admitted as much; when Douglas showed signs of being politically ambitious, however, Frankfurter became obsessed with his behavior and never ceased talking about how politics and judging did not mix.

Projections such as these help protect the individual against self-hatred. To admit his own faults would damage his self-esteem; to rationalize those faults and to magnify their significance in others allows the individual to function with his self-image intact.[18]

• • •

Given the presence of so many similarities between Frankfurter's behavior and both Horney's general neurotic personality type and the specific style of the narcissistic personality, it is difficult to avoid the conclusion that he fits the Horneyan model of neurosis. Although some of the traits I have listed are present to some degree in less neurotic individuals, the fact that *all* of these traits are present in Frankfurter's behavior, and that they are present in such intensity, strongly supports my contention. There is a nearly precise fit between Frankfurter and the neurotic personality type; although any single piece of evidence I have presented could perhaps be accounted for in a different manner, the cumulative weight of the evidence makes such alternative explanations doubtful and lends support to my hypothesis.

Thus it becomes difficult not to interpret Frankfurter's Court behavior within the framework of this explanation. The style Frankfurter displayed on the Court, and the self-image which supported that style, were rooted in the conflicts of his past; his reaction to his opponents when he failed to lead the Court was part of this syndrome. The heat and excessive preoccupation with which Frankfurter reacted to the behavior and doctrines of his "enemies" were a function of unconscious self-anger and self-doubt. For the first time in his long and successful life, Felix Frankfurter was not who and what he said he was, he was not the undisputed leader of the Roosevelt Court.

His state of mind influenced his jurisprudence. The passion with which Frankfurter defended his position on judicial self-restraint, the extent to which he was willing to stretch that philosophy, and the degree to which he ignored countervailing claims within his own belief system, were a function of his attitude toward his liberal opponents. I have argued that because of his anger at his opponents, Frankfurter ignored the distinction in his own thinking between fundamental values and absolute values; that he ignored his own commitment to the existence of a hierarchy of values in the Constitution in favor of a strengthened concept of judicial self-restraint; that he might have been willing to endorse the concept of preferred freedoms—in a form less absolute than that of his colleagues, to be sure—if it had not been first presented by a man he did not respect and in a case that touched him on a number of different levels—his need to appear "disinterested," his patriotism, his belief in the importance of national symbols, his very personal sense of the importance of public schools for the creation of national unity. Having taken his stand in *Gobitis*, he could only defend it further in *Barnette*, given the added impetus of his anger at the liberals for deserting him and his sense of himself as the true interpreter of Holmes. Yet despite this all-out commitment to judicial deference, Frankfurter at times used the concept of fundamental values (without endorsing it), thereby opening himself to the charges of logical contradiction and hypocrisy. He did so, I have argued, for values that were psychologically important to him: separation of church and state, and academic freedom.

Of course, it would be possible to account for Frankfurter's votes and opinions on the Court without reference to his personality. One could view his commitment to judicial self-restraint as consistent with his pre-Court philosophy and explain his abandonment of "preferred freedoms" as a realization that he held contradictory beliefs; self-restraint was more vital to him and thus he rationally chose to make it the touchstone of his judicial career and to jettison anything inconsistent with it. His votes and opinions—so the argument would run—logically followed.

But judicial behavior is more than votes and opinions. A simple, "rational" explanation cannot account for Frankfurter's personal style on the Court; it cannot explain his obsession with or anger at his opponents; it cannot explain the extent to which he projected his own characteristics onto his brethren. Judicial outcomes cannot be wrenched out of the context of a man's life; a member of the Court is not a composite of juridical abstractions but a complex individual of flesh and blood. His behavior on the bench must be understood within the framework of his life history; he comes to the Court with a personality and a style as well as with an ideology.

It is true that the ideological core of Frankfurter's judicial creed was a choice of values made early in life, but that choice of values was itself influenced by Frankfurter's personal relationships with his mentors, which cannot be understood without reference to Frankfurter's need for acceptance and a sense of belonging. Moreover, the manner in which that core of beliefs was expanded, the manner in which conflicting threads were sorted out, the style in which his beliefs were presented, and the passion with which they were defended, all were profoundly influenced by Frankfurter's personality needs. Too much is left unexplained by a simple "rational" explanation of Frankfurter's judicial behavior.

In this study, it must be emphasized again, I have not claimed that Frankfurter's judicial behavior was solely a function of ego-defensive personality factors. My purpose has been to present hypotheses that complement and expand a purely "jurisprudential" understanding of Frankfurter's behavior, not to reduce his life history to a psychiatric case history. The hypotheses presented here are plausible; they are consistent with accepted and clinically tested psychological models; they fit the information we have about Frankfurter's life; they explain aspects of his behavior left unaccounted for in other interpretations. These, finally, are the standards to which psychological hypotheses about historical figures must be held. This study has attempted to provide an explanation that enables us to understand Frankfurter in his full complexity. If it makes him any less magnificent, it does so, I would argue, only by making him more human.

NOTES

Key to Citations

The following abbreviations are used to indicate manuscript collections:

LC   The Felix Frankfurter papers, Manuscript Division, Library of Congress

HLSL   The Felix Frankfurter papers, Harvard Law School Library

LHP   The Felix Frankfurter–Learned Hand correspondence in the Hand papers, Harvard Law School Library

OWHP   The Oliver Wendell Holmes papers, Harvard Law School Library

COHC   The Columbia Oral History Collection

In citations to the Frankfurter letters, initials are used to indicate prominent individuals. In LC and HLSL citations, folder and box numbers follow the location reference. In LC citations, the first number indicates the folder number, and the second number indicates the box number. Thus "LC 53–7" indicates Folder 53 in Box 7 at the Library of Congress. In the Harvard citations, the first number indicates the box number; thus "HLSL 9–43" indicates Folder 43 in Box 9 at Harvard. These references are consistent with the different indexing practices at the two libraries. During his first years on the Court, Frankfurter bound together correspondence and memoranda in large scrapbooks. These books are part of the Harvard collection and are cited by term year—for example, HLSL 1940. Copies of some, but not all of this material are at the Library of Congress.

Any letters dated from internal evidence are enclosed in brackets—for example, 4/13/[35].

Notes

Chapter 1

1. Within the discipline of political science, the behavorial revolution of the 1950s and 1960s generated numerous untested assertions concerning the importance of personality in an institution that gives its members great powers of decision, free from the sanctions attached to most political offices. Yet there have been very few detailed, scholarly examinations of judicial personality and its effects on judicial behavior, and judicial biographers have been reluctant to use personality as an explanatory variable. (There is, however, a major exception to this generalization in the case of Mr. Justice Holmes. See Yosal Rogat, "The Judge as Spectator," *University of Chicago Law Review* 31 [1964], and Catherine Drinker Bowen, *Yankee From Olympus* [Boston: Little, Brown, 1944], both of whom analyze Holmes's personality in a suggestive, if unsystematic, manner.) J. Woodford Howard, Jr., has written of the "biographical neglect of the personality roots of judicial behavior. Not only does personality generate a relatively small number of propositions, but they are overwhelmingly superficial rather than in-depth observations drawn from psychological models" ("Judicial Biography and the Behavioral Persuasion," *American Political Science Review* 65 [1971]: 711). After systematically examining the major judicial biographies, Howard concludes that "the least satisfactory state of biographical knowledge concerns the relation of personality to judicial behavior" (p. 712). Several scholars have, nevertheless, recently begun to examine the importance of personality for the Court. Howard has argued that the collegiality of the Court greatly limits the degree to which a justice's ideology is translated into votes and opinions; he stresses intervening variables such as "socialization" and "style." See "On the Fluidity of Judicial Choice," *American Political Science Review* 62 (1968). Howard's biography of Frank Murphy emphasizes the importance of these variables for the behavior of one of the century's most interesting jurists and demonstrates that personality can be a variable of immense importance for determining judicial outcomes. See *Mr. Justice Murphy: A Political Biography* (Princeton: Princeton University Press, 1968). Walter F. Murphy, in his description of the process of reaching agreement within the Court, suggests that personality is one variable determining how a justice will interact with his brethren and offers several examples. See *Elements of Judicial Strategy* (Chicago: University of Chicago Press, 1964). David Danelski has emphasized the special importance of the personality of the Chief Justice for decision-making processes. See "The Influence of the Chief Justice in the Decisional Process," in *Courts, Judges and Politics*, ed. Walter F. Murphy and C. Herman Pritchett (New York: Random House, 1961).

2. Fred I. Greenstein provides an analysis of different variables affecting the probability that personality will enter the decision-making process; he argues that ambiguous and fluid situations "leave room for personal variability to manifest itself." See *Personality and Politics* (New York: Norton, 1975), pp. 50–51.

3. For a description of the anti-Semitism of the American bar prior to the New Deal, see Jerold S. Auerbach, *Unequal Justice: Lawyers and Social Change in Modern America* (New York: Oxford University Press, 1976).

4. Max Freedman, ed., *Roosevelt and Frankfurter: Their Correspondence, 1928–1945* (Boston: Little, Brown, 1967).

5. Joseph Lash, ed., *From the Diaries of Felix Frankfurter* (New York: Norton, 1975).

6. See my article, "Clio on the Couch," *World Politics* 32 (April 1980): 406–24.

7. James David Barber, *The Presidential Character: Predicting Performance in the White House* (Englewood Cliffs: Prentice-Hall, 1972). For a cogent criticism of Barber's work, see Alexander L. George, "Assessing Presidential Character,"

Notes

World Politics 26 (1974): 234–82. Despite George's critique of many aspects of Barber's analysis, he finds the concept of "style" an important theoretical formulation. See especially p. 242ff.

8. James David Barber, "The Interplay of Presidential Character and Style: A Paradigm and Five Illustrations," in *A Source Book for the Study of Personality and Politics*, ed. Fred I. Greenstein and Michael Lerner (Chicago: Markham, 1971), p. 386.

9. Barber, *Presidential Character*, p. 7.

10. George comments that "the possible lack of fit between an individual's personality and the demands of his role has long been recognized as one of the sources of 'role strain,' but it has not been easy to find satisfactory ways of studying it. . . . Barber's conceptualization of style is therefore an important theoretical contribution." See "Assessing Presidential Character," p. 244.

11. Perhaps the best recent example of tension between role requirements and personal style is Lyndon Johnson, who could not adapt his highly successful style as Senate Majority Leader to the different demands of the White House. See George, "Assessing Presidential Character," p. 243; Barber, *Presidential Character*, Part 2; and Doris Kearns, *Lyndon Johnson and the American Dream* (New York: Harper and Row, 1976), pp. 369–400.

12. The phrase is Barber's. See *Presidential Character*, p. 10.

13. George, "Assessing Presidential Character," p. 242.

14. For a discussion of the need to ground psychological interpretations in clinically tested theories, see Greenstein, *Personality and Politics*, passim. The choice of a psychological theory for the biographer poses a difficult problem. Both Erik H. Erikson and Karen Horney have been applied to political biography with impressive success; see Erikson, *Young Man Luther* (New York: Norton, 1958) and *Gandhi's Truth* (New York: Norton, 1969), as well as Robert C. Tucker, *Stalin as Revolutionary* (New York: Norton, 1973). Excursions into Freudian analysis, however, have produced more uncertain results; compare, for example, the stilted interpretation of Woodrow Wilson offered by Freud and William C. Bullitt in *Thomas Woodrow Wilson: A Psychological Study* (Boston: Houghton Mifflin, 1967) to the far more convincing arguments of Alexander and Juliette George in *Woodrow Wilson and Colonel House* (New York: John Day, 1956). One reason for this difference, of course, is purely practical: the evidence required for Freudian analysis is often completely absent or, at best, scanty, while ego psychology considers the entire process of maturation and does not place nearly so much emphasis upon early childhood. It is one thing to apply gingerly the theories of Erikson and/or Horney to a figure's early-adult identity crisis—which may be rather well documented—and to hypothesize about the psychological functions of that individual's political style; it is another matter entirely to "explain" a historical subject's adult behavior as the inevitable outcome of some early childhood trauma. Indeed, it is tempting to ask whether ego psychology as a general intellectual movement within clinical psychology developed, at least in part, in reaction to the often overwhelming problem of evidence in Freudian theory. Whether this is in fact the case, it must be kept in mind that hypotheses based upon the theories of ego psychology can be understood as complementary to traditional Freudian analysis, rather than as a refutation of them. Erikson himself has always emphasized his closeness to Freud. For a discussion of the relation between Erikson and Freud, see Paul Roazen, *Erik H. Erikson: The Power and Limits of a Vision* (New York: The Free Press, 1976).

15. Karen Horney, *Neurosis and Human Growth* (New York: Norton, 1950), p. 22.

16. The idea of compensation is central to the thought of Harold D. Lasswell, whose work did much to stimulate interest in psychology among political scientists. Lasswell conceptualizes "political man" as someone who uses power to overcome low estimates of the self. See especially *Power and Personality* (New York: Norton, 1948), pp. 39ff. For a criticism of Lasswell's formulation and a discussion of the relationship between Lasswell and Horney, see Robert C. Tucker,

Notes

"The Georges' Wilson Reexamined: An Essay on Psychobiography," *American Political Science Review* 71 (June 1977): 606–618.

17. George, "Assessing Presidential Character," p. 253.

18. Erik H. Erikson, "The Problem of Ego Identity," *Journal of the American Psychoanalytic Association* 4 (1956): 98. See also the seminal work by Daniel Levinson and his associates, *The Seasons of a Man's Life* (New York: Knopf, 1978).

Chapter 2

1. See, for example, FF to MD, 3/10/19, LC 53–6.

2. FF to MD, 5/?/19, LC 60–7; FF to MD, 3/?/19, LC 52–6.

3. Helen Shirley Thomas, *Felix Frankfurter: Scholar on the Bench* (Baltimore: Johns Hopkins Press, 1960), p. 3.

4. Matthew Josephson, "Profile: Jurist," *The New Yorker*, 12/7/40, p. 37.

5. Harlan B. Phillips, ed., *Felix Frankfurter Reminisces* (New York: Reynal, 1960), p. 4. This book is a heavily edited version of the complete transcript of Frankfurter's recollections for the Columbia Oral History Collection.

6. Liva Baker, *Felix Frankfurter* (New York: Coward-McCann, 1969), p. 19; Irving Howe, *World of Our Fathers* (Simon and Schuster, 1976), p. 131.

7. Baker, *Felix Frankfurter*, p. 19. According to Thomas, Leopold was a retail fur merchant. I have been unable to verify his occupation through any of the sources available to me and have therefore relied upon Baker, who had access to family members.

8. Josephson, "Profile: Jurist," p. 37. There is a curious absence of letters in Frankfurter's files between him and his brothers. Considering the fact that he was an avid correspondent, and that he saved most of his letters (including very intimate correspondence with his wife), it is at least a plausible conjecture that Frankfurter destroyed, or did not save, his correspondence with his brothers. Like his efforts to avoid the subject of conflict within his family in his recorded reminiscences (see pp. 16ff) this perhaps suggests the presence of less than complete harmony within the Frankfurter family.

9. The major split was between German and Russian Jews, and it should be noted that the Frankfurters' German origins made them socially superior, in a subtle but important way, to Russian immigrants. For a recent description of the difference between the two subcultures, see Howe, *World of Our Fathers*, passim.

10. Phillips, *Felix Frankfurter Reminisces*, pp. 3–5.

11. Ibid., p. 5.

12. Ibid.

13. Ibid., p. 6.

14. Ibid.

15. Josephson, "Profile: Jurist," p. 35. See also Joseph Lash, ed., *From the Diaries of Felix Frankfurter* (New York: Norton, 1975), p. 3. Lash, in his highly perceptive introductory essay, makes a similar assessment of Frankfurter's parents.

16. Howe, *World of Our Fathers*, pp. 254, 172ff.

17. FF to MD, 4/29?/19, LC 59–7. See also FF-COHC, pp. 36–38.

18. FF-COHC, pp. 21–22.

19. Ibid., p. 38.

20. Phillips, *Felix Frankfurter Reminisces*, p. 9.

21. Ibid., p. 11.

22. Ibid.

23. The move from religious observance to agnosticism was a common one for Jewish adolescents at this time. For an excellent discussion of this phenomenon, see David A. Hollinger, *Morris R. Cohen and the Scientific Ideal* (Cambridge: M.I.T. Press, 1975), p. 20.

24. FF-COHC, p. 36.

Notes

25. Baker, *Felix Frankfurter*, p. 20.
26. Lash, *From the Diaries of Felix Frankfurter*, p. 3.
27. Ibid.
28. Phillips, *Felix Frankfurter Reminisces*, p. 13.
29. Ibid., p. 15.
30. Ibid., p. 16.
31. Ibid., p. 17.
32. Ibid., p. 18.
33. Ibid., pp. 18–19.
34. Ibid., p. 19.
35. Ibid.
36. Ibid., pp. 26–27.
37. Ibid.
38. Ibid., p. 30.
39. Ibid., pp. 20–21.
40. Ibid., p. 24.
41. Ibid., p. 35.
42. Ibid., pp. 35–36.
43. Ibid., p. 36.
44. Ibid.
45. Ibid., pp. 36–37.
46. Ibid., p. 37.
47. Ibid., p. 38.
48. Erik H. Erikson, "The Problem of Ego Identity," *Journal of the American Psychoanalytic Association* 4 (1956):56–121. It is important to note that although Erikson finds that, in most individuals, the "completion" of an identity is accomplished by the early twenties, delays are not uncommon. "The sequence of stages," he writes, "represents a successive development of the component parts of the psychosocial personality. Each part exists in some form . . . before the time when . . . 'its' psychosocial crisis is precipitated both by the individual's readiness and by society's pressure. . . . Individual make-up and the nature of society determine the rate of development of each of them . . ." (p. 76). In another work, Erikson writes of the "variations in tempo and intensity" of each individual's progression through the stages of development (*Childhood and Society* [New York: Norton, 1963], p. 271). My hypothesis is that Frankfurter was unable to "complete" his identity until very late in his life because of several unresolved emotional issues, and thus faced severe psychological consequences. See especially pp. 23ff.
49. Phillips, *Felix Frankfurter Reminisces*, p. 39.
50. Lash, *From the Diaries of Felix Frankfurter*, p. 5, quoting Phillips, *Felix Frankfurter Reminisces*, p. 43.
51. Phillips, *Felix Frankfurter Reminisces*, p. 42.
52. Ibid., p. 43.
53. Ibid., p. 45.
54. Ibid., p. 47.
55. Ibid., p. 51.
56. For a discussion of the difference between the New Nationalism and the New Freedom, see Arthur S. Link, *Woodrow Wilson and the Progressive Era* (New York: Harper, 1954), pp. 1–25; and C. B. Forcey, *The Crossroads of Liberalism* (New York: Oxford University Press, 1961), especially pp. xiii–xxix.
57. Daniel J. Levinson et al., *The Seasons of a Man's Life* (New York: Knopf, 1978). It is important to note that Levinson's clinical studies demonstrate that a firm psychological identity may not be completed until an individual's mid-thirties. He writes: "The process of entering into adulthood is more lengthy and complex than has usually been imagined. It begins at around age 17 and continues until 33 (plus or minus two years at either end). A young man needs about fifteen years to emerge from adolescence, find his place in adult society and commit himself to a more stable life" (p. 71). Levinson also finds that "unresolved

adolescent problems" may make this process more difficult. The evidence indicates, I believe, the presence of such unresolved problems in Frankfurter's case. See especially pp. 47ff.

58. Levinson, *The Seasons of a Man's Life*, p. 100.
59. Levinson et al., "The Psychosocial Development of Men in Early Adulthood and the Mid-Life Transition," in *Life History Research in Psychotherapy*, vol. 3., ed. D. F. Ricks, A. Thomas, and M. Roff (Minneapolis: University of Minnesota Press, 1974), p. 251.
60. Phillips, *Felix Frankfurter Reminisces*, p. 48.
61. E. Morrison, *Turmoil and Tradition: A Study of the Life and Times of Henry L. Stimson* (New York: Atheneum, 1964), p. 163.
62. Ibid. and passim.
63. Phillips, *Felix Frankfurter Reminisces*, p. 48.
64. Ibid.
65. FF to HLS, 11/16/08, LC 2173-104.
66. See HLS to FF, 6/8/11, LC 2144-103.
67. HLS to FF, 6/30/11, LC 2144-103.
68. HLS to FF, 7/1/11, LC 2144-103. In the same letter Stimson wrote: "By the way, you could have had offered to you the position of Assistant Attorney General in charge of Customs. . . . The Attorney General consulted me about you, and I took the responsibility of saying that in spite of the large salary I did not think that you should be wasted on that work."
69. Phillips, *Felix Frankfurer Reminisces*, p. 56.
70. Ibid., p. 59.
71. Ibid., p. 62.
72. FF to HLS, 9/9/11, LC 2173-104.
73. Ibid.
74. Lash, *From the Diaries of Felix Frankfurter*, p. 102.
75. Ibid., p. 110.
76. FF to Emory R. Buckner, 9/26/11, LC 510-30.
77. Frankfurter was also, at times, aware of the need for Jews not to be overly suspicious; he writes:

> Difficult case of alleged discrimination against Jewish cadet at West Point— probably unduly suspicious but [two words illegible] articles bring out anew the deep causes for such susceptibility and suspicion—at my suggestion Stimson dispatched a Jewish officer of capability to West Point to investigate. [Lash, *From the Diaries of Felix Frankfurter*, p. 117]

78. Ibid.
79. Ibid., p. 120.
80. Ibid., p. 108. Emphasis added.
81. FF to Emory R. Buckner, 9/26/11, LC 510-30.
82. Lash, *From the Diaries of Felix Frankfurter*, pp. 103-4.
83. Phillips, *Felix Frankfurter Reminisces*, p. 58.
84. FF to OWH, 2/10/12, OWHP 30-15. It is interesting to note that Frankfurter in this letter refers to "our" Puritanism; this suggests his strong desire to identify with the Brahmin culture represented by Holmes.
85. OWH to FF, 3/8/12, OWHP 29-2.
86. Felix Frankfurter, "Herbert Croly and American Political Opinion," *New Republic*, 7/16/30, p. 247.
87. Herbert Croly, *The Promise of American Life* (Indianapolis: Bobbs-Merrill, 1965), p. 22.
88. FF to HLS, 4/30/12, LC 2174-104.
89. FF to LH, 9/23/12, LC 1217-63.
90. FF to HLS, 9/10/12, LC 2174-104.
91. HLS to FF, 9/19/12, LC 2174-104.
92. FF to Emory R. Buckner, 8/2/12, LC 513-30.

93. Emory R. Buckner to FF, 3/?/12, LC 511-30.
94. See Stimson Diaries, Yale University Library; vol. 2, p. 31, microfilm edition.
95. See FF to Emory R. Buckner, 1/6/12, LC 511-30.
96. FF to Emory R. Buckner, 3/11/13, LC 514-30.
97. FF to Emory R. Buckner, 3/26/13, LC 514-30.
98. See Lash, *From the Diaries of Felix Frankfurter*, p. 10.
99. See FF to HLS, 5/19/13, LC 2174-104.
100. Phillips, *Felix Frankfurter Reminisces*, pp. 106–7.
101. Ibid., p. 109.
102. Frankfurter's correspondence and oral history are full of derogatory remarks about Wilson. See, generally, Phillips, *Felix Frankfurter Reminisces*, chap. 8.
103. Winfred Dennison to Edward H. Warren, 6/12/13, quoted in Baker, *Felix Frankfurter*, p. 41. A copy of this letter is in Frankfurter's files, LC 952-51.
104. Frankfurter phrased Harvard's inquiry this way: "Suppose a new professorship is established for criminology or other or further subjects, largely in control of Pound; suppose that the professorship were to become effective for the Academic Year 1914–1915, and were offered to you, would you accept it?"
105. FF to HLS, 6/26/13, LC 2145-103.
106. HLS to FF, 6/28/13, LC 2145-103.
107. LH to FF, 7/3/13, LC 1218-63.
108. Quoted in Baker, *Felix Frankfurter*, p. 42.
109. See LH to FF, 7/18/13, LC 1218-63.
110. FF to HLS, 7/7/13, LC 2174-104.
111. FF to HLS, 4/8/14, LC 2175-104.
112. FF to OWH, n.d., OWHP 30-15.
113. Laura C. Rosenfield, *Portrait of a Philosopher: Morris R. Cohen in Life and Letters* (New York: Harcourt Brace and World, 1962), p. 242.
114. FF to HLS, 12/9/13, LC 2174-104.
115. FF to HLS, 5/19/13, LC 2174-104.
116. FF to OWH, 9/6/13, OWHP 30-15.
117. FF to OWH, 1/14/16?, OWHP 30-9.
118. FF to OWH, 5/18/?, OWHP 30-9.
119. FF to OWH, 1/25/?, OWHP 30-12.
120. FF to OWH, 3/17/?, OWHP 30-10.
121. FF to OWH, 10/2/?, OWHP 30-11.
122. FF to OWH, 1/7/?, OWHP 30-11.
123. OWH to FF, 3/9/15, OWHP 29-2.
124. FF to HLS, 11/4/14, LC 2175-104.
125. Josephson, "Profile: Jurist," p. 24.
126. FF to MC, 3/9/12, quoted in Rosenfield, *Portrait of a Philosopher*, p. 241.
127. Emory R. Buckner to FF, 11/5/14, LC 517-30.
128. LDB to Philip P. Wells, 7/21/13, in Melvin I. Urofsky and David W. Levy, eds., *The Brandeis Letters*, vol. 3 (Albany: State University of New York Press, 1972–78), p. 146.
129. Frankfurter's involvement in Zionist affairs despite his lack of personal religious feeling was not completely contradictory; it was, in fact, common for men of his generation of Jewish immigrants who considered themselves "liberal." David Hollinger's comments concerning Morris Cohen are an excellent analysis of this phenomenon: "It was an abstract liberalism that Cohen employed to justify his participation in Jewish affairs. His concern for 'Jewish survival' was always a defense of Jews, as human beings, against genocide, persecution, and discrimination; it was never an attempt, consciously at least, to perpetuate Jewish identity" (Hollinger, *Morris R. Cohen and the Scientific Ideal*, p. 212).
130. LDB to FF, 11/19/16, LC 403-26.
131. 11/14/16, LC 403-26.
132. FF to LDB, 6/16/16, LC 487-29.
133. FF to HLS, 12/8/14, LC 2175-104.
134. Phillips, *Felix Frankfurter Reminisces*, p. 92.

135. Bunting v. Oregon, 243 U.S. 426 (1917).
136. Stettler v. O'Hara, 243 U.S. 629 (1917).
137. Phillips, *Felix Frankfurter Reminisces*, pp. 99–100.
138. Ibid., p. 101.
139. Ibid., p. 102.
140. Ibid., p. 78.
141. It is interesting to note that this is the precise age at which Levinson finds the process of "entering adulthood" to have normally come to an end. See chapter 2, note 57 herein.
142. FF to HLS, 3/18/16, LC 2176-104.
143. FF to MD, 4/6/17, LC 35-5.
144. FF to Harold Laski, 11/17/41, LC 1503-75.
145. FF to HLS, 4/29/16, LC 2176-104.
146. FF to MD, 10/14/19, LC 85-9.
147. See FF to MD, 7/21/16, LC 33-5.
148. FF to OWH, n.d., OWHP 30-13.
149. I am basing this interpretation on the general tone of the letters from Frankfurter to Marion, and on the following letter, written one year after his father's death:

> After a visit to the cemetary yesterday (it's a year since Father died and a year since you got health) Mother had to be told the news. She took it with sheer bravery—the strength and wisdom of much endurance and much faith. Had you seen *her* throughout the evening you would know why praise of me by people so often arouses almost morbid discomfort, and almost always a sense of its irrelevance. But then—you know anyhow. [FF to MD, 2/27/17, LC 34-5]

150. MD to FF, early October 1916, LC 33-5.
151. FF to MD, 10/3/16, LC 33-5.
152. FF to HLS, 10/26/16, LC 2176-104.
153. Copy in LC 2176-104.
154. FF to HLS, 11/2/16, LC 2176-104.
155. FF to MD, 7/23/18, LC 39-5.
156. Phillips, *Felix Frankfurter Reminisces*, p. 114.
157. Lash, *From the Diaries of Felix Frankfurter*, p. 21, quoting *New York Times*, 6/20/17.
158. FF to MD, 6/21/17, LC 35-5.
159. Phillips, *Felix Frankfurter Reminisces*, p. 147.
160. Ibid., pp. 148–49.
161. Ibid., p. 151.
162. FF to WL, 11/22/17, LC 1557-77.
163. See, for example, *Felix Frankfurter Reminisces*, p. 123. Frankfurter's analysis of the labor situation was that of a typical Progressive. His primary goal was the successful prosecution of the war effort, although he sympathized with the workers' complaints against conditions and lack of security. From Arizona he wrote Marion:

> It's about this way: there is no security of work, because there is no machinery of protection in which the men have a part, hence unemployment (resulting in this part of the country in the "hobo mind") and irregularity of employment; there is no security of output, because the men can and do resort to strike, as the only effective means of safeguarding their interests, legitimate or felt to be legitimate. In other words autocracy and anarchy . . . are the basic evils. It's the same old story. One of the English Commissions on Industrial Unrest very recently spoke of the feeling of the men, that "they are regarded as instruments of the community and not members of it"—and there you are! All the evils flow from that source. [FF to MD, 10/9/17, LC 36-5]

164. Phillips, *Felix Frankfurter Reminisces*, pp. 136–37.

165. Ibid.
166. Ibid., p. 130.
167. Frankfurter cabled Emory Buckner:

VERY URGENT . . . EVIDENTLY SOME ONE HAS BEEN DRAWING ON TR'S GOOD NATURE AND PATRIOTISM TO GET HIM LINED UP IN THIS LOCAL FIGHT FOR HIS OWN SAKE HE OUGHT NOT TO MIX IN AT LONG RANGE BECAUSE IT MUDDIES THE WATER CONSIDERABLY FROM THE POINT OF VIEW OF CREATING THE RIGHT KIND OF WAR SPIRIT ON THE COAST PLEASE SEE THE COLONEL AND TELL HIM THAT I AM HERE INVESTIGATING THE SITUATION AND GOING TO THE BOTTOM OF THE THING THAT HE OUGHT NOT TO ALLOW HIMSELF TO BE MADE USE OF AND THAT THE ISSUE IS NOT WHAT HE HAS BEEN TOLD IT IS TO MAKE HIM REALIZE THAT I AM WIRING THIS SOLELY FROM THE POINT OF VIEW OF THE MOST EFFECTIVE PROSECUTION OF THE AIMS WHICH HE HAS MOSTLY IN MIND. [Copy in LC 2643-127]

168. The letter is dated 12/19/17.
169. FF to TR, 1/7/18, LC 3116-154.
170. FF to WL, 10/3/17, LC 1557-77.
171. FF to MD, 12/16/18, LC 44-6.
172. FF to MD, 5/7/18, LC 38-5.
173. FF to MD, 11/12/18, LC 43-6.
174. FF to MD, 8/18/18, LC 40-5. On the first anniversary of the marriage proposal, Frankfurter writes to Marion: "I know too well how poor 'the job' I made of it a year ago—the struggle, the torture, the incoherence, the aloofness of it, all were the final stage of the inner tussle of years" (FF to MD, 5/6/19, LC 61-7). Although he proposes to Marion in May of 1918, he does not tell his mother they will be married until his return from Paris in the fall of 1919. See FF to MD, 10/14/19, LC 85-9.
175. To his friend Eustace Percy, Frankfurter wrote of the importance of his new position, to which Wilson had considered appointing Brandeis:

You see I have changed to a new activity. After a great deal of talking the divergent and manifold labor activities have finally been focused and I find myself at the direction of things. It is not what I though[t] should have been done—I thought L.D.B. the man—but I am not wasting much thought or energy in idle questioning. [FF to Percy, 6/3/18, LC 1830-89]

176. FF to MD, 5/17/18, LC 38-5.
177. In late July he reports to Marion a dinner at the Brandeises:

He took me back to my office and said "take good care of yourself" . . . as though he were bidding his own child farewell. You hi[t] him hard, the very first time he saw you—he has a quick and wise eye. . . . And yet when you think how bothered he would be by you-me you can get some measure of what the racial symbol means to my mother. Gosh!! . . . . My very anchorage is your "we'll work it out." [FF to MD, 7/26/18, LC 39-5]

178. FF to MD, 8/18/18, LC 40-5.
179. FF to MD, 8/2/18, LC 40-5. In the same letter, Frankfurter speaks of having "unspent personality—since childhood days." In another letter meant to reassure Marion, Frankfurter describes his feelings about women in a passage spilling over with Freudian implications:

I suppose I was a child, I suppose also that tempermentally—by the very nature of my being, by the discipline of tradition and my own convictions, above all by the grace of God—I enjoyed immunities which made relations with women (you know the exceptions) really and truly not essentially, so far as my consciousness goes not at all, different from those with men. . . . The fact is that the cleavage between men and women is more than it need be . . . while we are dealing with the dominant impulse (after hunger) and so deal with dynamite, the process of civilization is its domestication. . . . [FF to MD, 7/31/18, LC 39-5]

180. FF to MD, 10/29/19, LC 42-5.
181. FF to MD, 9/8/18, LC 41-5.
182. FF to MD, 10/26/18, LC 42-5.
183. Phillips, *Felix Frankfurter Reminisces*, pp. 141–42.
184. FF to MD, 9/20/18, LC 41-5.
185. FF to MD, 3/2/19, LC 52-6.
186. FF to MD, 5/9/19, LC 61-7.
187. FF to MD, 5/12/19, LC 62-7.
188. FF to MD, 6/25/29, LC 70-8.
189. FF to MD, 3/18/19, LC 54-6.
190. FF to WW, 5/8/19, LC 3609-189.
191. FF to MD, 8/13/19, LC 78-9.

Chapter 3

1. FF to Herbert Croly, n.d., LC 926-50.
2. FF to Julian Mack, 10/25/27, LC 1638-81.
3. FF to Herbert Croly, n.d., LC 926-50.
4. FF to MD, 5/15/19, LC 63-7. Pound's letter to Frankfurter is dated 4/28/19, LC 1869-90.
5. FF to MD, 6/21/19, LC 70-8.
6. Harlan B. Phillips, ed., *Felix Frankfurter Reminisces* (New York: Reynal, 1960), pp. 168–69.
7. A. Lawrence Lowell to Julian Mack, 3/14/22, LC 1635-81.
8. A. Lawrence Lowell to Julian Mack, 6/14/22, LC 1635-81. Frankfurter kept typed copies of most notes and letters concerning this incident.
9. Draft of letter, FF to Lowell, 6/14/22, LC 1635-81. The volleys continued. Lowell responded:

I do not pretend to know anything about your ideas on the subject of Jewish students. I only know the insistence with which Judge Mack has urged your appointment to the Committee gives the impression that he looks upon you as an advocate of his views. I have tried to select a committee that would not advocate anyone's views, but approach the question in a large and open-minded spirit. [ALL to FF, 6/20/22, LC 2620-126]

To which Frankfurter replied:

I greatly regret that my note should have carried an implication which was wholly absent from its purpose. I had not the slightest idea even of appearing to urge my appointment on your Committee. But you were quoted to me as regarding my views on the pending question as "extreme" and "violent" and I deemed it appropriate to bring this report directly to your attention.

I'm surprised to have you indicate that on such an issue I would be apt to advocate anyone's views but my own. But what gives me real concern about your letter is its clear implication that you do not wish on your Committee anyone who shares the kind of views on this question which Judge Mack entertains. That, if I may say so, does not seem to me to be dealing with the matter "in a large and open-minded spirit." [FF to ALL, 6/21/22, LC 2620-126]

10. Seymour Martin Lipset, "Political Controversies at Harvard, 1636 to 1974,"

in *Education and Politics at Harvard*, ed. Seymour Martin Lipset and David Riesman (New York: McGraw-Hill, 1975), p. 147.

11. Ibid.

12. Phillips, *Felix Frankfurter Reminisces*, pp. 175–76.

13. To Stimson, who was critical of Chafee, Frankfurter wrote:

I know all about this affair. It was one of the most outrageous and absurd incidents of the post-war hysteria. I am aware that a minority of the members of the visiting Committee found that Chafee's article on the Abrams case contained "erroneous statements of fact". But I also know well that all the members of the Visiting Committee, and even distinguished scholars, were not immune from the prevelent hysteria . . . Chafee, as I told you before, is one of the best things the school has. . . . [FF to HLS, 10/4/23, LC 2151-103]

Frankfurter elsewhere accused Stimson of harboring resentment against Chafee because of his legal work for corporations Chafee had criticized. See FF to Augustus Hand, 9/28/23, LC 1213-63, in which Frankfurter says that "Stimson, of course, is deep in coal as counsel for the operators. . . . "

14. Phillips, *Felix Frankfurter Reminisces*, p. 177.

15. FF to Alexander Meiklejohn, 6/20/23, LC 2616-126.

16. FF to *New Republic*, 7/6/23, LC 2616-126.

17. Phillips, *Felix Frankfurter Reminisces*, pp. 172–73.

18. Roger Baldwin, COHC, p. 133.

19. Phillips, *Felix Frankfurter Reminisces*, p. 174.

20. FF to HLS, 3/22/21, LC 2150-103. He makes similar comments in his reminiscences: "I told them I thought it was very undesirable for me to preside, that they ought to get a good respectable Beacon Hill Yankee to preside." Phillips, *Felix Frankfurter Reminisces*, p. 174.

21. Phillips, *Felix Frankfurter Reminisces*, p. 175.

22. FF to LDB, n.d., LC 491-29.

23. The disagreement is usually described as one between Brandeis the pragmatist and Weizmann the utopian. See Liva Baker, *Felix Frankfurter* (New York: Coward-McCann, 1969), pp. 98–99.

24. In his reminiscences, Frankfurter said:

I saw that very early. I became thick with Weizmann early and realized that through circumstances this jealousy would develop without anyone wanting it to develop. The temperaments were different. I saw early that they would clash since each naturally felt that he was a master of his respective situation. [Phillips, *Felix Frankfurter Reminisces*, pp. 179–80]

25. Baker, *Felix Frankfurter*, p. 99.

26. Beck's letter is dated 10/12/21.

27. Draft of Frankfurter letter, n.d., LC 3117-154.

28. Ibid.

29. Several letters congratulating Frankfurter for his triumph over Beck are in LC 3118-155. Herbert Croly wrote: "I decided not to publish several letters which we had received in which our correspondents had jabbed pins into Beck and asked him whether he did not feel humiliated at the exposure which you had made of him" (Croly to FF, 1/30/22, LC 3118-155).

30. HLS to FF, 3/17/21, LC 2150-103.

31. FF to HLS, 3/22/21, LC 2150-103. To Holmes, who also expressed concern about the mounting attacks on him, Frankfurter wrote:

Be entirely at ease. Nothing *is* happening to me, and nothing will (bold as that sounds). Only time is needlessly wasted. Otherwise I'm not ruffled in the least, partly, I suspect, because of my buoyant vitality, partly because men's foolishness does not too much surprise me.

I verily believe I'm an occasional target because I worship no sacred cow, and because I do regard it the business of the mind to inquire, altho neither advocating nor expecting any sudden or upsetting changes, and loving what America means passionately. . . .

It's not to be wondered at that after an upheaval such as the war and its aftermath reason is not wholly enthroned, tho it is a bit surprising that some of the most "educated" are the least self-possessed. But then—their "education" is a very small part of them. [FF to OWH, 12/1/21, OWHP 30-17]

It is important to note that Frankfurter's tone to Holmes is much gentler than his tone to Stimson, suggesting that the justice was by now a more important relationship to Frankfurter. By this point in his life, Frankfurter had cut his emotional dependence upon Stimson, and replaced it, in part, by his relationship to Holmes.

32. FF to Buckner, 4/?/23, LC 525-31.
33. FF to HLS, 3/22/21, LC 2150-103.
34. Phillips, *Felix Frankfurter Reminisces*, pp. 190–91.
35. FF to MDF, 7/9/24, LC 122-12. Walter Lippmann, now an editor of *The World*, supported Davis, and carried on a long battle with Frankfurter over the merits and demerits of the candidates. Frankfurter finally ended their discussion:

You and I are taking very different roads in this campaign, and I shan't be bothering you anymore, politically, till November, for controversial correspondence isn't one of your favorite sports, and you have the responsibility of guiding a Democratic newspaper. But a final word about Davis and his "liberalism". . . . I think I know Davis' career intimately, his actions, his abstentions, his controlling views and feeling about things social and economic—Davis is as "liberal," barring the tariff as Coolidge. [FF to Lippmann, 7/11/24, LC 1560-77]

36. FF to Croly, 4/18/24, LC 924-50.
37. The piece appeared in the *New Republic* on 10/22/24 and is reprinted in *Law and Politics: Occasional Papers of Felix Frankfurter 1913–1938*, ed. Archibald MacLeish and E. F. Prichard, Jr. (New York: Harcourt Brace, 1939), pp. 314f. Frankfurter continued:

The Republican Party is frankly standpat—things are all right. To the Democracy, also, things are all right, only those who administer them are not. . . . I welcome LaFollette as a fit symbol of the movement which he leads. I do not believe in all his specifics; I am indifferent to others. But specifics by a party out of power are really unimportant because necessarily they are somewhat academic and artificial. . . . What matters in a statesman is his direction, his general emphasis and outlook. Senator LaFollette's direction is revealed by forty years of public service. His aim has been consistently to give deeper meaning and scope to the masses of men, to make the commonwealth more secure and enduring by resting it on a broad basis of independent, trained, and contented citizens. These are his aims. He has pursued them with unflagging devotion to the resources of reason.

38. FF to MDF, 7/9/24, LC 122-12.
39. See ibid.
40. Phillips, *Felix Frankfurter Reminisces*, p. 194.
41. Baker, *Felix Frankfurter*, p. 109; Alpheus T. Mason, *Harlan Fiske Stone: Pillar of the Law* (New York: Viking Press, 1956), chaps 10 and 12. Senate supporters of Wheeler threatened to hold up Stone's appointment to the Supreme Court. See Mason, pp. 193ff.
42. Ibid., p. 829.
43. Mason reprints this correspondence in ibid., pp. 189f.
44. FF to Mack, 6/11/24, LC 1636-81.
45. FF to Lippmann, 1/3/25, LC 1561-77.
46. A copy of the memo is in LC 1559-77. Frankfurter also prepared an unsigned editorial for the *New Republic* on the subject, in which he denounced "the preposterous assumption that an investigation into the conduct of public officials who are suspected of wrong doing should be conducted under all the limitations

of a criminal trial." Quoted in Arthur E. Sutherland, *The Law at Harvard* (Cambridge, Mass: Belknap Press, 1967) pp. 301–2.

47. FF to Buckner, 6/10/24, LC 526-31.
48. FF to Buckner, 6/12/24, LC 526-31.
49. Ibid.
50. FF to MDF, 6/23/24, LC 118-12.
51. Both Emory Buckner and Learned Hand suggest to Frankfurter that he may be overreacting to Stone. Buckner's attitude can be inferred from Frankfurter's reply to him. Hand's attitude is expressed in a letter dated 4/7/26, LC 1222-63.
52. FF to HLS, 9/16/21, LC 2178-104.
53. FF to HLS, 10/20/22, LC 2178-104.
54. MDF to FF, 12/4/23, LC 108-11.
55. MDF to FF, 11/25/24, LC 133-13.
56. MDF to FF, 5/20/25, LC 137-13.
57. MDF to FF, 6/18/25, LC 138-13.
58. MDF to FF, 7/1/25, LC 140-13.
59. Joseph Lash, ed., *From the Diaries of Felix Frankfurter* (New York: Norton, 1975), p. 31.
60. Gardner Jackson, COHC, pp. 295–96. Dr. Alfred Cohn, a medical researcher and intimate friend of the Frankfurters, felt that Frankfurter had a tendency to misunderstand Marion's troubles. When the Frankfurters spent the academic year of 1933 to 1934 at Oxford, Cohn wrote a letter of introduction to a London doctor.

Mrs. Frankfurter has been psychoanalyzed—she is wholly conscientious in what she tells you, but may emphasize or heighten sensations or emotions. She is not unduly, but is nevertheless, given to phobias. Felix is sympathetic and is liable to be quixotic and not adequately critical of his wife's experiences; he may indeed go so far as to misinterpret them, thinking she is going on gallantly when in fact she is on the verge of a break. [Alfred E. Cohn to Francis F. Fraser, 11/16/33, LC 826-46]

61. MDF to FF, 12/17?/34, LC 162-14.
62. FF to MDF, n.d., LC 178-15.
63. MDF to FF, 7/17/25, LC 143-14.
64. FF to MDF, 7/12/24, LC 123-12.
65. See Lash, *From the Diaries of Felix Frankfurter*, p. 102; Phillips, *Felix Frankfurter Reminisces*, p. 183.
66. Lash, *From the Diaries of Felix Frankfurter*, p. 109.
67. FF to MDF, 6/24/24, LC 118-12.
68. FF to MDF, 8/1/24, LC 128-13.
69. See FF to LDB, 9/29/24, LC 488-29. The letter in which Frankfurter first asked Brandeis for help with these expenses is undated, LC 493-29. In this letter, Frankfurter said:

After considerable self-debate, I have concluded that it is unfair . . . to withhold from you a personal problem. To carry out the therapy prescribed by Dr. Salmon for Marion will mean additional expenditure of about 1500 per academic year for this and the following year. There is little doubt that I could fill the gap through odd jobs for some of my New York lawyer friends. But I begrudge the time and thought that would take from intrinsically more important jobs—and so I put the situation to you. Marion knows, of course, of the extent to which you make possible my efforts of a public concern and rejoices over it. But I'm not telling her of this because her sensitiveness might be needlessly burdened where our private interests are involved.

70. LDB to MD, 11/3/19, LC 405-26.
71. FF to MDF, 7/2/24, LC 120-12.
72. FF to MDF, 7/7/24, LC 121-12. Frankfurter made notes of these conversations, transcripts of which are in LC 257.

73. FF to MDF, 7/30/24, LC 127-12. See also FF to MDF, 6/21/19, LC 70-8, in which Frankfurter quotes Brandeis as saying that Holmes "is as innocent as a sixteen year old girl as to the facts of human conduct. I've had great fun in awakening Holmes to the facts." On the Brandeis-Holmes relationship, see Alpheus T. Mason, *Brandeis: A Free Man's Life* (New York: Viking Press, 1946), chap. 32.

74. FF to MDF, 3/12/23, LC 107-11.

75. FF to OWH, 3/5/21, OWHP 30-16.

76. FF to MDF, 7/13/25, LC 142-13.

77. FF to Lippmann, 11/22/28, LC 1564-77.

78. Gardner Jackson, COHC, pp. 226–27.

79. Ibid.

80. Mrs. Howe is quoted by Lash, *From the Diaries of Felix Frankfurter*, pp. 54–55.

81. Ibid. Howe produced two volumes before his death in 1967.

82. Marion is quoted by Garsin Kanin in *Felix Frankfurter: A Tribute*, ed. Wallace Mendelson (New York: Reynal, 1964), p. 56.

83. Lippmann to FF, 6/13/29, LC 1565-77.

84. FF to Hand, 10/3/24, LC 1221-63. Frankfurter is referring to LaFollette's proposal for a constitutional amendment that would empower Congress to override a Supreme Court decision by a two-thirds vote. Frankfurter opposed the proposal.

85. Laski is quoted by Lash, *From the Diaries of Felix Frankfurter*, p. 41.

86. FF to Croly, 4/17/25, LC 925-50.

87. FF to Buckner, 1/25/22, LC 524-31.

88. FF to Laski, 3/1/29, LC 1492-74.

89. FF-COHC, pp. 281, 311.

90. For example, Frankfurter carried on a long correspondence with Harlan Stone, praising his judicial outputs, while most of his private comments were, to say the least, uncomplimentary to Stone. The praise is documented in Mason, *Brandeis*.

91. FF-COHC, p. 144.

92. Garrison is quoted by Lash, *From the Diaries of Felix Frankfurter*, p. 76.

93. Quoted in Albert M. Sacks, "Felix Frankfurter," in *The Justices of the United States Supreme Court*, vol. 3, ed. Leon Friedman and Fred L. Israel (New York: Chelsea House, 1969), p. 2403.

94. Ibid.

95. See, for example, Isaiah Berlin's account of Frankfurter at Oxford in Wallace Mendelson, *Felix Frankfurter: A Tribute*.

96. Morris Cohen calls attention to these traits in a letter to Frankfurter dated 1/1/37. Laura C. Rosenfield, *Portrait of a Philosopher: Morris R. Cohen in Life and Letters* (New York: Harcourt Brace and World, 1962), pp. 281–82.

97. "He was not what is known as a good listener," according to Isaiah Berlin. Mendelson, *Felix Frankfurter: A Tribute*, p. 26.

98. Phillips, *Felix Frankfurter Reminisces*, pp. 210–11.

99. Ibid., p. 212.

100. Ibid., p. 213.

101. Frankfurter never publicly acknowledged Gates's contribution to the article. See Baker, *Felix Frankfurter* (citing interview with Gates), p. 119; see also FF to MDF, 11/18/26, LC 151-14.

102. Frankfurter himself compared his involvement with Sacco-Vanzetti to his experience in the Mooney case in a letter to Judge Mack, 10/25/27, LC 1638-81.

103. Phillips, *Felix Frankfurter Reminisces*, pp. 216–17. In a letter to Charles Wyzanski, Frankfurter claimed that his source for Lowell's words was Norman Hapgood who "repeated these words to me within half an hour after seeing Lowell" (FF to Wyzanski, 6/8/48, LC 2376-113). It is not possible to verify Lowell's words; what is significant, however, is that Frankfurter perceived this as a very personal fight, and that Frankfurter felt that Lowell shared this perception.

Notes

104. Phillips, *Felix Frankfurter Reminisces*, p. 202.
105. FF to RP, 8/22/27, LC 1871-90.
106. Phillips, *Felix Frankfurter Reminisces*, p. 203.
107. Daniel Levinson and his associates, in their psychological study of the adult life cycle, have found that their clinical subjects have selected, in their early forties, an event in their life as a key episode.

> At about age 40 . . . most of our subjects fix on some key event in their careers as carrying the ultimate message of their affirmation or devaluation by society. . . . This event is given a magical quality. If the outcome is favorable, one imagines, then all is well and the future is assured. If it is unfavorable, the man feels that not only his work but he as a person has been found wanting and without value. [Levinson et al., "The Psychological Development of Men in Early Adulthood," in *Life History Research in Psychotherapy*, vol. 3, ed. D. F. Ricks, A. Thomas, and M. Roff (Minneapolis: University of Minnesota Press, 1974), p. 253]

Sacco-Vanzetti was such an event for Frankfurter.
108. Phillips, *Felix Frankfurter Reminisces*, p. 203.
109. FF to Lippmann, 7/13/27, LC 1563-77.
110. FF to Mack, 10/15/27, LC 1638-81.
111. FF to Mack, 10/25/27, LC 1638-81.
112. FF to Lippmann, 7/13/27, LC 1563-77.
113. FF to Lippmann, 7/25/27, LC 1563-77.
114. FF to LH, 4/13/27, LHP.
115. FF to RP, 10/23/27, LC 1871-90.
116. FF to Mack, 10/25/27, LC 1638-81.
117. FF to RP, 8/23/27, LC 1871-90.
118. Sutherland, *The Law at Harvard*, p. 262.
119. See Phillips, *Felix Frankfurter Reminisces*, p. 177. Julius Rosenwald, a wealthy Jewish businessman and friend of Frankfurter, made a large contribution to Harvard after the Sacco-Vanzetti affair. He set up a $10,000 fund for publications under Frankfurter's direction. At first, Rosenwald wanted the fund to be under the sole direction of Frankfurter, but President Lowell objected. See correspondence in LC 1639-81. Frankfurter wrote to Judge Mack:

> I told [Pound] that I had nothing to do with Rosenwald's offer and that the matter was of no concern to me. I only added that I was sure that if the offer had been made for a fellowship to Professor X, rather than to me, there would have been no more difficulty. To which Pound replied, "Why, of course not." [FF to Mack, 12/19/28, LC 1640-81]

120. FF to MDF, 7/16/25, LC 143-14.
121. FF to MDF, 10/20/25, LC 147-14.
122. FF to OWH, 11/11/?, OWHP 30-9; FF to Croly, 10/7/19, LC 922-50.
123. FF to LDB, 4/22/27, LC 497-29. Again, it is Frankfurter's attitude here that is crucial, whether or not the incident actually took place.
124. See LC 1870-90 and 1871-90.
125. FF to RP, 12/9/25, LC 1870-90.
126. FF to RP, 12/8/26, LC 1871-90.
127. FF to RP, n.d., LC 1872-90.
128. Landis's doctoral thesis—"Constitutional Limitations on the Congressional Power of Investigation"—contained, according to Sutherland, views remarkably similar to those Frankfurter had expressed in a *New Republic* editorial. See Sutherland, *The Law at Harvard*, pp. 301-2.
129. Lash, *From the Diaries of Felix Frankfurter*, pp. 124-140.
130. FF to RP, 7/3/28, LC 1872-90.
131. Lash, *From the Diaries of Felix Frankfurter*, p. 130.

132. FF to HLS, 4/7/24, LC 2152-103.
133. FF to Mack, 10/25/27, LC 1638-81.
134. FF-COHC, p. 331.
135. Ibid., p. 120.

Chapter 4

1. Max Freedman, ed., *Roosevelt and Frankfurter: Their Correspondence, 1928–1945* (Boston: Little, Brown, 1967), pp. 10–11.
2. Ibid., p. 12.
3. FF to MDF, 6/26/24, LC 119-12.
4. FF to FDR, quoted in Freedman, *Roosevelt and Frankfurter*, p. 56.
5. FF to Lippmann, quoted in Freedman, *Roosevelt and Frankfurter*, p. 52.
6. FF to CCB, 6/29/32, quoted by Joseph Lash, ed., *From the Diaries of Felix Frankfurter* (New York: Norton, 1975), p. 42.
7. FF to LH, 11/9/32, LHP.
8. Freedman, *Roosevelt and Frankfurter*, p. 76.
9. One of these friends has written:

I think Frankfurter knew what we were up to, but he made no effort to stop us. Either he thought nothing would come of it or that if it did an offer to make him a high justice was important whether he accepted it or not. [Phillip Ehrmann in *Felix Frankfurter: A Tribute*, ed. Wallace Mendelson (New York: Reynal, 1964), p. 111]

10. Brandeis advised him against accepting the offer. LDB to FF, 6/26/32, LC 461-28.
11. FF to Alfred Cohn, 7/18/32, LC 822-46.
12. FDR to FF, 8/28/32, quoted in Freedman, *Roosevelt and Frankfurter*, p. 85.
13. Lash attributes Berle's dislike of Frankfurter to "a touch of resentment at having been excluded from Frankfurter's little elite group of student disciples at Harvard when he had been a student there in 1916" (*From the Diaries of Felix Frankfurter*, p. 44). Berle's hostility to Frankfurter was more than reciprocated. See, for example, Frankfurter's comments to Brandeis: "I don't mind saying that Berle—whatever his use—is about the most offensive and obstructive egoist I know" (FF to LDB, 3/29/33, LC 489-29).
14. Lash, *From the Diaries of Felix Frankfurter*, p. 44.
15. FF to LDB, 8/7/32, LC 494-29.
16. FF to MDF, 10/20/32, LC 160-13.
17. In the memorandum he prepared of their conversation, Frankfurter quoted Roosevelt as saying:

I think there is a great deal in what you say. I'm not at all sure it isn't true that you can be of more use to my Administration outside of office than you could as Solicitor General. But there is another consideration, and I am going to talk Dutch to you. I am going to talk frankly to you, as a friend. You ought to be on the Supreme Court, and I want you to be there. One can't tell when it will come—it may come in my time or not—but that's the place where you ought to be. Now you have, of course, a national reputation, a national recognition. But you know—and I said I was going to talk Dutch to you—that there are also objections to you. For a good many years now you have been a professor (smiling), you haven't actively practiced law, you've never held judicial office (again smiling), you've been the man who has refused to be a judge, then there is the Sacco and Vanzetti case (again smiling) and (this time with grave countenance) your race. I can't put you on the Supreme Court from the Harvard Law School. But once you are Solicitor General, these various objections will be forgotten or disappear.

Notes

Frankfurter quoted himself as replying:

> Of course I very deeply appreciate not only what you say but the friendship that makes you say it. You know what any American lawyer thinks about the Supreme Court and a place on it, but so far as that goes, that matter will have to take care of itself, if ever the time may come. . . . I do not think it is a wise way of life to take a job I don't want because it may lead to another, which also I'm not all that sure I'd want. All that must be left to the future. [Freedman, *Roosevelt and Frankfurter*, pp. 112–13]

18. OWH to Harold Laski, 11/7/32, quoted in Liva Baker, *Felix Frankfurter* (New York: Coward-McCann, 1969), p. 152.
19. Memorandum of talk with LDB 12/8/33 by Harry Shulman, LC 467-28. (Copy also in HLSL 188-8.) Frankfurter had several copies of this memo duplicated.
20. Lash, quoting FDR's secretary Grace Tully, *From the Diaries of Felix Frankfurter*, p. 46.
21. Albert M. Sacks, "Felix Frankfurter," in *The Justices of the United States Supreme Court*, vol. 3, ed. Leon Friedman and Fred L. Israel (New York: Chelsea House, 1969), p. 2405.
22. Freedman, *Roosevelt and Frankfurter*, p. 27.
23. See, for example, the following letters, in which Frankfurter criticizes Roosevelt's economic policies: FF to LDB, 7/6/[33], LC 495-29; FF to LDB, 8/25/33, LC 495-29; FF to LDB, 2/8/[34], LC 494-29.
24. Freedman, *Roosevelt and Frankfurter*, p. 311.
25. Ibid., p. 354.
26. Ibid., p. 357.
27. Stimson diaries, 1/4/41, vol. 32, p. 80, Yale University Library.
28. FF to MDF, 4/8/33, LC 161-14.
29. FF to LDB, 8/31/[35]?, LC 492-29.
30. FF to FDR, 5/24/41, quoted in Freedman, *Roosevelt and Frankfurter*, p. 599.
31. FF to Walter Lippmann, 3/11/33, quoted in Freedman, *Roosevelt and Frankfurter*, p. 116.
32. FF to FDR, 12/13/34, quoted in Freedman, *Roosevelt and Frankfurter*, p. 248.
33. Telegram FF to FDR, 5/23/34, quoted in Freedman, *Roosevelt and Frankfurter*, p. 220.
34. FF to FDR, 5/11/39, quoted in Freedman, *Roosevelt and Frankfurter*, p. 492.
35. FF to C. C. Burlingham, 6/9/37, quoted in *Roosevelt and Frankfurter*, p. 401.
36. Jerome Frank, COHC, p. 87.
37. FF to Frank, 1/18/36, LC 1053-55.
38. See the account of and correspondence concerning Hugh Johnson's attack on Frankfurter's role in the administration in Freedman, *Roosevelt and Frankfurter*, pp. 288ff.
39. See, for example, FF to LDB, 11/28/?, LC 496-29: ". . . you had better cross off Richberg. . . ." Donald Richberg was a labor expert, advisor to FDR, and the temporary chairman of the NIRA in 1935.
40. FF to FDR, 1/18/37, quoted in Freedman, *Roosevelt and Frankfurter*, p. 377.
41. FF to Charles Wyzanski, 12/30/38, LC 2375-113.
42. FF to OWH, 11/26/26?, OWHP 30-17.
43. Arthur M. Schlesinger, Jr., *The Politics of Upheaval* (Boston: Houghton Mifflin, 1960), p. 227.
44. Ibid., p. 229.
45. FF to MDF, n.d., LC 179-15.
46. FF to MDF, 8/18/35, LC 166-15.
47. Schlesinger, quoting Jay Franklin, *The Politics of Upheaval*, p. 235. In 1941, a feud developed between Frankfurter and Corcoran that never healed. Corcoran wanted the post of solicitor general; Frankfurter supported Charles Fahy for the job. Their mutual friends attempted to bring them together, but could not. Frankfurter wrote to FDR that "for a combination of reasons Tom lacks mental

Notes

health just now. He is, therefore, in great danger of making a wrong turning, with possibilities of vast harm to himself and of undoubted serious damage to the present national effort." (FF to FDR, 1/8/41, quoted in Freedman, *Roosevelt and Frankfurter*, p. 577).

48. James Landis COHC, p. 15. See also Baker, *Felix Frankfurter*, p. 174, and Lash, *From the Diaries of Felix Frankfurter*, p. 48.

49. Freedman, *Roosevelt and Frankfurter*, p. 331.

50. Baker, *Felix Frankfurter*, p. 155.

51. Raymond Moley, *After Seven Years* (New York: Harper and Bros., 1939), p. 180.

52. Their bill had to compete with a Senate version, which Frankfurter was able to torpedo by convincing Roosevelt to endorse the work of his protégés. Baker, *Felix Frankfurter*, p. 158.

53. "I am confident," he wrote, "that the future historian will find that my profession bears a heavy responsibility for the course of events in furthering and investing corporate and financial practices that were socially unhealthy. I recall in sorrow that 'eminent law firms of the highest character' found equally disastrous every sane effort of the last half-century to conserve our capitalist system by reforming it" (FF to Arthur Perry, 9/13/33, LC 2785-135).

54. FF to Ellery Sedgwick, 12/19/33, LC 2472-118.

55. FF to Howe, 9/13/33, LC 2785-135.

56. FF to Seligman, 5/10/33, LC 2782-135. Seligman responded: "I am a sadder but wiser man. I had hoped notwithstanding what I had heard from mutual acquaintances to the contrary, that it might be possible to conduct an objective discussion with you on a matter where we did not entirely agree. I realize that this is not the case and that you prefer personalities and invective to reasoned arguments" (Seligman to FF, 5/15/33, LC 2782-135).

57. HLS to FF, 1/26/34, LC 2159-103.

58. Schlesinger, *The Politics of Upheaval*, p. 234.

59. See, for example, the remarkable letter written by Corcoran, signed "Tom and Ben," in which Frankfurter's two protégés discuss the anti-Semitic attacks in the press against Frankfurter and describe the general chaos within the administration. The letter is dated 4/22/34, LC 2432-116.

60. They had met briefly at the Paris Peace Conference in 1919.

61. Robert L. Heilbroner, "The New Deal," in *The New Deal: Doctrines and Democracy*, ed. Bernard Sternsher (Boston: Allyn and Bacon, 1966), pp. 101-3.

62. FF to Keynes, 12/9/33, LC 2449-117. Keynes wrote an open letter to FDR for the *New York Times*. Frankfurter sent Roosevelt an advance copy of the letter.

63. FF to Corcoran, 5/7/34, LC 2432-116.

64. Schlesinger, *The Politics of Upheaval*, p. 405.

65. This is the interpretation of James MacGregor Burns. "A Keynesian solution," Burns writes, "involved an almost absolute commitment, and Roosevelt was not one to commit himself absolutely to any political or economic method" (*Roosevelt: The Lion and the Fox* [New York: Harcourt Brace & World, 1956], p. 335).

66. The letter is dated 6/18/34 and is quoted by Lash, *From the Diaries of Felix Frankfurter*, p. 54, and by Freedman, *Roosevelt and Frankfurter*, pp. 223-25.

67. FF to LDB, 5/1/[34], LC 494-29.

68. William E. Leuchtenburg provides the best analysis of the first New Deal and the 1935 transition. See *Franklin D. Roosevelt and the New Deal: 1932-40* (New York: Harper and Row, 1963), pp. 143ff.

69. FF to LDB, 5/6/[35], LC 492-29.

70. Baker, *Felix Frankfurter*, p. 193. There was a great deal of administration infighting over the choice of a proper test case. Donald Richberg and Hugh Johnson, chief administrators of the NRA, wanted the *Belcher* case, dealing with the lumber industry code. Frankfurter and Stanley Reed (at this time serving as solicitor general) thought it a bad test case, and managed to have it dropped. The lumber code was one of the earliest NRA codes and contained production

230

quotas, "a device which the NRA itself was unwilling to defend in 1935." Schlesinger, *The Politics of Upheaval*, p. 276.

71. Typed copy of telegram, Corcoran to FDR, LC 906-49.

72. This paragraph draws upon Schlesinger, *The Politics of Upheaval*, p. 278. Arthur Krock of the *New York Times* mistakenly published a column in which he blamed Frankfurter for choosing the *Schecter* case.

73. LC 472-28. On the bottom of the memo Frankfurter wrote: "Given me by B.V.C. in Washington Tuesday, May 28, 1935."

74. Leuchtenburg, *Franklin D. Roosevelt and the New Deal*, p. 149.

75. FF to LDB, 7/21/[35], LC 492-29.

76. Because Frankfurter wrote Marion almost daily, his activities in Washington are extremely well documented.

77. FF to MDF, 8/16/35, LC 165-15.

78. Ibid.

79. FF to MDF, 8/19/[35], LC 166-15.

80. FF to MDF, 8/27/35, LC 166-15.

81. FF to MDF, 8/29/35, LC 167-15.

82. FF to MDF, 9/1/[35], LC 167-15.

83. Leuchtenburg, *Franklin D. Roosevelt and the New Deal*, p. 163. The "true" ideological meaning of the second New Deal—and whether there was in fact a sharp break in 1935—has been a continuing source of debate among historians. The general consensus seems to be that in 1935 there *was* a move to the right, toward the free-market ideology and emphasis on decentralization of the Brandeisian program. See Leuchtenburg, pp. 163f; Schlesinger, *The Politics of Upheaval*, p. 398.

84. The administration blamed "monopolists" for the recession. See Eugene O. Golub, *The "Isms": A History and Evaluation* (New York: Harper and Bros., 1954), pp. 125-45; Ellis W. Hawley, *The New Deal and the Problem of Monopoly: A Study in Economic Ambivalence* (Princeton: Princeton University Press, 1966), pp. 383ff.

85. FF to Frank, 6/10/35, LC 1053-55.

86. FF to Frank, 1/18/36, LC 1053-55.

87. FF to MDF, 4/22/36, LC 169-15.

88. FF to LDB, 12/18/[33], LC 496-29.

89. FF to MDF, 8/29/35, LC 167-15.

90. FF to MDF, 8/31/35, LC 167-15.

91. Ibid.

92. FF to MDF, 8/21/35, LC 166-15.

93. FF to MDF, 8/24/35, LC 166-15.

94. FF to Corcoran, 5/7/34, LC 2432-116.

95. Schlesinger, *The Politics of Upheaval*, p. 285.

96. FF to LDB, 6/3/35, LC 490-29. In 1952, Frankfurter wrote to Sam Rosenman (FDR's chief speechwriter) about the incident: "I never had any doubt that it was one of those occasions where he purposely did not talk with me because he respected that my views wouldn't accord with his. What awful ignorant advice he had on that subject from those who were in on the secret" (FF to Rosenman, 5/27/52, LC 2028-99).

97. The consensus among historians is that the plan was largely the idea of Attorney General Homer Cummings, with advice from Donald Richberg, Sam Rosenman, and Stanley Reed. See Schlesinger, *The Politics of Upheaval*, p. 256; Freedman, *Roosevelt and Frankfurter*, p. 371; Lash, *From the Diaries of Felix Frankfurter*, pp. 60-61.

98. FDR to FF, 1/15/37, quoted in Freedman, *Roosevelt and Frankfurter*, p. 377.

99. FF to FDR, 1/18/37, quoted in Freedman, *Roosevelt and Frankfurter*, p. 378.

100. Lash writes:

Roosevelt's failure to consult Frankfurter in the field of his special competence demonstrated what all those around the President understood—he used men and women for *his* purposes, not theirs, but for someone like Frankfurter who needed the feeling that Roosevelt's countenance was not turned away from him, the exclusion must have been dismaying, and like courtiers usually, and there were elements of the courtier in Frankfurter's relationship to Roosevelt, the desire to be on the inside caused him to redouble his efforts to gain his principal's favor. [*From the Diaries of Felix Frankfurter*, pp. 60–61]

Frankfurter was, in many ways—but especially in his relationship with FDR—a perfect example of the "court Jew," a phenomenon best described by Judith N. Shklar:

The court Jew, as a social type, identifies himself with whatever upper class he may encounter, and does so in the hope of overcoming his despised, actual self. As a cure for self-hatred this is pure poison. All that flattering . . . and self-deceiving can only irritate an already inflamed wound. . . . It is also poor policy, for there is no safety up there. For every tolerant *grand seigneur* there are a dozen uppercrust bigots.

Why then do so many talented and able Jews acquire these useless and self-defeating habits? Why will they risk their personal honor to imagine that they are Athenian heroes, or English gentlemen, or Boston Brahmins, or anything except what they are, middle-class Jews? . . . Because they hate themselves, many Jews hate their social origins. In every generation since their emancipation, there have been many who simply could not face the prospect of becoming dry-goods merchants or usurers. The liberal professions offered a morally acceptable way out. But for some even this option is inadequate, for they crave an aristocratic ethos of honor as a substitute for a despised bourgeois rectitude. Rampant in all European societies and even in America, these aspirations were simply absorbed in the general process of assimilation. Zionism once owed much to them, in all fairness, and to give the aristocratic political imagination its due. But the role of the court Jew is psychologically fatal, nevertheless, since it ensures both personal insecurity and public disgrace. For the court Jew does not say "no" to anti-Semitism, he says "no" to himself as a Jew. [Judith N. Shklar, book review, *New Republic*, 4/5/80, pp. 34–35]

101. Freedman, *Roosevelt and Frankfurter*, p. 372. Freedman is, presumably, repeating the version of the events given to him by Frankfurter.
102. Lash, *From the Diaries of Felix Frankfurter*, p. 61.
103. MDF to FF, 2/25/37, LC 170-15.
104. Ibid.
105. FF to MDF, 2/?/37, LC 170-15.
106. FF to Burlingham, 3/6/37, LC 579-34.
107. FF to Burlingham, 3/9/37, LC 579-34.
108. FF to Clark, 3/6/37, LC 2925-142.
109. Freedman, *Roosevelt and Frankfurter*, p. 400; Lash, *From the Diaries of Felix Frankfurter*, p. 61.
110. FF to Clark, 4/14/37, LC 783-44.
111. Only Brandeis signed the letter. Hughes claimed that he did not have enough time to obtain the signatures of the other associate justices.
112. LC 477-28.
113. At the top of the letter, Frankfurter wrote: "Draft of letter to L.D.B. re/letter of Chief Justice Hughes, in which L.D.B. concurred, dated March 26, 1937. I did not send this."
114. For example, Frankfurter wrote to Judge Mack that "I greatly deplore that L.D.B. should have lent himself to the Chief's statement" (FF to Mack, 3/24/37, LC 1649-81).
115. Cohen to FF, 10/11/37, LC 479-28.
116. Matthew Josephson, "Profile: Jurist," *New Yorker*, 12/14/40, p. 26.
117. Lash, *From the Diaries of Felix Frankfurter*, pp. 63–64.
118. Ibid.
119. Harold L. Ickes, *Secret Diary*, vol. 2 (New York: Simon and Schuster,

Notes

1953), pp. 539–40. Quoted in Lash, *From the Diaries of Felix Frankfurter*, p. 64, and in Helen Shirley Thomas, *Felix Frankfurter: Scholar on the Bench* (Baltimore: Johns Hopkins Press, 1960), p. 35.

120. Lash, *From the Diaries of Felix Frankfurter*, p. 64.

121. Ibid., citing Alpheus T. Mason, *Harlan Fiske Stone: Pillar of the Law* (New York: Viking Press, 1956), p. 482.

122. HLS to FF, 8/30/38, LC 2163-104.

123. Lash, *From the Diaries of Felix Frankfurter*, p. 64.

124. Ickes, *Secret Diary*, vol. 2, p. 533, quoted in ibid., p. 66.

125. Cohn to FF, 1/31/39, LC 839-47.

Chapter 5

1. FF to Charles Wyzanski, 2/19/44, LC 2376-113.

2. See, for example, FF to LH, 10/21/40, LC 1233-64.

3. Sanford V. Levinson, "Skepticism, Democracy, and Judicial Restraint: An Essay on the Thought of Oliver Wendell Holmes and Felix Frankfurter" (Ph.D. dissertation, Harvard University, 1969), pp. 218f.

4. FF to Jack E. Brown, 2/3/56, HLSL 170-7.

5. Alpheus T. Mason, *Brandeis: A Free Man's Life* (New York: Viking Press, 1946), p. 573. See also Samuel J. Konefsky, *The Legacy of Holmes and Brandeis: A Study in the Influence of Ideas* (New York: Macmillan, 1956), passim.

6. See Levinson, "Skepticism, Democracy, and Judicial Restraint," part 1.

7. Mason, *Brandeis*, p. 576.

8. See Sanford V. Levinson, "The Democratic Faith of Felix Frankfurter," *Stanford Law Review* 25 (February 1973): 431.

9. Ibid.

10. Levinson, "Democratic Faith," p. 432.

11. Grant Gilmore, *The Ages of American Law* (New Haven: Yale University Press, 1977), pp. 48–49.

12. Gary J. Jacobsohn, "Felix Frankfurter and the Ambiguities of Judicial Statesmanship," *New York University Law Review* 49 (April 1974): 9.

13. See Mason, *Brandeis*, pp. 573ff. Mason writes that "certain prejudices and certain special preferences formed a picture of an ideal society and predetermined his stand" (p. 578).

14. FF to LH, 4/?/21, LHP.

15. FF to LH, 1923, LHP.

16. See chapter 4 herein.

17. See Mason, *Brandeis*, p. 578, and Konefsky, *The Legacy of Holmes and Brandeis*, p. 265.

18. Whitney v. California, 274 U.S. 357 (1927).

19. Brandeis wrote:

Those who won our independence believed that the final end of the State was to make men free to develop their faculties. . . . They believed that freedom to think as you will and to speak as you think are means indispensable to the discovery and spread of political truth. . . . They recognized the risks to which all human institutions are subject. But they knew that order cannot be secured merely through fear of punishment . . . that it is hazardous to discourage thought, hope and imagination; that fear breeds hate; that hate menaces stable government . . . and that the fitting remedy for evil counsels is good ones. . . .

Fear of serious injury cannot alone justify suppression of free speech and assembly. Men feared witches and burnt women. It is the function of speech to free men from the bondage of irrational fears. To justify suppression of free speech there must be reasonable ground to fear that serious evil will result if free speech is practiced. There must be reasonable ground to believe that the evil to be prevented is a serious one. . . . The wide difference between advocacy and incitement, between preparation and attempt, between assembling and conspiracy, must be borne in mind. In order to support a finding of clear and present danger it must be shown either that violence was to be expected or was advocated, or that the past conduct furnished reasons to believe that such advocacy was then contemplated.

Those who won our independence by revolution were not cowards. They did not fear political change. They did not exalt order at the cost of liberty. . . . If there be time to expose through discussion the falsehood and fallacies, to avert the evil by the processes of education, the remedy to be applied is more speech, not enforced silence. Only an emergency can justify repression. . . . [274 U.S. at 375-77]

20. Schenck v. United States, 249 U.S. 47 (1919). Schenck and others were charged with conspiracy to obstruct the draft and other violations of the Espionage Act of 1917. Their specific offense was printing and distributing leaflets opposed to the war and to the draft.
21. Abrams v. United States, 250 U.S. 616 (1919). The case involved the Sedition Law of 1918; Abrams had distributed pamphlets opposing the allied intervention in Russia after the Bolshevik Revolution.
22. 250 U.S. at 624. The relationship between Holmes's opinion in *Schenck*, where he first presents the clear-and-present-danger doctrine, and this dissent in *Abrams* has been examined in detail by Gerald Gunther, the biographer of Learned Hand. Gunther writes:

The correspondence between Hand and Holmes confirms what revisionist commentators have recently suggested: that Holmes was at that time [*Schenck*] quite insensitive to any claim for special judicial protection of free speech; that the Schenck standard was not truly speech-protective; and that it was not until the fall of 1919, with his famous dissent in Abrams . . . that Holmes put some teeth into the clear and present danger formula, at least partly as a result of probing criticism by acquaintances such as Learned Hand. ["Learned Hand and the Origins of Modern First Amendment Doctrine: Some Fragments of History," *Stanford Law Review* 27 (1975): 720]

23. 262 U.S. 390 (1923).
24. Holmes wrote:

It is with hesitation and unwillingness that I differ from my brethren with regard to a law like this but I cannot bring my mind to believe that in some circumstances, and circumstances existing it is said in Nebraska, the statute might not be regarded as a reasonable or even necessary method of reaching the desired result. The part of the act with which we are concerned deals with the teaching of young children. Youth is the time when familiarity with a language is established and if there are sections in the State where a child would hear only Polish or French or German spoken at home I am not prepared to say that it is unreasonable to provide that in his early years he shall hear and speak only English at school. But if it is reasonable it is not an undue restriction of the liberty either of teacher or scholar. No one would doubt that a teacher might be forbidden to teach many things, and the only criterion of his liberty under the Constitution that I can think of is "whether, considering the end in view, the statute passes the bounds of reason and assumes the character of merely arbitrary fact." . . . I think I appreciate the objection to the law but it appears to me to present a question upon which men reasonably might differ and therefore I am unable to say that the Constitution of the United States prevents the experiment being tried. [262 U.S. at 412]

25. Frankfurter wrote:

Before one can find in [these] case[s] proof of the social value of the Supreme Court's scope of judicial review a balance must be struck of all cases that have been decided under the Fourteenth Amendment. In rejoicing over [these] . . . cases, we must not forget that a heavy price has to be paid for these occasional services to liberalism. The New York bakeshop case, the invalidation of anti-trade union laws, the sanctification of the injunction in labor cases, the veto of minimum wage legislation, are not wiped out by [this] decision. They weigh heavily in any full accounting of the gains and losses to our national life due to the Supreme Court's control of legislation by the states that does not involve an arbitrament between state and national powers, such as arises when purely state legislation encroaches upon the commerce powers of the federal government. . . .

For ourselves, we regard the cost of this power of the Supreme Court on the whole as greater than its gains. After all, the hysteria and chauvinism that forbade the teaching of German in Nebraska schools may subside, and with its subsidence bring repeal of the silly measure. . . .

This editorial is reprinted in Felix Frankfurter, *Law and Politics,* ed. Archibald MacLeish and E. F. Prichard, Jr. (New York: Harcourt, Brace, 1939), p. 196ff.

26. Ibid.

27. Frankfurter, *Mr. Justice Holmes and the Supreme Court* (Cambridge: Harvard University Press, 1938), pp. 49–51. In his personal correspondence Frankfurter often emphasized Holmes's sensitivity to civil liberties, as when he wrote Grenville Clark in 1938 that "it is a fact that, as a result of the espionage cases and the post war period frenzies, he came to have a more acute realization of the threats to civil liberties" (FF to Clark, 11/16/38, LC 784-44).

28. Typed transcripts of Frankfurter's notes of his conversations with Brandeis are in LC Box 257.

29. Emphasis added.

30. 304 U.S. 144 (1938).

31. 304 U.S. at 152–53. See Alpheus T. Mason, *Harlan Fiske Stone: Pillar of the Law* (New York: Viking Press, 1956), chap. 31.

32. FF to Burlingham, 4/29/37, LC 580-34.

33. MacLeish forward to Frankfurter, *Law and Politics,* ed. Archibald MacLeish and E. F. Prichard, Jr. (New York: Harcourt Brace, 1939).

34. Typescripts of FF-LDB conversations, LC 257.

35. For example, Frankfurter reports the following exchange about Holmes:

L.D.B.: "Truth of matter is that he takes joy in the trick of working out what he calls 'a form of words' in which to express desired result. He occasionally says, 'I think I can find a form of words' to which I reply 'of course you can—you can find a form of words for anything.' "

FF.: "He goes along carefully, moderately, step by step and every once in a while he indulges himself at large; he goes on a spree."

36. Upon his appointment as chairman Douglas wrote Frankfurter:

Your three generous letters gave me more pleasure than the chairmanship did or could. Approbation and understanding from those whose friendship, standards and ideals I cherish and respect as highly as I do yours surpass all else, because of the abiding and deep inner satisfaction which they bring.

For all of your teachings, including those of humility, I am eternally grateful. [WOD to FF, 9/30/37, LC 965-52]

37. FF to Wyzanski, 3/22/39, LC 2375-113.

38. FF to CCB, 9/9/37, LC 581-34.

39. See Gerald T. Dunne, *Hugo Black and Judicial Revolution* (New York: Simon and Schuster, 1977), passim.

40. FF to CCB, ca. 9/7/37, LC 581-34.

41. See Mason, *Stone,* p. 469.

42. HFS to FF, 2/8/38, quoted in Mason, *Stone*, p. 469. For a description of the tension between Stone and Black, see Dunne, *Hugo Black*, p. 189.

43. FF to LDB, 5/20/38, LC 481-29. Brandeis was still on the Court at the time of this letter.

44. FF to Mack, 3/9/39, LC 1650-81.

45. FF to LH, 2/16/39, LC 1232-64.

46. Frankfurter's correspondence before his Court appointment is full of comments critical of Hughes, whom he often referred to as "Charles the Baptist." He was highly critical of Hughes's leaving the Court in 1916 to pursue the presidency, and, when Hughes was reappointed to the Court in 1930, Frankfurter wrote C. C. Burlingham:

> As for Hughes on the merits, I wish he had not been confirmed. It would have been an impressive precedent in the country's history against a man going off the Bench for politics and then going on again. I have yet to hear anybody defend his conduct in going off the Court in 1916. Since he has been off he has behaved precisely along those lines of political motives which led him to get off, and so he should have been kept off. I don't suppose so self-righteous a man as Hughes can for a moment understand why all this hullabaloo. [FF to CCB, 2/19/30, LC 567-33]

"I'm grateful for every show of courage and statesmanship by Charles the Baptist," Frankfurter wrote Charles Wyzanski in 1932. "But at this term he has a few deeds to his account that he will not easily explain away at Judgment Day" (FF to Wyzanski, 5/25/32, LC 2372-113). In later years, Frankfurter readily admitted having changed his opinion about Hughes after his own appointment to the Court. In 1959 he wrote:

> I should be greatly surprised if I made any derogatory remark about Hughes after I came on the Court and had opportunities to watch him from the inside. I was, on occasion, critical of him as I viewed him from Cambridge and I am not ashamed to have changed my opinion on the kind of intimate knowledge that we cannot possibly have from the outside. . . . [FF to CCB, 4/2/59, LC 646-38]

47. Hughes is often described as an ideal chief justice; the political science literature portrays him as having exerted both "social" and "task" leadership as chief justice. David Danelski, "The Influence of the Chief Justice in the Decisional Process," in *Courts, Judges, and Politics*, ed. Walter F. Murphy and C. Herman Pritchett (New York: Random House, 1961). See also Walter F. Murphy, *Elements of Judicial Strategy* (Chicago: University of Chicago Press, 1964), pp. 82–90, especially p. 87; and Mason, *Stone*, pp. 788–790.

48. CEH to FF, 1/17/39, LC 1339-68.

49. On the slip opinion for Lane v. Wilson, 307 U.S. 268 (1939), Hughes wrote: "I have doubts—on the point I stated in Conference—but I am not disposed to express them. I shall acquiesce." All of the slip opinions quoted here are bound in Frankfurter's scrapbooks in the Harvard Law School Library.

50. FF to CEH, 4/6/39, LC 1339-68. They are discussing Frankfurter's opinion in Rochester Telephone v. United States, 307 U.S. 125 (1939).

51. Ibid.

52. FF to CEH, 12/5/39, LC 1339-68.

53. For example, Frankfurter wrote Hughes concerning the latter's opinion in Pittman v. H.O.L.C., 308 U.S. 21 (1939), subtly threatening to write a concurrence.

> Forgive me for troubling you with two reservations in your disposition of No. 10. There is such thorough agreement amongst us all regarding the merits of this particular case and the immediately applicable doctrines that I hope we can avoid expression on the theoretical differences that are not likely to have practical importance except in breeding litigation. [FF to CEH, 10/31/39, LC 1339-68]

Hughes responded:

> I am surprised that exception should be taken to the statements in the paragraphs you mention in your letter. . . . While I think the opinion will not be as complete and well-rounded without them, I am willing in the interest of harmony to make the omission you suggest. [CEH to FF, 11/1/39, LC 1339-68]

54. For example, Frankfurter wrote Reed about Neirbo v. Bethlehem Shipbuilding, 308 U.S. 165 (1939):

> If I understand your difficulty in No. 38, it relates to opposition against coercive action by a state to achieve the surrender of a federal right. I have thought conscientiously, I believe and certainly extensively, about this difficulty and perhaps you will let me tell you briefly why I think that the problem that confronts us . . . does not involve the difficulty you pose.

There followed an analysis of the principles of the case, with the concluding remark that "authority and reason—practical good sense and fairness in the administration of justice—alike discredit" a conclusion contrary to Frankfurter's. (FF to SR, 10/23/39, LC 1921-92).

55. FF to SR, 11/28/29, HLSL 1939. The case is Ford Motor v. Beauchamp, 308 U.S. 331 (1939).

56. See SR to FF, 11/29/39, LC 1921-92; SR to FF, 11/30/39, HLSL 1939; and FF to SR, 11/30/39, HLSL 1939.

57. FF to SR, 11/30/39, HLSL 1939.

58. For example, on Frankfurter's slip opinion in Keifer and Keifer v. RFC, 306 U.S. 381 (1939), Stone wrote: "You see this is a damned good opinion even if you have fallen into the bad (for judicial opinion) academic habit of putting your important citations into footnotes." In an early case in which Frankfurter wrote a concurrence, Driscoll v. Edison, 307 U.S. 104 (1939), Stone attempted to dissuade him from filing his opinion. See HFS to FF, 4/13/39, HLSL 1938. Frankfurter responded that despite "the garnered wisdom of your experience here," he felt strongly about his point. FF to HFS, 4/14/39, HLSL 1938.

59. FF to HFS, 11/9/39, HLSL 1939. The case is Neirbo v. Bethlehem.

60. FF to HFS, 12/12/39, LC 2196-105. The case is American Federation of Labor v. National Labor Relations Board, 308 U.S. 401 (1940), involving the Wagner Act.

61. FF to HFS, 3/12/40, LC 2197-105.

62. Rochester Telephone v. United States, 307 U.S. 125 (1939). HLSL 1938.

63. Palmer v. Massachusetts, 308 U.S. 79 (1939); Neirbo v. Bethlehem Shipbuilding, 308 U.S. 165 (1939). HLSL 1939.

64. Palmer v. Massachusetts. HLSL 1939.

65. FF to HLB, 10/31/39, HLSL 169-2. There is no indication of the context in which this letter was sent, or of any response from Black.

66. FF to HLB, 12/15/39, HLSL 1939.

67. The case—Board of County Commissioners v. United States, 308 U.S. 343 (1939)—involved the issue of whether an Indian tribe could collect interest on tax money wrongfully collected by the state. Frankfurter and Black agreed that they could not. Frankfurter rested his conclusion upon an interpretation of "appropriate considerations of public convenience"; Black, upon the silence of Congress on the issue.

68. Deputy v. DuPont, 308 U.S. 488 (1940).

69. 308 U.S. at 499.

70. HLSL 1939. It is, of course, possible that Frankfurter added these notes after the case was handed down.

71. FF to HFS, 11/30/39, HLSL 1939. The case is Ford Motor v. Beauchamp, 308 U.S. 331 (1939).

72. Minersville School District v. Gobitis, 310 U.S. 586 (1940).

73. "You probably have heard me quote Holmes's epigram, 'we live by symbols.' Marion says I quote it so often that she wishes Holmes had never said it, but I

said I quote it so often because it is so often applicable" (FF to Alexander Bickel, 10/20/64, LC 359-24).

74. I am grateful to Professor Richard Danzig for calling this point to my attention. An intriguing letter from Alfred Cohn, one of Frankfurter's closest friends, underscores the extent to which the issues raised by the flag salute were highly emotional for Frankfurter, reflecting his own past.

> I want to hear more of the flag salute opinion. . . . To us, who know you and have heard of the pride with which you learned and performed the ceremony, just what you thought was in fact anticipated. But how you managed the argument was very exciting. [Cohn to FF, 6/9/40, LC 844-47]

75. 310 U.S. at 591, 593-94.
76. 310 U.S. at 596-97.
77. 310 U.S. at 599-600.
78. Notes taken by Justice Murphy at conference indicate that Frankfurter's opinion in *Gobitis* followed closely the outline of the case presented by Chief Justice Hughes. Personal communication of author with J. Woodford Howard, Jr.
79. Howard reports that Murphy's first reaction had been to prepare a dissent, but that several factors, including his newness to the bench, induced him to concur. See Howard, *Mr. Justice Murphy* (Princeton: Princeton University Press, 1968), pp. 250ff.
80. 310 U.S. at 610.
81. Mason, *Stone*, p. 526.
82. FF to HFS, 5/27/40, LC 2197-105. Mason reprints this letter in an appendix to *Security Through Freedom* (Ithaca: Cornell University Press, 1955).
83. HFS to FF, n.d., HLSL 1939. Quoted in Mason, *Stone*, p. 527.
84. Joseph Lash, ed., *From the Diaries of Felix Frankfurter*, (New York: Norton, 1975) p. 73.
85. Mason, *Stone*, p. 532.
86. Ibid.
87. For example, in the following cases: Federal Communications Commission v. CBS, 311 U.S. 132 (1940); Wisconsin v. J. C. Penney, 311 U.S. 435 (1940); Sibbach v. Wilson, 312 U.S. 1 (1941).
88. Railroad Commission of Texas v. Rowan and Nichols Oil Co., 311 U.S. 570 (1941).
89. Sibbach v. Wilson.
90. For a description of Murphy's slow pull away from Frankfurter, see Howard, *Mr. Justice Murphy*, chaps. 11 and 12. Howard attributes Murphy's shift, at least in part, to Frankfurter's tactics:

> Justice Murphy . . . came to regard Justice Frankfurter's professorial habits as tiresome and tangential. The former law professor's campaigns for "self-restraint" and "law as the embodiment of reason," he found hard not to dismiss as masks for the same use of personal convictions that Frankfurter so readily condemned in others. . . . Frankfurter appeared to be offended by Murphy's rejection of his leadership . . . but his sharpness in intellectual exchange, and his occasional resorts to flattery and sarcasm as if the recipient were unable to perceive either, pricked Murphy's abundant pride. Long after his early fascination with "F. F." was over, Murphy might readily dismiss Frankfurter's scholarly output as "elegant bunk." But not many battles were required before their differences became tinged with bitterness. [P. 269]

Dunne suggests that "a complicating interaction of personality" contributed to the Frankfurter-Black split. Dunne, *Hugo Black*, p. 251 and passim.
91. Milk Wagon Drivers Union of Chicago v. Meadowmoor Dairies, 312 U.S. 287 (1941).
92. 310 U.S. 88 (1940).
93. See Howard, *Mr. Justice Murphy*, p. 248.

94. Dunne, *Hugo Black,* p. 206.
95. 312 U.S. at 301-2. Stone, the originator of the preference doctrine, voted with Frankfurter. Pritchett comments that

> Stone presents an interesting case. His lone dissent in the first flag salute decision might have seemed to mark him as the most ardent of the Court's members in his concern for the protection of individual liberties of conscience and action, but his record reveals only 44 per cent support for these claims. He did maintain rather consistently his support for Jehovah's Witnesses. . . . But in the other categories his vote was usually in favor of the challenged federal or state restriction. [C. Herman Pritchett, *The Roosevelt Court* (New York: Macmillan, 1948), pp. 130–31]

One of the most fascinating aspects of the change in the Court during these years is the degree to which Stone came to occupy the ideological center when his own doctrines were extended by the justices who came to occupy the Court's left wing. For this development, and documentation of Stone's exasperation with the unorthodox behavior of the liberals, see Mason, *Stone,* chaps. 35 through 42.
96. See Howard, *Mr. Justice Murphy,* pp. 254f.
97. FF to FM, 2/7/41, LC 1762-85. During their correspondence on this case, Frankfurter could not help instructing Murphy. "As bearing on the appropriate way of reading an injunction," he wrote, "please take a look at Brandeis's opinion in Swift and Company v. U.S. . . . " (FF to FM, 2/11/41, LC 1762-85).
98. Phelps Dodge Corporation v. National Labor Relations Board, 313 U.S. 177 (1941).
99. See Howard, *Mr. Justice Murphy,* pp. 263, 268. The case involved the Wagner Act. The Court held that under the Act a corporation can be required to "instate" applicants for employment never previously employed by a company, who were denied jobs because of their union activities and affiliations, and also can be required to give them back pay from the time they applied for work until they were offered jobs. Pritchett, *The Roosevelt Court,* pp. 200–201.
100. FF memorandum to conference, 4/3/41, HLSL 1940.
101. Howard, *Mr. Justice Murphy,* p. 268.
102. FF to Laski, 5/11/41, LC 1503-75.
103. See Mason, *Stone,* pp. 566–67.
104. Walter F. Murphy writes that "since he had felt frustrated by Hughes's methods, the new Chief Justice refused to cut off discussion—indeed, he joined in angry wrangling with his associates, something which Hughes considered beneath his station. Long, acrimonious harrangues, which often stretched from Saturday until Wednesday, marked the Stone conferences" (Murphy, *Elements of Judicial Strategy,* p. 88).
105. Edwards v. California, 314 U.S. 160 (1941).
106. See Mason, *Stone,* pp. 578–80.
107. FF to JFB, 10/28/41, HLSL 169-9. Frankfurter followed this up with another letter, analyzing the history of the clause. FF to JFB, 11/1/41, LC 711-41.
108. FF to RHJ, 10/28/41, HLSL 170-1; copy in LC 1367-69.
109. The letter reads as follows:

> Dear Frank: *In re* "privileges or immunities" I hope that you can find time to read:
>   Slaughter House Cases . . .
>   Colgate v. Harvey . . .
>   Madden v. Kentucky . . .
>   Hague v. C.I.O. . . . .
> And remember that free speech cases for *Gitlow* . . . To your *Thornhill* case, did *not* go on privileges and immunities. [FF to FM, 11/1/41, LS 1762-85]

110. Jackson was not convinced either, and also filed a concurrence endorsing the "privileges and immunities" basis of the decision.
111. Bridges v. California, 314 U.S. 252 (1941).

112. Robert G. McCloskey, *The Modern Supreme Court* (Cambridge: Harvard University Press, 1972), p. 13.
113. Howard, *Mr. Justice Murphy*, pp. 262–63.
114. Murphy wrote Frankfurter: "The still-new robe never hangs heavier than when my conscience confronts me. Months of reflection and study convince me to give it voice. And so I have advised the Chief Justice and Justice Black that my vote . . . must be in reversal" (FM to FF, 5/29/41, HLSL 1941; quoted in Howard, *Mr. Justice Murphy*, p. 263).
115. HLSL 1941. It has not been possible to verify this story.
116. McCloskey, *The Modern Supreme Court*, pp. 14–15.
117. 314 U.S. at 279.
118. SR to FF, n.d., HLSL 1941.
119. FF to SR, 12/2/41, HLSL 1941. In another note to Reed, Frankfurter made sarcastic reference to the *Bridges* case, in which Reed had voted with his opponents: "Dear Brother Reed: Perhaps now you will reconsider whether the right to commit contempt of Court is really one of Mr. Bridges' privileges and immunities" (FF to SR, 11/4/41, LC 1921–92).
120. JFB to FF, n.d., HLSL 1941.
121. FF to WOD, 11/5/41, HLSL 1941.
122. FF to SR, 11/10/41, LC 1921–92.
123. FF to SR, 12/2/41, LC 1921–92.
124. FF to HFS, 11/5/41, LC 2198-105.
125. FF to RHJ, 10/22/41, LC 1367-69. The case is Indianapolis v. Chase Bank, 314 U.S. 63 (1941), involving diversity jurisdiction.
126. FF to RHJ, 2/5/42, LC 257.
127. FF to RHJ, 2/24/42, LC 1368-69.
128. FF to SR, 2/25/42, LC 1922-92. The case is Pearce v. Commissioner, 315 U.S. 543 (1942).
129. FF to SR, 3/12/42, LC 1922-92.
130. FF to SR, 2/9/42, LC 1922-92.
131. 316 U.S. 584 (1942).
132. "The break with Frankfurter," Howard comments, "was now complete." Howard, *Mr. Justice Murphy*, p. 289.
133. 316 U.S. at 623-24. The trio first circulated this paragraph in late May. Pasting it into his scrapbook, Frankfurter wrote on the side:

This was circulated on Saturday, May 30, 1942. It was the first intimation that I had (and I consulted Reed and Roberts and they heard nothing before this circulation, and I assume the same is true of the others except these three) that the *Gobitis* case would be raised. That case was *not* challenged in the argument and its relevance to this case . . . never discussed or alluded to in Conference!

134. 316 U.S. 455 (1942).
135. Pritchett, *The Roosevelt Court*, pp. 39–40.
136. FF to FDR, 12/3/42, Max Freedman, ed., *Roosevelt and Frankfurter: Their Correspondence, 1928–1945* (Boston: Little, Brown, 1967), p. 673.
137. FM to FF, 11/6/42, LC 1763-85.
138. Adams v. United States ex rel. McCann, 317 U.S. 269 (1942).
139. Howard, *Mr. Justice Murphy*, p. 280.
140. An excellent example of Frankfurter's style is the following letter to Jackson concerning a tax case in which Jackson had been assigned the majority opinion:

Dear Bob:

I am very happy that Eisner v. Macomber was assigned to you. For I know that your opinion will be infused with that intimacy of knowledge of the fiscal practicalities that you have beyond any man on this Court. I also know that you will forestall as well as can be forestalled all the meretricious opportunities that the occasion will afford.

And so it is not out of any mood of concern that there bubbled up in me this morning some words that I have put on paper conveying ideas which I know in some form or other will turn up in your opinion. But I knew that you would not mind my sending them to you. [FF to RHJ, 12/15/42, HLSL 170-1]

141. Pendergast v. United States, 317 U.S. 412 (1943) and Johnson v. United States, 318 U.S. 189 (1943).
142. Lash, *From the Diaries of Felix Frankfurter*, p. 179.
143. Ibid., pp. 179–80.
144. Ibid., p. 175.
145. Ibid.
146. Ibid.
147. United States v. Monia, 317 U.S. 424 (1943).
148. FF memorandum, 1/9/43, LC 4021-218. Black and Murphy joined Roberts's majority opinion. Douglas, however, "to my great surprise handed me my *Monia* dissent with 'I agree' two minutes before Conference" (ibid).
149. SEC v. Chenery Corporation, 318 U.S. 80 (1943).
150. FF to SR, 1/29/43, HLSL 1942. In another case in which Reed joined Black's opinion rather than his concurrence, Frankfurter recorded the following:

After I circulated my concurring opinion . . . Reed J. phoned and said "I am very glad you wrote what you did, because you put in words what I tried inadequately to express to Black to indicate my dissatisfaction with his opinion."

FF "But I understand that you are going with him."

Reed "That's right"

FF "In other words, you are going with Black because he is not expressing your views, and you're not going with me because I *am* expressing your views."

Reed "That's a funny but fair way of stating the situation." [HLSL 1942. The case is Tiller v. Atlantic Coast Line Railroad, 318 U.S. 54 (1943)]
151. Lash, *From the Diaries of Felix Frankfurter*, p. 174.
152. Ibid., pp. 175–76.
153. See Lash, *From the Diaries of Felix Frankfurter*, p. 239. See also Michael A. Kahn, "The Politics of the Appointment Process: An Analysis of Why Learned Hand was Never Appointed to the Supreme Court," *Stanford Law Review* 25 (1973): especially 281.
154. Murdock v. Pennsylvania, 319 U.S. 105 (1943).
155. Mason, *Stone*, p. 599.
156. 319 U.S. 141 (1943).
157. HLSL 1942. Frankfurter filed his opinion, which he labeled neither a concurrence nor a dissent.
158. HLSL 1942.
159. Lash, *From the Diaries of Felix Frankfurter*, p. 234.
160. Ibid., p. 197.
161. Schneiderman v. United States, 320 U.S. 118 (1943); West Virginia State Board of Education v. Barnette, 319 U.S. 624 (1943).
162. Howard, *Mr. Justice Murphy*, p. 309.
163. Ibid.
164. Lash, *From the Diaries of Felix Frankfurter*, p. 211.
165. Ibid., p. 212.
166. Ibid., p. 209.
167. FF to HFS, 5/31/43, LC 1763-85.
168. FF to SR, 6/2/43, LC 1763-85.
169. FF to FM, 5/31/43, LC 1763-85.
170. FF to FM, n.d., LC 1763-85.
171. FM to FF, 6/2/43, LC 1763-85. Frankfurter describes in his diary discord between Murphy and Douglas over Douglas's concurrence in *Schneiderman*. Frankfurter records trying hard to get Murphy to change his mind, using Mur-

phy's anger at Douglas as a wedge. See Lash, *From the Diaries of Felix Frank-furter*, pp. 257ff. In the Japanese curfew case. Hirabayashi v. United States, 320 U.S. 81 (1943), Murphy was once again Frankfurter's target; this time, however, Frankfurter was successful in persuading Murphy to change his proposed dissent to a concurrence. See Howard, *Mr. Justice Murphy*, p. 308.

172. Frankfurter documents several conversations with Jackson in his diary in which Jackson expresses hostility toward Black, Douglas and Murphy. See Lash, *From the Diaries of Felix Frankfurter*, pp. 174, 250.

173. FF to RHJ, 4/9/43, HLSL 1942; quoted in Howard, *Mr. Justice Murphy*, p. 294.

174. Jackson wrote:

The compulsory flag salute and pledge requires affirmation of a belief and an attitude of mind. . . . It is now a commonplace that censorship or suppression of expression of opinion is tolerated by our Constitution only when the expression presents a clear and present danger of action of a kind the State is empowered to prevent and punish. It would seem that involuntary affirmation could be commanded only on even more immediate and urgent grounds than silence. But here the power of compulsion is invoked without any allegation that remaining passive during a flag salute ritual creates a clear and present danger that would justify an effort even to muffle expression. To sustain the compulsory flag salute we are required to say that a Bill of Rights which guards the individual's right to speak his own mind, left it open to public authorities to compel him to utter what is not in his mind. [319 U.S. at 633–34]

175. 319 U.S. at 638.

176. Lash, *From the Diaries of Felix Frankfurter*, p. 253.

177. FF to RHJ, 6/4/43, LC 1369-69.

178. 319 U.S. at 646-47.

179. 319 U.S. at 647.

180. 319 U.S. at 662.

181. Stone had voted to dismiss similar cases several times before *Gobitis*, for lack of a substantial federal question. Mason, *Stone*, p. 526.

182. 319 U.S. at 664. Frankfurter singled out Stone for a special jibe; he threw Stone's own words back at him: "Not so long ago we were admonished that 'the only check upon our own exercise of power is our sense of self-restraint' " (319 U.S. at 647, quoting Stone in United States v. Butler, 297 U.S. 1, 79).

183. 319 U.S. at 649.

184. 319 U.S. at 663.

185. 319 U.S. at 667. The extent to which Frankfurter has now dismissed any conception of a hierarchy of values is revealed in his correspondence over the years with Zechariah Chafee. Not only does he maintain that there is no judicially enforceable ranking of values within the Constitution; when pressed by Chafee, Frankfurter maintains that civil liberties and economic rights are equal in value to the life and dignity of the individual, a position it is very difficult to imagine Frankfurter defending in the years before his appointment to the Court. For example, Frankfurter wrote Chafee in 1956:

The coal-diggers who live under the "yellow-dog" regime, which the Supreme Court sanctified by invalidating legislation against it, got very little comfort out of the fact that they were allowed to read the edifying pieces in The Atlantic Monthly or even perchance my own writings against the labor injunction. . . . I, who am . . . in a manner of speaking an emeritus professor, do not deny that there is analytic relevance in the distinction that you make between the two kinds of "liberties." I do insist, however, that in the actual life of an individual—if you please, the fulfillment of his dignity and the expression of his personality—the distinction asserts a differentiation that is rather empty. [FF to Chafee, 12/3/56, LC 751-42]

186. 319 U.S. at 653.

187. FF to FDR, 5/3/43, Freedman, *Roosevelt and Frankfurter*, p. 699.
188. FF to Bliven, 5/5/43 and 5/7/43; FF to Buxton, 5/5/43. HLSL 178-14.
189. FF to Griswold, 6/3/43, LC 1151-59.
190. FF-COHC, p. 309. This passage was pointedly excised from the public version of Frankfurter's reminiscences. Mason has indicated that he believes Brandeis may not have wholeheartedly approved of Frankfurter's opinion in *Gobitis*. Mason was present at the Brandeis home during a family discussion of the case. Personal communication of author with Alpheus T. Mason. For a discussion of Brandeis's position on civil liberties, see pp. 133ff.

Chapter 6

1. See, generally, Joseph Lash, ed., *From the Diaries of Felix Frankfurter*, (New York: Norton, 1975) pp. 309-38.
2. Ibid., p. 11.
3. FF to MDF, 9/14/44, LC 175-159.
4. FF to WOD, n.d., LC 967-52.
5. FF to WOD, 6/2/58, LC 967-52.
6. WOD to FF, 11/12/47, HLSL 19-8. The case is Shapiro v. United States, 335 U.S. 1 (1948).
7. FF to WOD, 2/25/48, LC 966-52.
8. 332 U.S. 46 (1947).
9. LC 550-32.
10. FF to LH, 3/5/54, LHP.
11. FF to LH, 11/30/52, LHP.
12. There are a number of warm exchanges between Frankfurter and Black in the early sixties, before Frankfurter's death. See, for example, HLB to FF, 12/22/64, LC 257, in which Black effusively thanks Frankfurter for one of *his* letters. Hugo Black, Jr., has written a perceptive account of his father's relationship with Frankfurter, and of some of the differences between them.

When FF came on the Court, I believe that he expected to form an army which would include Daddy as a lieutenant. After all, FF could have thought, with some justification, This Black is a liberal and a Southerner from a common family with very little formal education who would be impressed by my associations; and this Black supported my appointment and has openly expressed admiration for me. So no sooner was FF appointed than he began to woo Daddy as well as Mama and all of us kids.

And, of course, no sooner was FF appointed than Daddy decided to win him over to *his* views. . . . But this mutual enterprise was doomed to failure, for by nature neither Hugo nor FF had it in him to be a lieutenant. It was inevitable that each should eventually go his separate way. . . . And, of course, every time thereafter that the two agreed, each hoped that the other had finally become convinced of the error of his ways. . . .

With all his brilliance, charm and strategems, however, FF could not really match Daddy in picking up converts. Even though their passionate conviction of the righteousness of their positions was equal, there was one important difference. . . . FF had gained his reputation in an academic system, where he was mainly concerned with instructing, not persuading. But Hugo had gotten ahead by convincing ordinary citizens . . . that was right. When out to persuade, FF was likely to try to instruct his brethren by presenting an intellectual tour de force, often in language that was more a display of his exceptional vocabulary than a means of communication. FF tended to believe that he was a member of an intellectual elite, and before long some of his colleagues came to believe that FF did not consider them to be of this elite and may have resented this attitude. Hugo, on the other hand, believed in no elite of any kind. [Hugo Black, Jr., *My Father: A Remembrance* (New York: Random House, 1975), pp. 224–28]

13. FF to LH, 1/16/52, LHP.

14. Frankfurter's relationship with Murphy took some complex turns. After Murphy's death, Frankfurter recorded his feelings in a letter to Harold Laski:

Poor Frank Murphy! He was a strange mixture of mystic aspirations and as extreme a case of self-love as I have experienced. His deep fear of coming on the Court was well-founded and I think it's fair to say his decade in it was unabated inner tension. As for "the candidate" (as Frank called Bill, whom he despised) he became more and more of a mommser as the year went on. [FF to Laski, 7/27/49, LC 1509-75. "Mommser" is a Yiddish term carrying connotations of "bastard."]

Frankfurter also notes in his diary that Murphy attempted to warn him that Black and Douglas were "trying to poison" Chief Justice Vinson against him. Lash, *From the Diaries of Felix Frankfurter*, p. 329. J. Woodford Howard, Jr., discusses the Murphy-Frankfurter relationship at length; see *Mr. Justice Murphy* (Princeton: Princeton University Press, 1968), passim. Commenting upon this Frankfurter letter to Laski, Howard has indicated in private correspondence that he found no evidence that Murphy despised Douglas and that he suspects Frankfurter is projecting his own feelings toward Douglas onto Murphy, an interpretation I share. Frankfurter's ultimate judgment about Murphy was less harsh than about Black and Douglas. In 1960 he wrote Learned Hand that "to an extent," Frank Murphy was a man of principle, but that such a judgment "emphatically cannot be said of Hugo and Bill" (FF to LH, 8/18/60, LHP).

15. FF to LH, 2/13/58, LC 1255-65.

16. FF to LH, 6/30/57, LHP.

17. FF to LH, 11/7/54, LHP.

18. FF to LH, 4/2?/56, LHP.

19. Frankfurter wrote his most candid letters during this period to Learned Hand. See, generally, LC Box 65.

20. See, for example, FF to Hand, 10/10/55, LC 1251-65.

21. FF to Bickel, 3/18/63, LC 359-24.

22. James Landis makes a similar assessment of the Frankfurter-Roberts relationship in his Oral History Reminiscences. Landis, COHC, p. 95.

23. C. Herman Pritchett, *The Roosevelt Court* (New York: Macmillan, 1948) p. 40.

24. Ibid., p. 42.

25. Lash, *From the Diaries of Felix Frankfurter*, p. 227.

26. Mahnich v. Southern Steamship Company, 321 U.S. 96, 113 (1944). The press took Roberts's dissent—and Frankfurter's willingness to join it—as a sign of the developing split within the Court. See Mason, *Harlan Fiske Stone*, p. 611.

27. HLSL 1944. The case is Williams v. Kaiser, 323 U.S. 471 (1945).

28. Note passed from OR to FF in Screws v. United States, 325 U.S. 91 (1945). HLSL 1944.

29. For example, see HLSL 1944. Thomas v. Collins, 323 U.S. 516 (1945).

30. Alpheus T. Mason, *Harlan Fiske Stone: Pillar of the Law* (New York: Viking Press, 1956), pp. 765–769. Mason comments: "Why did honorable, busy men make such a furor over a merely formal matter? . . . Black and Frankfurter stubbornly refused to treat it as a ceremonial formality. . . . This trifling incident parodies the working Court."

31. FF to LH, 6/15/53, LHP.

32. FF to FMV, 4/25/49, LC 2268-108.

33. FF to SR, 6/5/45, LC 1924-92.

34. Jewell Ridge Coal Corp. v. Local 6167 UMW, 325 U.S. 161 (1945).

35. Howard, *Mr. Justice Murphy*, pp. 392–93. See also Mason, *Stone*, chap. 38, and Gerald T. Dunne, *Hugo Black and the Judicial Revolution* (New York: Simon and Schuster, 1977), chap. 11.

36. Pritchett *The Roosevelt Court*, pp. 260–61 and passim.
37. Mason, *Stone*, p. 643.
38. FF to RHJ, 6/9/45, HLSL 170-2.
39. FF to LH, 6/27/46, LC 1238-64.
40. RHJ to FF, 8/6/[49], HLSL 170-4.
41. RHJ to FF, 4/8/48, LC 1374-69.
42. FF to RHJ, 4/2/51, LC 1376-70.
43. FF to RHJ, n.d., HLSL 28-7. The case is McComb v. Jacksonville Paper Co., 336 U.S. 187 (1949).
44. FF to RHJ, 6/4/47, HLSL 170-3.
45. RHJ to FF, 1/27/49, HLSL 26-3. The case is Foley Bros. v. Filardo, 336 U.S. 281 (1949).
46. For example, see RHJ to FF, 3/30/49, HLSL 28-20, concerning Nye and Nissen v. United States, 336 U.S. 613 (1949).
47. FF to LH, 11/7/54, LHP.
48. FF to JMH, 2/22/56, HLSL 169-14.
49. FF to SM, 5/28/54, HLSL 170-10.
50. SM to FF, ca. November 1953, HLSL 170-9.
51. FF to HHB, 1/17/46, HLSL 169-6.
52. FF to SM, 5/27/50, HLSL 32-8.
53. FMV to FF, 6/26/46, LC 2267-108.
54. FF to FMV, 2/7/47, LC 2267-108.
55. FF to FMV, 5/26/49, HLSL 24-13. The case is Commissioner v. Culbertson, 337 U.S. 733 (1949).
56. FF to LH, 7/4/61, LHP.
57. FF to LH, 2/2/59, LC 1256-65.
58. FF to JMH, 6/11/57, HLSL 169-15.
59. The analysis in this section draws upon Sanford V. Levinson, "Skepticism, Democracy, and Judicial Restraint: An Essay on the Thought of Oliver Wendell Holmes and Felix Frankfurter" (Ph.D. dissertation, Harvard University, 1969) chap. 5; and Helen Shirley Thomas, *Felix Frankfurter: Scholar on the Bench* (Baltimore: Johns Hopkins Press, 1960), chaps. 3 and 10. Levinson convincingly argues that contradictions such as those into which Frankfurter fell are inherent in the essentially empty formula of Thayer: "The so-called 'reasonableness test' becomes a device for blocking discussion just where it should begin" (p. 283). My point is that Frankfurter did not realize this before he was appointed to the Court, and that, after his appointment, the interpersonal situation on the Court and Frankfurter's psychological state made it impossible for him to realize or admit any contradictions or faults in his own beliefs, and forced him to harden his commitment to Thayer and to ignore his own belief in fundamental values.
60. Everson v. Board of Education, 330 U.S. 1 (1947).
61. The Court divided five to four. Black, Douglas, Murphy, Reed, and Vinson formed the majority; Frankfurter, Rutledge, Jackson, and Burton dissented. Rutledge and Jackson filed dissents, both of which Frankfurter joined. Howard points out that "however committed ideologically, most Justices paused before the implications of *Everson*. Attitudes were inchoate and options highly fluid" (Howard, *Mr. Justice Murphy*, p. 449). Frankfurter tried to get Murphy to vote with the dissenters by appealing to his conscience as a Catholic.

Dear Frank:

You have some false friends—those who flatter you and play on you for *their* purposes, not for your good. What follows is written by one who cares for your place in history, not in tomorrow's columns, as lasting as yesterday's snow. At least your sister and your brother would acquit me of anything but disinterestedness. I am willing to be judged by them.

The short of it is that you, above all men, should write along the lines—I do not say with the phrasing—of Bob's opinion in *Everson*. I know what you think of the great American doctrine of Church and State—I also know what the wisest men of the Church, like Cardinal Gibbons thought about it. You have a chance to do for your country and your Church such as never come to you before—and may never again. The things we most regret—at least such is my experience—are the opportunities missed. For the sake of history, for the sake of your inner peace, don't miss. No one knows better than you what *Everson* is about. Tell the world—and shame the devil.

Anyhow—this comes to you from one who writes because the truth within him is insistent. [FF to FM, ca. 2/10/47, LC 1765-86.]

62. Illinois ex rel. McCollum v. Board of Education, 333 U.S. 203 (1948).
63. Lash, *From the Diaries of Felix Frankfurter*, p. 343.
64. 333 U.S. at 219.
65. 333 U.S. at 225.
66. Thomas, *Felix Frankfurter: Scholar on the Bench*, p. 63.
67. 333 U.S. at 214.
68. 333 U.S. at 231.
69. Ibid.
70. FF to Burlingham, 4/13/51, LC 622-36. In another released-time case in 1952, the Court voted to uphold a New York program in which school facilities were not used. Zorach v. Clauson, 343 U.S. 306 (1952). Black, Jackson, and Frankfurter dissented; each filed a separate opinion. Frankfurter endorsed Jackson's opinion but not Black's.
71. 354 U.S. 234 (1957).
72. 354 U.S. at 262.
73. 354 U.S. at 265.
74. Ibid.
75. 354 U.S. at 266–67.
76. 333 U.S. at 216–17.
77. 347 U.S. 483 (1954).
78. McLaurin v. Oklahoma State Regents, 339 U.S. 637 (1950).
79. HLSL 34-3.
80. For a thorough description of the decision-making process in *Brown*, and Frankfurter's crucial role in that process, see Richard Kluger, *Simple Justice* (New York: Knopf, 1976), especially pp. 564ff.
81. 354 U.S. at 261–62.
82. This paragraph cites the cases used by Raoul Berger in *Government by Judiciary* (Cambridge: Harvard University Press, 1977), pp. 259–265.
83. Louisiana ex rel. Francis v. Resweber, 329 U.S. 459, 471 (1947).
84. Haley v. Ohio, 332 U.S. 596, 603 (1948).
85. Rochin v. California, 342 U.S. 165, 169 (1952). The practice in question was the use of a stomach pump to retrieve evidence of narcotics. Douglas concurred only with Frankfurter's holding; he pointed out that the practice in question "would be admissible in the majority of states where the question has been raised" and thus did not violate the " 'decencies of civilized conduct' . . . formulated by responsible courts with judges as sensitive as we are" (342 U.S. at 177–78). See Berger, *Government by Judiciary*, note 57, p. 262.
86. Arthur Sutherland, quoted in Berger, *Government by Judiciary*, pp. 262–63.
87. Louis Jaffe, quoted in Berger, *Government by Judiciary*, note 62, p. 263.
88. Berger, *Government by Judiciary*, p. 260.
89. Dennis v. United States, 341 U.S. 494 (1951).
90. 369 U.S. 186 (1962).
91. Levinson, "Skepticism, Democracy, and Judicial Restraint," pp. 257–58.
92. 341 U.S. at 550–51.
93. 369 U.S. at 270.
94. FF to Stone, 5/27/40, LC 2179-105.
95. FF to Freund, 6/3/64, LC 1072-56.
96. FF to Kurland, 1/31/64, LC 1465-73.

97. Frankfurter had written an article in 1955 in which he tried to resurrect the reputation of Roberts. Frankfurter had urged Roberts to record his version of the events of 1937; Roberts, when he resigned from the Court, gave Frankfurter a memorandum "to be used at his discretion." The facts of the situation are complex and are summarized by Freedman, *Roosevelt and Frankfurter*, pp. 392ff. Freedman also prints the text of the Roberts memorandum.

98. Clear-and-present-danger might have been a "great idea," Frankfurter wrote Learned Hand in 1949, but "great thoughts and little minds (to paraphrase Burke) go ill together" (FF to LH, 9/3/49, LHP).

99. FF to Howe, 8/22/63, LC 1328-68.

100. FF to Howe, 9/4/63, LC 1328-68.

Chapter 7

1. Karen Horney, *Neurosis and Human Growth*, (New York: Norton, 1950) p. 22.

2. Ibid., p. 23.

3. Ibid., p 24.

4. Alexander L. George, "Some Uses of Dynamic Psychology in Political Biography: Case Materials on Woodrow Wilson," in *A Source Book for the Study of Personality and Politics*, ed. Fred I. Greenstein and Michael Lerner (Chicago: Markham, 1971), pp. 84–85.

5. Horney, *Neurosis and Human Growth*, p. 191.

6. Ibid., pp. 194–95.

7. Ibid., p. 18.

8. Ibid, p 297.

9. Erik H. Erikson, "The Problem of Ego Identity," *Journal of the American Psychoanalytic Association* 4 (1956): 79.

10. James David Barber, "The Interplay of Presidential Character and Style," in *A Source Book for the Study of Personality and Politics*, p. 387.

11. See Fred I. Greenstein, *Personality and Politics* (New York: Norton, 1975), p. 65f.

12. George, "Some Uses of Dynamic Psychology in Political Biography," p. 85.

13. Ibid., pp. 88–89.

14. FF-COHC, p. 59.

15. FF to Burlingham, 5/24/45, LC 607-35.

16. George, "Some Uses of Dynamic Psychology in Political Biography," p. 87.

17. FF to MD, 6/21/19, LC 70-8.

18. See especially Horney, *Neurosis and Human Growth*, chap. 12.

INDEX

Abrams v. *United States,* 70, 133, 137, 234
Acheson, Dean, 90, 109, 126
Adamson v. *California,* 179
Adkins v. *Children's Hospital,* 71
American Federation of Labor v. *National Labor Relations Board,* 237
American Zionist Organization, 11
Ames, James Barr, 21, 22, 24, 96
Auerbach, Jerold S., 214

Baker, Liva, 223, 226, 230
Baker, Newton D., 52
Baker v. *Carr,* 197–98
Baldwin, Roger, 71
Barber, James David, 6, 205*n*, 214
Barron v. *Baltimore,* 145*n*
Beck, James M., 73–74, 223
Berger, Raoul, 196, 246
Berle, A. A., 102, 104, 228
Berlin, Isaiah, 226
Betts v. *Brady,* 161
Bickel, Alexander, 83, 183, 198
Black, Hugo, 4, 139–41, 145, 146, 147, 153, 154, 155, 156, 157, 158, 161, 162, 164, 165, 166, 167, 169–70, 173, 177–80, 182, 183, 184, 185–86, 189, 190, 192, 193, 236, 237, 238, 241, 242, 243, 244, 245, 246

Black, Jr., Hugo, 243
Bliven, Bruce, 175
Board of County Commissioners of Jackson County v. *United States,* 237
Bowen, Catherine Drinker, 214
Brandeis, Louis D., 10, 11, 12*n*, 31–32, 36, 51, 70*n*, 71*n*, 80, 85–87, 95, 103, 104, 105, 106, 107, 109, 113, 114, 115, 116, 118, 120, 123, 124, 127–37, 138, 139, 140, 144, 158, 159, 175, 181, 198, 200, 207, 221, 223, 225, 226, 228, 232, 233, 236, 243; appointment to Supreme Court, 45–46, 47, 48, 49, 69; and civil liberties, 129–30, 133–37; and Zionism, 44, 62–63, 73.
Brennan, William, 180, 188, 190, 193
Bridges v. *California,* 157–59
Broun, Heywood, 88
Brown v. *Board of Education,* 195*n*, 246
Buckner, Emory R., 31, 35, 36, 44, 71*n*, 75, 80, 81, 221, 225
Bullitt, William C., 215
Burlingham, C. C., 101, 122, 137, 139, 193, 236
Burns, James MacGregor, 230
Burton, Harold, 188, 189, 245
Butler, Pierce, 41*n*, 71*n*, 139
Buxton, Frank, 175
Byrnes, James F., 139, 155*n*, 156, 157, 159, 160, 162, 178

Index

Cardozo, Benjamin, 124, 125, 181, 198
Chafee, Zechariah, 70, 233, 242
City College of New York, 17–19, 40n
Clark, Grenville, 122, 235
Clark, John H., 71n
Clark, Tom C., 188
Cohen, Benjamin V., 111, 113, 114, 116, 124
Cohen, Morris L., 40, 43, 219, 226
Cohn, Alfred, 126, 225, 238
Commissioner v. *Culbertson*, 245
Corcoran, Thomas, 98, 110, 113, 114, 115, 116, 124, 125, 229, 230
Croly, Herbert, 33, 45, 66, 67, 78, 89, 94, 95, 207, 223
Cummings, Homer, 115, 231

Danelski, David, 214, 236
Danzig, Richard, 238
Daugherty, Harry M., 78
Davis, John W., 76–77, 81, 94, 224
Day, William, 71n
Dennis v. *United States*, 197–98
Dennison, Winfred, 38
Donovan, William J., 78
Douglas, William O., 4, 125, 139, 141, 145, 146–47, 150, 153, 154, 155, 156, 157, 159, 161, 162, 163, 164, 165, 166, 167, 173, 177–80, 182, 183, 184, 187, 189, 190, 193, 235, 241, 242, 244, 245, 246
Driscoll v. *Edison Light and Power*, 237
Dunne, Gerald T., 236, 238

Edwards v. *California*, 156
Ehrmann, Phillip, 228
Erikson, Erik, 7–8, 203–4, 215, 217
Everson v. *Board of Education*, 191–92

Fahy, Charles, 229
Federal Communications Commission v. *CBS*, 238
Flag salute cases: *See West Virginia State Board of Education* v. *Barnette* and *Minersville School District* v. *Gobitis*
Foley Bros. v. *Filardo*, 245
Forcey, C. B., 217
Ford Motor Co. v. *Beauchamp*, 237
Frank, Jerome, 109, 118
Frankfurter, Leopold (father), 13, 47–48
Frankfurter, Marion Denman (wife), 11–12, 15, 37, 39, 47, 48, 49–51, 52, 53, 58–61, 62, 64, 68, 77, 81–85, 86, 87, 88, 100, 103, 110, 116, 117, 119, 120, 121, 178, 204, 206, 208–9, 220, 221, 225, 226, 237
Freedman, Max, 106, 111n, 120n, 229, 231, 232, 247
Freud, Sigmund, 215
Freund, Paul, 109, 198
Fuller, Alvan T., 92, 95n

Gates, Sylvester, 91, 226
George, Alexander, 9, 202, 206n, 209, 214–15
George, Juliette, 215
Gilmore, Grant, 130
Golub, Eugene, 231
Greenstein, Fred, 206n, 214, 215
Griswold, Erwin, 175
Gunther, Gerald, 234

Hand, Learned, 34, 38, 39, 80, 87n, 89, 93, 101, 129, 132, 141, 160, 162, 166, 175, 179–80, 181, 182, 185, 186, 225, 234, 244
Hapgood, Norman, 226
Harlan, John Marshall, 181–82, 188, 194

Index

Harvard Law School, 6, 10, 11, 19–25, 32, 38–40, 43, 47, 50, 55, 58, 64, 66–71, 90, 94, 96, 97, 100, 133, 138, 175, 204, 206, 207, 208n, 236
Hawley, Ellis W., 231
Hillman, Sidney, 71, 78
Hirabayashi v. *United States*, 242
Hiss, Alger, 98, 108
Hollinger, David A., 216, 219
Holmes, Oliver Wendell, 10, 21, 31–33, 38, 39, 40, 41, 42–43, 47, 85–87, 95, 104, 110, 127, 128–37, 138, 152, 157, 158, 159, 171, 181, 198, 199–200, 206, 218, 223, 224, 226, 234, 235; and civil liberties, 129–31, 133–37, 174
Hopkins, Harry, 106, 124, 125
Horney, Karen, 7–8, 62, 201–11, 215
Howard, Jr., J. Woodford, 155, 168, 186n, 214, 238, 240, 244
Howe, Irving, 15, 112, 216
Howe, Mark DeWolfe, 88, 198, 199–200, 226
Howe, Mrs. Mark D., 88
Hughes, Charles Evans, 51, 80, 123, 142, 147, 150, 155, 157, 175, 199, 232, 236, 237, 238, 239

Ickes, Harold, 78, 106, 125, 126
Illinois ex rel. McCollum v. *Board of Education*, 192–93, 195.
Indianapolis v. *Chase Bank*, 240

Jackson, Gardner, 83
Jackson, Robert H., 4, 125, 139, 155n, 156, 157, 159, 160, 163, 166, 171–73, 175, 182, 183, 185–88, 198, 199, 239, 240, 242, 245, 246
Jacobsohn, Gary, 131
Jaffe, Louis, 196
Jewell Ridge Corp. v. *Local 6167 UMW*, 185n, 186

Johnson, Hugh, 106, 229, 230
Johnson, Lyndon, 215
Jones v. *Opelika*, 161
Josephson, Matthew, 14–15, 43

Kahn, Michael A., 241
Kaufman, Andrew, 198
Kearns, Doris, 215
Keifer and Keifer v. *RFC*, 237
Keynes, John Maynard, 113–14
Kluger, Richard, 246
Krock, Arthur, 231
Kurland, Philip, 198

LaFollette, Robert, 76–78, 226
Landis, James M., 96–97, 98, 109, 111, 227, 244
Lane v. *Wilson*, 236
Lash, Joseph P., 83, 102, 121, 152, 177, 216, 218, 228, 231–32, 242, 244
Laski, Harold, 48, 89, 153, 155, 244
Lasswell, Harold D., 215
Leuchtenberg, William, 116n, 230, 231
Levinson, Daniel, 27, 216, 217–18, 220, 227
Levinson, Sanford V., 130, 245
Link, Arthur S., 217
Lippmann, Walter, 54, 58, 64, 78, 79, 88, 100, 111n, 224
Lowell, A. Lawrence, 67, 68–70, 92–93, 94, 95n, 206, 222, 226, 227
Lowenthal, Max, 55

Mack, Julian, 68–69, 78, 80, 94, 141, 226, 227, 232
MacLeish, Archibald, 137n, 235
Mahnich v. *Southern Steamship Company*, 244

Margold, Nathan, 96
Martin v. Struthers, 166–67
Mason, Alpheus T., 129, 226, 233, 239, 243, 244
McCloskey, Robert G., 157
McComb v. Jacksonville Paper Co., 245
McReynolds, James C., 46, 139, 146, 155n
Meiklejohn, Alexander, 70–71
Mencken, H. L., 78
Mendelson, Wallace, 226, 228
Meyer v. Nebraska, 133–35, 137
Milk Wagon Drivers Union of Chicago v. Meadowmoor Dairies, 153–54
Minersville School District v. Gobitis, 147–52, 161, 171–73, 175, 184, 211, 242
Minton, Sherman, 188, 189
Moley, Raymond, 104, 111
Mooney, Tom, 55–57, 73, 91, 226
Moors, John F., 92
Morgenthau, Henry, 53, 54, 63, 66, 206
Morrow, Dwight, 22
Murdock v. Pennsylvania, 166
Murphy, Frank, 4, 125, 139, 150, 153, 154, 155, 157, 158, 159, 161, 162–63, 164, 165, 166, 167, 173, 179, 180, 181, 184, 186, 238, 240, 241, 242, 244, 245
Murphy, Walter F., 214, 236, 239

National Consumer's League, 45, 46
NRA (National Industrial Recovery Administration), 106n, 114, 115, 230–31
Neirbo v. Bethlehem Shipbuilding, 237
New Republic, 33, 45, 71, 73, 77, 89n, 134, 175, 224, 227, 232
New School for Social Research, 66
Nye and Nissen v. United States, 245

Paris Peace Conference, 11, 53, 62–63, 205
Pearce v. Commissioner, 240
Pearson, Drew, 187
Percy, Eustace, 54, 55, 64, 221
Phelps Dodge Corporation v. National Labor Relations Board, 154–55
Phillips, Harlan P., 219
Pitney, Mahlon, 71n
Pittman v. H.O.L.C., 236
Pound, Roscoe, 38, 43–44, 63, 67, 79, 92, 94–97, 111n
Powell, Thomas Reed, 89
Prichard, Jr., E. F., 235
Pritchett, C. Herman, 162, 236, 239

Rayburn, Sam, 111
Reed, Stanley F., 115, 139, 142–44, 147, 157, 159, 160–61, 165, 166, 170, 183, 184–85, 230, 231, 237, 240, 245
Richberg, Donald, 115, 229, 230, 231
Roazen, Paul, 215
Roberts, Owen, 123, 145, 146, 147, 150, 157, 161, 163, 166, 167, 170, 183, 184, 199, 241, 244, 247
Rochester Telephone v. United States, 236
Rochin v. California, 246
Rogat, Yosal, 214
Roosevelt, Franklin D., 4, 5, 6, 25, 98, 99–126, 155n, 162, 163n, 166, 175, 178, 186, 207, 229–30
Roosevelt, Theodore, 24, 25–26, 27, 34, 36, 51, 55, 56, 58
Rosenfield, Laura C., 226
Rosensohn, Sam, 231
Rosenwald, Julius, 227
Rutledge, Wiley, 166, 179, 185n, 245

Sacco and Vanzetti, 56n, 58, 83, 90–94, 163n, 206, 207, 226, 227

Sacks, Albert M., 105
Sanford, Edward T., 71*n*
Schechter case (*Schechter Poultry Corp. v. United States*), 114, 115, 116, 119, 231
Schenck v. *United States*, 133, 234
Schlesinger, Jr., Arthur M., 110, 114, 231
Schneiderman v. *United States*, 168–71, 241
SEC v. *Chenery Corporation*, 165
Securities Bill of 1933, 111–12
Seligman, Eustace, 112, 230
Shapiro v. *United States*, 243
Shattuck, Henry L., 97
Shklar, Judith N., 232
Sibbach v. *Wilson*, 238
Smith, Al, 100, 101
Stewart, Potter, 188
Stimson, Henry L., 10, 24–31, 34, 35, 36, 38, 39, 44, 45, 48, 51, 52, 63, 74–76, 85, 89, 91, 97, 103, 112, 125, 206, 218, 223, 224
Stone, Harlan Fiske, 76, 78–81, 95, 125, 136, 139, 144, 147, 150–51, 152, 153, 155–56, 157, 160, 161, 163, 166, 170, 172, 173, 184, 189, 199, 224, 225, 226, 236, 237, 239, 242
Sutherland, Arthur E., 196, 225, 227
Sutherland, George, 71*n*, 134*n*
Sweezy v. *New Hampshire*, 193, 195–96

Taft, William Howard, 26, 31, 34, 35, 71*n*
Thayer, Ezra, 97
Thayer, James Bradley, 128–29, 132, 191
Thomas, Helen Shirley, 216, 245
Thomas, Norman, 78
Thompson, William G., 90–91
Thornhill v. *Alabama*, 153
Tiller v. *Atlantic Coast Line Railroad*, 241
Truman, Harry, 186*n*, 187

Tucker, Robert C., 215
Tugwell, Rexford G., 104, 113

United States v. *Butler*, 242
United States v. *Carolene Products*, 136, 150–51, 198
United States v. *Monia*, 164

VanDevanter, William, 122–23
Vinson, Fred M., 185, 186*n*, 188, 189–90, 244, 245

War Labor Policies Board, 58–59, 100
Warren, Earl, 180, 182, 188, 190, 193
Warren, Edward H., 38
Weizmann, Chaim, 21*n*, 63, 73, 223
West Virginia State Board of Education v. *Barnette*, 168, 171–76, 193, 211
Wheeler, Burton K., 78, 224
White, Edward D., 46, 66, 71*n*
White, William Allen, 78
Whitney v. *California*, 133
Whittaker, Charles E., 188
Wigmore, John H., 92
Williams v. *Kaiser*, 244
Wilson, Woodrow, 36, 38, 51, 53, 55, 56, 58, 63, 76, 219, 221
Wisconsin v. *J. C. Penney*, 238
Wolman, Leo, 71
Wyzanski, Charles, 98, 109, 113, 139, 226, 236

Zorach v. *Clauson*, 246